Blogging My Religion

Religion in Europe is currently undergoing changes that are reconfiguring physical and virtual spaces of practice and belief, and these changes need to be understood with regards to the proliferation of digital media discourses. This book explores religious change in Europe through a comparative approach that analyzes Atheist, Catholic, and Muslim blogs as spaces for articulating narratives about religion that symbolically challenge the power of religious institutions.

The book adds theoretical complexity to the study of religion and digital media with the concept of hypermediated religious spaces. The theory of hypermediation helps to critically discuss the theory of secularization and to contextualize religious change as the result of multiple entangled phenomena. It considers religion as being connected with secular and post-secular spaces, and media as embedding material forms, institutions, and technologies. A spatial perspective contextualizes hypermediated religious spaces as existing at the interstice of alternative and mainstream, private and public, imaginary and real venues.

By offering the innovative perspective of hypermediated religious spaces, this book will be of significant interest to scholars of religious studies, the sociology of religion, and digital media.

Giulia Evolvi is a Research Associate in Religion and Media at Ruhr University, Germany. Her research interests include religion and materiality, secularization, Islam, and Islamophobia. She has published various articles and chapters on these subjects in publications such as *Media History, Social Compass*, and *Information, Communication & Society*.

Routledge Studies in Religion and Digital Culture

Edited by Heidi Campbell, Mia Lövheim, and Gregory Price Grieve

For more information about this series, please visit: www.routledge.com/religion/series/RDC

Blogging My Religion
Secular, Muslim, and Catholic Media Spaces in Europe

Giulia Evolvi

Routledge
Taylor & Francis Group

LONDON AND NEW YORK

First published 2019
by Routledge
2 Park Square, Milton Park, Abingdon, Oxon OX14 4RN

and by Routledge
52 Vanderbilt Avenue, New York, NY 10017

First issued in paperback 2020

Routledge is an imprint of the Taylor & Francis Group, an informa business

© 2019 Giulia Evolvi

The right of Giulia Evolvi to be identified as author of this work has been asserted by her in accordance with sections 77 and 78 of the Copyright, Designs and Patents Act 1988.

British Library Cataloguing-in-Publication Data
A catalogue record for this book is available from the British Library

Library of Congress Cataloging-in-Publication Data
Names: Evolvi, Giulia, author.
Title: Blogging my religion : secular, Muslim, and Catholic media spaces in Europe / Giulia Evolvi.
Description: New York : Routledge, 2018. | Series: Routledge studies in religion and digital culture | Includes bibliographical references and index.
Identifiers: LCCN 2018031148 | ISBN 9781138562110 (hardback : alk. paper) | ISBN 9781351357210 (pdf) | ISBN 9781351357203 (epub) | ISBN 9781351357197 (mobi)
Subjects: LCSH: Europe—Religion—21st century. | Blogs. | Social media—Social aspects.
Classification: LCC BL695 .E96 2018 | DDC 200.94/09051—dc23
LC record available at https://lccn.loc.gov/2018031148

ISBN 13: 978-0-36-758487-0 (pbk)
ISBN 13: 978-1-138-56211-0 (hbk)

Typeset in Sabon
by Apex CoVantage, LLC

To my parents, Cristina Comotti and Luigi Evolvi

Contents

Figures

Acknowledgments

Writing this book has been a long but fun and interesting process. It is based on my doctoral dissertation, and I wrote it during the first two years of my postdoctoral research, so its publication is both the best conclusion of my Ph.D. and – hopefully – the first step of my academic career.

My thanks go, first and foremost, to my Ph.D. adviser, Nabil Echchaibi, who is not only a brilliant mind but also a kind and compassionate person who pushed me to become the best scholar I could be. I would like to thank also the members of my dissertation committee: Stewart Hoover, the example of how extremely smart scholars can also be supportive and caring; Shu-Ling Chen Berggreen, who has been for me a wonderful mentor and a friend; Michela Ardizzoni, a strong and passionate professor who is a constant inspiration; Peter Simonson, who is an intellectual guide and whose refined rhetoric I will never end to admire. I am also very grateful to Janice Peck, Andrew Calabrese, Paul Voakes and all the professors and graduate students at the College of Media, Communication, and Information at the University of Colorado Boulder who have helped and inspired me during my Ph.D. A special mention goes to Martha LaForge, who has always been there for graduate students in any way possible.

I would also like to thank all the members of the Center for Media, Religion, and Culture at the University of Colorado Boulder for providing me with an intellectually challenging and friendly environment to conduct my research. I thank Krissy Peterson for being such a smart and wonderful friend and Samira Rajabi for always inspiring me with her strength. Thanks to Susanne Stadlbauer, who has been my friend and colleague in both Colorado and Germany. I would like to mention in particular also Deborah Whitehead, Art Bamford, Ryan Bartlett, Patrick Johnson, Rachel Liberman, William Ramsey, Nathan Schneider, Brad Breiten, Henrik Reintoft Christensen, Laurens de Rooij, Brooke Edge, Ahammed Junaid, Raoof Mir, Jin Kyu Park, Fazlul Rahman, Lei Su, Sara Souza, Adriana do Amaral, Hugo Cordova. I thank Seung Soo Kim, Rianne Subijanto, Ashmi Desai for supporting me until the end, when I defended my dissertation. My Ph.D. was particularly pleasant thanks to Megan Hurson and Tyler Rollins, the best cohort for whom I could have hoped. Special thanks to Lynn Schofield

Clark, who is the first person who suggested that I apply to CU Boulder for my Ph.D. and has been an inspiration ever since.

Furthermore, I would like to thank my friends and colleagues from the Center for Religious Studies at Ruhr University, which was my intellectual home while writing this book. Thanks to Volkhard Krech, Alexandra Cuffel, and Kianoosh Rezania for providing a great leadership to the Käte Hamburger Kolleg (KHK) project of which I am part. I would like to mention my KHK colleagues Tim Karis, Jessie Pons, Eduard Iricinschi, Licia Di Giacinto, Knut Martin Stünkel. I also thank my media and religion people, in particular Frederik Elwert, Anna Neumaier, Samira Tabti. I would like to thank in particular Adam Knobler, who edited my book and was the first person to read the full manuscript.

I am grateful for the support and feedback of the editors of the Routledge Studies in Religion and Digital Culture: Mia Lövheim, Heidi Campbell, and Gregory Price Grieve, three scholars whose work I greatly admire. Warm thanks also to everyone at Routledge, especially Joshua Wells and Jack Boothroyd for working on my manuscript. I also appreciate the suggestions of the anonymous reviewers who read my book proposal. I am grateful to family and friends in Italy, Germany, the US, and all over the world for believing in me. To all the people who accepted to be interviewed for this book and helped me with my research: thank you for blogging your religion.

The most special thanks to Mauro. Writing this book often meant being apart, but also getting closer to the moment we can be together.

Introduction

Discussing religious change in Catholic Europe

In an episode of Paolo Sorrentino's dramatic television series *The Young Pope*, fictional Pope Pius XIII, played by actor Jude Law, meets the Italian Prime Minister. The golden-embroidered papal vest of the Pope covers almost entirely the white chair where he sits and sharply contrasts with the sober black suit of the Prime Minister, played by actor Stefano Accorsi. In the episode, the Pope and the Prime Minister have disagreements on the relationship the Vatican should sustain with the Italian government. Pius theatrically shows a mirror to the Prime Minister and asks him to describe what he sees. The Prime Minister glances at his image and that of the Pope in the mirror and answers, with a smile, that he sees "two young men, one who is dressed in a slightly odd style." However, Pius has another answer in mind: "I, on the other hand, see two media events." Oscar-winning filmmaker Paolo Sorrentino, in his series *The Young Pope*, depicts an arrogant, conservative, and extravagant Pope. Pius XIII refuses to appear in public because he is aware of the power of the media and the expectations he can build by eschewing media attention, like some celebrities do. In describing himself as a "media event," he displays a deep knowledge of media logics and media power.

The character played by Jude Law is hardly a truthful depiction of real popes. Pope Francis, elected in 2013, often appears on various media platforms, which describe him as friendly and full of humanity. However, real and fictional popes have also something in common: they understand the power of media. Pope Francis arguably sustains a celebrity status, which not only attracts the attention of media worldwide but also inspires international television series such as *The Young Pope* – even if they might not offer a very flattering portrayal of the papacy. When I started designing my research about religion and media in Catholic Europe, I visited the editorial office of the Italian Catholic magazine *Famiglia Cristiana* (Christian Family, 12 June 2013). A journalist showed me a blackboard full of pictures of Pope Francis kissing children, hugging people with disabilities, and blessing elderly believers. The journalist explained that it is easy to find something to put on the cover of *Famiglia Cristiana* because the engaging and friendly attitude of Pope Francis always provides sources for media stories.

In looking at the pictures of Pope Francis on the blackboard, I asked myself some questions: which are the stories that magazine covers do not tell? And which media tell the stories that are not (yet) media events?

There are many examples of religious media events. Pope Francis proved to be a media event – to employ Sorrentino's language in *The Young Pope* – on various occasion. For example, the first papal visit outside Rome, on 8 July 2013, was to Lampedusa, the island that many migrants from North Africa try to reach with dinghy boats, often meeting a cruel death by drowning in the Mediterranean Sea. Dressed in plain white, Pope Francis threw flowers in the sea to commemorate migrants who lost their lives near the shores of Lampedusa and blessed a cross made from the wood of shipwrecked boats that had carried migrants (Napolitano, forthcoming). In his speech, he condemned the "globalization of indifference" that prevents people from understanding and alleviating the sorrows of others. Pope Francis spoke in Italian (which is, in contrast to what *The Young Pope* depicts, the language of the Catholic clergy), but he probably aimed at reaching people beyond the Italian borders. The choice of visiting Lampedusa, internationally famous for being one of the migrants' access points to Europe, likely underscores the attention of the Catholic Church to global cultural and political issues. Meeting Lampedusa mayor Giuseppina Nicolini, the Pope symbolically demonstrated how Catholic and secular institutions can have a dialogue on these issues. Greeting Muslim migrants living in Lampedusa's refugee camps, Pope Francis attested his acceptance of other faiths in Europe, notably Islam.

Pope Francis' visit to Lampedusa was a media event because of its worldwide resonance. The news was not only talked about on Vatican media, for example, through a live stream of the channel Vatican News on YouTube in multiple languages, but also by non-religious newspapers and media outlets, from the Italian *Corriere della Sera*, to the French *Le Figaro*, to the British BBC. The story was also told through social media. The Pope, indeed, sustains a regular Twitter presence, started by Benedict XVI with the account @Pontifex. The day of his visit to Lampedusa, Pope Francis – or, supposedly, his communication office – tweeted in various languages, "We pray for a heart which will embrace immigrants. God will judge us upon how we have treated the most needy." The speech the Pope gave in Lampedusa, therefore, did not only occur on the small Mediterranean island, but also on television, newspapers, and digital spaces. According to Daniel Dayan and Elihu Katz (1994), media events are breaks of the media routine that embed quasi-religious elements such as a sense of reverence and ceremony. In the case of the visit to Lampedusa, different media platforms told the same story: the Pope, who is the leader of the Catholic Church and embodies Catholic values, welcomes Muslims arriving in Europe and discusses the issue of migration with secular institutions.

The Pope is a media event for this ability to switch between media platforms and to attract the attention of a global public that does not necessarily only include Catholic believers. The ways in which Pope Francis comfortably interacts with secular politics and with other faiths suggest that the Catholic Church occupies a privileged social and media position within European society. Rhetoric about European civilization often favors Christianity at the expenses of other faiths, writes Talal Asad (2003). Indeed, Christian history is "being re-invoked in secular language as the foundation of an ancient identity" (164). By considering Christianity as a historical presence and a resource for ethics and morality, many European secular discourses justify and welcome the public display of Christian values. In the Italian context, this paradoxical compromise of secularism and Christianity has been defined as "Catholic secularism" (Frisina 2011; Vilaça et al. 2014), a term I extend in this book to greater Catholic Europe. The speech of Pope Francis in Lampedusa, which commented on European society through Christian values, can be considered as an example of Catholic secularism. However, Catholic secularism can easily become ambiguous. Asad mostly criticizes it for excluding Muslims from the construction of European identities, but the model of Catholic secularism can dissatisfy also atheists and Catholics who wish to live in a society where the role of religion is less – or more – public.

While Pope Francis visits Lampedusa, maintains an active Twitter profile and, perhaps, enjoys watching Sorrentino's *The Young Pope*, other religious events occur in Europe. A video created by Muslim students born in France becomes viral because it criticizes Islamic-inspired terrorist attacks and shows that Islam can exist in harmony with European culture. In Italy, atheist groups oppose the presence of the Catholic crucifix in public schools, claiming the importance of state secularism in a series of blog posts and official statements. In a number of European countries, Italy and France in particular, informal Catholic groups gather in squares and remain still, silently protesting against same-sex unions and the so-called "gender ideology," and diffuse their messages mainly through the internet. These events, and many others, usually do not become media events such as the Pope's visit in Lampedusa. They also tell different stories, which often contrast with the concept of Catholic secularism as described above: Muslims are not only those who arrive by boat in Lampedusa; atheists do not necessarily welcome the presence of the Pope in certain secular spaces; and conservative attitudes of Catholic groups that are against gender theory remind more of fictional Pius XIII in *The Young Pope* than Pope Francis blessing the poor in Lampedusa.

The aim of this book is to tell these stories. It will not focus on the media status of the real Pope Francis or of the fictional Pope Pius XIII, even if it contributes providing a cultural and social framework where these stories are told. Rather, the book will describe how Pope Francis' presence on magazine covers, newspaper articles, and social networks is only a part of European religiosity. It will talk about how certain groups try to discuss religion through mediated actions and discourses that arguably aspire to become media events. In the following chapters, I will tell these stories by analyzing the blogs, written in French and Italian, of certain groups of Muslims, atheists, and Catholics. These groups constitute an important facet of European religiosity because they symbolically and implicitly refuse to accept the concept of Catholic secularism, even if in antithetical ways from each other: they imagine a more multicultural society, a more secular society, or a more religious society. In so doing, they force a re-thinking of European religious identities.

These stories are often overlooked by many media platforms, but can be told in non-institutionalized and non-conventional spaces, such as the internet. In contemporary Europe, the internet is pervasive and conditions many aspects of culture and society, including religion. This book proposes to employ the theory of hypermediation to understand internet-mediated religious changes in Europe. Building on the theory of mediation, hypermediation describes the contemporary media moment where the proliferation of digital technologies intensifies human interactions in terms of speed and emotions (Scolari 2015). When they have access to digital technologies, people approach everyday life in an interconnected way. This book presents the theory of hypermediation in relation to religion, which stands in a fluid relationship with the secular and the post-secular. Media embed simultaneously material, institutional, and technological characteristics. Indeed, religious discourses continuously intersect with non-religious narratives, and most instances of everyday life involve some forms of media. The theory aims at capturing this complex character of mediated religion: the discourses of the Pope and the actions of other religious groups are, today, hypermediated. The theory of hypermediation explains how certain Muslim, atheist, and Catholic groups employ blogs to blur the boundaries between various media platforms and tell stories that aspire to have the same public relevance of those that see the Pope as the main character.

Religious change often occurs in terms of space. "Hypermediated religious spaces" are those digital venues that are relevant to understand religious change. The internet allows discussions about the space that religion and the secular should – or should not – occupy within the public sphere. Digital spaces can amplify actions that occur in physical spaces, create online communities, and help people discuss their religiosity. A focus on space allows exploring embodied and tangible religious forms also in relation to internet practices. Space is analyzed through three dialectical pairings: mainstream and alternative spaces; public and private spaces; and real and imaginary spaces. These pairings represent lenses through which it is possible to analyze contemporary religious-related phenomena. Groups that perceive themselves as socially marginalized may try to establish their voices through the internet; groups that wish for religion to remain in the private sphere, or become more public, may write blogs to express their views; and groups that wish to change the society in which they live, may employ digital spaces to imagine a different reality. These groups create hypermediated religious spaces when they establish dynamics that would likely not exist in a purely physical community and address religion in ways that would probably not be possible without the internet.

This book explores how hypermediated religious spaces can help understanding religious change in contemporary Catholic Europe. Innovatively applying the theory of hypermediation to religion, the contribution this book aims at giving to the existing literature on religion and media is a new approach to digital religion. By focusing on Europe, and in particular on case studies in languages other than English, it analyzes geographical areas often overlooked by other studies, as addressed in the following section. In addition, it explains how blogs are ideal to understand questions of space as they offer venues to narratively articulate religious feelings and identities, as will be explained below. Then, the chapter addresses the methodology employed to study blogging practices and describes my experience in approaching them. Lastly, an outline of the book will briefly explain how the chapters are organized.

Why Catholic Europe?

Europe has been defined as "exceptional" because it is more secular than other parts of the world (Davie 2002; Torpey 2010). However, this does not mean that religion does not exist in Europe anymore. On the contrary, various instances of religious re-publicization and revival occur in contemporary Europe, making religion more public (and mediated) than it used to be (Herbert 2011). Indeed, religion in contemporary Europe "receives more attention now in public discourse than it did just a few decades ago" (Green 2010, 300). The social and media visibility of Christianity, as exemplified by the visit of Pope Francis to Lampedusa, shows how religion still occupies a role in the European public sphere and in media representations. Religion remains a relevant resource for identity articulation (Schnabel and Hjerm 2014), as the majority of the European population – 74.5 percent – self-identify as Christian (Masci 2015). The model of Catholic secularism, which exists in various European areas, provides venues to articulate – and resist – religious identities in between religion and the secular. Therefore, Europe can be defined as an "exception" not because it is entirely secular, but because it witnesses religious transformations that likely do not occur in the same way in other places. It is this exceptionalism that makes Europe an interesting area to understand interactions between religion and media.

The unique character of religion in Europe is the result of historical processes. Christianity had an important role in shaping European culture and society, establishing itself in connection with state power and within public spaces already in late antiquity. However, Christianity in Europe has always coexisted with other religions, such as Islam (Allievi 2003). In addition, Christianity is characterized by intestine differences, which culminated with the Reformation in the sixteenth century (Horsfield 2015).

Significant historical events after the Reformation substantially shaped contemporary European religiosity. On the one hand, the distinction of religion and the secular, started during the Reformation, was further elaborated by seventeenth-century intellectuals who advanced the idea that the secular could be applied to all spheres of society. This idea resulted in the concept of *laïcité* which characterized the Enlightenment and the French Revolution (Taylor 2007), and which today usually indicates the French model of state-church separation. On the other hand, the Peace of Westphalia sanctioned the end of religious conflicts in Europe, advancing the principle of *cuius regio eius religio* (whose realm, his religion). This event established the principle that religions are mutually exclusive and created the political model of state religion (Beyer 2016). Both the Enlightenment's conceptualization of secularism and the Westphalian intertwinement between religion and state power arguably provide a historical explanation for the current "exceptional" character of European religiosity.

The intertwining of religion and secularism assumes a peculiar character in Catholic countries because of the structure of the Catholic Church. After the Second Vatican Council, the Catholic Church left the private sphere of practice to enter the public sphere of civil society. Recognizing the principle of religious freedom and the modern doctrine of human rights, the Church established itself as a global and public institution (Casanova 1996). Catholicism – whose etymology comes from the Greek *Katholicos*, "universal" – aims at reaching the entire humankind because it is based on universal concepts such as the dignity of human existence. The public and international character of the Catholic Church arguably contributes to framing its relations with secular institutions, as in the case of Pope Francis' visit to Lampedusa. Religious and secular media contribute to the publicity of the Catholic Church. Therefore, a focus on the context of Catholic Europe allows reflecting on how religious identities are articulated alongside – and, sometimes, in contrast with – the influence of the Vatican, a strong religious institution with universalistic aspirations that often interacts with secular organizations.

Countries in Catholic Europe conceptualize the cultural and social role of the Catholic Church in different ways. While some countries enforce a strict separation of church and state, others sustain agreements with certain religions (Sandberg and Doe 2007; Torfs 2010). By looking at sources in French and Italian, this book focuses mostly – but not only – on two Catholic European countries: France and Italy. They both belong to the Southern European area, characterized by "the historical memory of tight bonds between a majority religion and state institutions" and a "specificity in the interactions between religion and politics" (Giorgi and Itçaina 2016, 276). Historically, the Catholic Church sustained a strong public presence in Southern Europe and continues to influence certain aspects of contemporary society and politics. However, France and Italy represent two antithetical models of state-church relations. In Italy, Catholicism holds an important public role because of the presence of the Vatican (as the series *The Young Pope* aptly reminds); in France, the concept of *laïcité* was elaborated and continues to inform national identity. It is for this reason that case studies from these two countries can help to understand various nuances of religion in Catholic Europe. Here below these countries' main characteristics in terms of religiosity are summarized.

Italy is a formally secular country, but the state has agreements – *concordato* – with a number of religious organizations with which it sustains cooperation (Willaime 2009). During the Fascist dictatorship of the 1920s, the 1930s, and 1940s, the Pope signed the Lateran Pacts which established the Catholic Church as state religion (Toronto 2008). The concordat with the Catholic Church remained in place until 1984, when the Italian government removed Catholic clergy from the state's payroll. In exchange, the state instituted the *otto per mille*, a tax system that allows citizens to support a religion of choice among those that have an agreement with the Italian government. However, not all religious institutions have a *concordato* with the Italian state, as, for example, Islam is not among the beneficiaries of the *otto per mille*. Despite the formal plurality of the Italian state, Catholicism maintains a central position in Italian society: 82.2 percent of Italians self-identify as Catholic (Pew Templeton 2017), and an even higher number of people receive Catholic baptism. As a result, the Catholic Church has a prominent role in civil society (Garelli 2007), exemplified by the presence of the crucifix in public spaces (such as city halls) and Catholic education in public schools (Frisina 2011; Leigh and Ahdar 2012; Ozzano and Giorgi 2013). In addition, because of this public role of Catholicism, Italian media and public discourses tend to frame Italian identity as fundamentally Catholic (Ardizzoni 2007).

France, different from Italy, enforces a regime of *laïcité*, which entails a strict separation of church and state. The law of 1905, while guaranteeing freedom of religion, states that the government does not recognize or support any religion (Bowen 2010; Kelly 2017). Despite the principle of state secularism, 72 percent of the French population is estimated to believe in a religion, with more than half this number – 60 percent – being Catholics (Pew Templeton 2017). In addition, religion still maintains a role in French civil society. For example, the principle of *laïcité* does not apply to all French regions, as the Alsace-Moselle and certain overseas territories have specific agreements with the Catholic Church (Menéndez 2005). *Laïcité* does not entail the non-interference of the state in religious matters; on the contrary, the government oversees religious activities and carries tasks on behalf of religions that it recognizes. For example, it finances public Sunday religious broadcast and subsidizes religious buildings built before 1905, which are mostly Christian (Bowen 2010). Moreover, the French colonial past and increasing migrations from Islamic countries has resulted in a growing Muslim minority, often deemed incompatible with *laïcité* because of the public visibility of Islamic dress (Ardizzoni 2004). As a result, the parliament reinforced the concept of *laïcité* by prohibiting religious symbols in educational establishments and requiring religious neutrality for government employees and civil servants (Maeder, Dempsey, and Pozzulo 2012; Kavakci and Kraeplin 2016). These laws have been often supported by anti-Islamic political and social groups, which sometimes advocate for a greater public role of Catholicism to oppose migrations (Davies 2010). Therefore, the French government, while not formally recognizing and supporting religions, is far from ignoring them or considering them unimportant in the public sphere.

Analyzing discourses in French and Italian media puts emphasis on these two national contexts, but it is not limited by national boundaries. Indeed, the blogs explored in this book often articulate discourses that have global aspirations and target other European countries where these languages are spoken or understood, sometimes translating posts in English or in other languages for an international audience. Therefore, the following chapters will talk about narratives that target and concern various countries in Europe, Belgium in particular. With French as one of its national languages and Catholicism as a majority religion, Belgium is, together with Italy and France, among the founders of the European Union. The capital of Belgium, Brussels, hosts the official seat of the European Commission, the Council of the European Union, and the European Council, thus being the *de facto* capital of the European Union and a strategic point for EU-related activity, including religious bodies that function as lobbies to the EU (Foret 2009). Because some of the analyzed groups are part of European-level networks, their discourses often directly or indirectly mention activities in Belgium in order to target European institutions.

Italy, France, and other Catholic European countries witness similar patterns of religious change. For example, the Muslim population is steadily increasing (Roy 2013); atheists tend not only to grow in numbers, but also to become more vocal about their ideas and create associations to diffuse *laïcité* (Taira and Illman 2012); certain Catholic groups engage in activism – for example, against same-sex unions – to diffuse a specific understanding of religious values, showing that religious change is also represented by increasing heterogeneity within the Catholic Church (Paternotte 2015). These three examples – the growth of Islam and atheism, and the increasing visibility of certain Catholic groups – do not represent the only trends of religious change in Catholic Europe. However, I explore them in this book because they, in ways often antithetical to each other, can create hypermediated spaces that symbolically oppose certain representations of Catholic secularism.

These groups are not religious *stricto sensu* and are not connected to religious institutions (in case of atheists, they articulate their values on the very rejection of religion); even if, for the sake of brevity, I sometimes name them as "religious groups," they are groups that discuss religion and religious identities. In so doing, they tell stories from innovative viewpoints:

European Muslims try to break existing stereotypes and show that they can conciliate different identities; atheist groups extensively talk about religion, suggesting that they need to be taken into account alongside religious groups in order to understand religious change; and Catholic anti-gender theory activism attests that social movements can be conservative rather than progressive, and take action beyond the authority of the Pope. Because of their innovative discourses, case studies based on these three phenomena can arguably be among the most interesting examples of religious hypermediation in the "exceptionalism" context of Catholic Europe.

The focus on Catholic Europe represents a novelty in the field of religion and media. While systematic analyzes in Europe have often interested Northern and Protestant countries (Hjarvard and Lovheim 2012), there is a lack of studies concerning the Southern Catholic area. The choice of exploring blogs in French and Italian aims at producing scholarship on sociolinguistic contexts that are often marginal in the literature on digital media. Blogs in various parts of the world seem to develop in ways that are different from US blogs, yet literature on blogging in non-English languages remains scarce (Russell and Echchaibi 2009). In addition, the variety of religious models in Europe – such as the French principle of *laïcité* or the Italian *concordato* – cannot be captured by studies that focus only on English-speaking countries. With this focus on languages other than English, this book aims at telling stories that can help to better understand the heterogeneity of Europe and its model of Catholic secularism. And, in telling these stories, it seeks to answer the following questions: Which discourses and actions contribute to religious change in Catholic Europe? How do different and competing religious groups conceptualize the space of religion in Catholic Europe? What kind of society do they wish to create, and what is their social impact? These questions are explored through the analysis of blogs, because they are spaces where people can discuss religion between media practices and social actions.

Why blogs?

Religion exists also on the internet. From faith forums to virtual churches and mosques on Second Life, from prayer apps to YouTube live streaming of religious events, it seems that contemporary religion increasingly occurs also in digital spaces. With the term "networked religion," Heidi Campbell (2012a) defines the ways in which cultural and social shifts occur in the online religious experiences, allowing negotiations of authorities and identities. The creation of religious spaces on the internet often results in changes within religious communities and in the experience of religion. Therefore, the internet is useful to understand contemporary religiosity and religious changes. This book focuses on blogs because they are good examples of how believers create religious spaces on the internet, mirroring and engaging with physical spaces. Blogs can thus be employed as examples of hyper-mediated religious spaces that contribute to religious change in Europe.

A "blog," short for "web log," is an online journal intended for a public audience (Campbell 2010), generally frequently updated and connected with other websites and social platforms (Schmidt 2007; Cheong, Halavais, and Kwon 2008). This book employs a flexible definition of blogs, which includes social networks and microblogging practices – such as Facebook pages and Twitter accounts – used to circulate blogs' posts (Keller 2015). The next chapters will talk about blogs that have different interfaces, which might or might not include comments, posts' authorship, and hyperlinks to other platforms. This broad definition allows taking into account blogs in their ability to interactively engage a community of readers and to blur the boundaries between producers and consumers (Wakeford and Cohen 2008). According to this definition, blogs constitute spaces where people write opinions and share experiences, ask and answer reciprocal questions, and often come to see each other as part of the same community.

Blogs are examples of hypermediated religious spaces because they blur "the lines between orality and literacy, corporeality and spatiality, public and private." (boyd 2006, 2). This means that they are based on writing, but they also reproduce oral expressions, thus mirroring conversations that normally happen in physical spaces. They exist online, but they discuss what happens in society, embedding pictures and videos that reproduce offline spaces. They are public spaces, but, at the same time, discuss private experiences of individuals and communities. Spatial metaphors, and in particular the concepts of "ethical space" (Lövheim 2011) and "third space" (Hoover and Echchaibi 2014), have been used to describe blogging practices. Blogs can constitute spaces where people discuss religion and form religious-like communities because of some characteristics they have.

First, they provide alternative venues for grassroots journalism (Russell and Echchaibi 2009). News-related blogs differ from traditional journalism as they can incorporate reader inputs, remain available in time, and confront matters from different sources (Graves 2007). Blogs that discuss religion may thus provide information by selecting news from religious and non-religious platforms, and by discussing issues that other media outlets overlook. Second, they can help define personal values and identities. Often created as public diaries, blogs allow for storytelling practices that make private experiences available in the public sphere (McCullagh 2008; Lövheim 2011). Therefore, they help the discursive articulation of the religious self through descriptions of everyday forms of religiosity (Cheong, Halavais, and Kwon 2008). Third, blogs allow for the creation of resistive discourses. Groups that do not belong to mainstream culture sometimes suffer from a lack of recognition and symbolic power (Couldry 2013). Blogging can help these groups find a voice and create discourses that challenge mainstream representations. While blogs can rarely provoke direct social change, they can contribute to a "cultural thickening" of the perception of religious identities that can impact long-term cultural change (Echchaibi 2013), thus establishing themselves as counter-hegemonic spaces.

This book analyzes blogs that function both as public spaces of alternative journalism and as venues to articulate private narratives. These blogs are online spaces that discuss religion as well as family life, politics, activism, and culture. Being multiauthored and aimed at reaching a large audience, they are not representative of all atheists, Muslims, and Catholics in Catholic Europe, but rather negotiate specific religious identities and religious spaces. Aware of the fact that digital practices are dependent on conditions of access, literacy, and technological skills, these blogs are examples of hypermediated religious spaces that connect with offline activity and produce religious-related discourses.

Studying religious blogs can add new perspectives to the existing literature on religion and media. Blogs attracted considerable scholarly attention, especially as they reached popularity in early 2000. While social networks have partially replaced blogging, they also enhance blogs' discourses by allowing greater circulation of posts (Tremayne 2006). However, blogging as a religious practice remains underresearched. Indeed,

> the presence of religious discourse in blogs calls for fresh thinking about the representation of believers and their faiths, motivations for religious storytelling, the constitution of religious practices, together with the interplay of online and offline connections among religious believers, nonbelievers, and seekers.
>
> (Cheong, Halavais, and Kwon 2008, 108)

Because religious blogging is a relevant practice that contributes to religious changes on various levels, it is beneficial to elaborate theories that can help in understanding this phenomenon. The scarcity of studies on religious-related blogs – with some notable exceptions, such as Heidi Campbell (2010, 2012a) and Mia Lövheim's (2011) works – elicits further reflections on the relationships between blogs and religion. Why do certain religious groups choose the internet to articulate their narratives? Would they be able to express themselves in the same way without the internet? Are they successful in using blogs to establish their voices? How does the internet change the understanding of religion within given groups? In exploring these questions, this book offers material for understanding various facets of digital religion besides blogging. In particular, it aims at providing a "fresh thinking" about religion and the internet through the theory of hypermediation, offering new theoretical and methodological reflections on digital religion.

The story of this book

For many people, it would be difficult to imagine life without the internet. Because of its pervasive character, the internet highlights most areas of life, social relationships, and identity discourses. Therefore, scholars are increasingly interested in methods to understand society through the study of the internet. Richard Rogers (2015) describes an approach leading to a "new era of internet research." He continues writing, "The issue no longer is how much of society and culture is online, but rather how to diagnose cultural change and societal conditions by means of the Internet" (21). With these words, Rogers conceptualizes the internet as both an object of study and a tool that can help scholars understand various aspects of society and culture.

This approach is useful to analyze hypermediated religious spaces. The groups I explore in this book employ the internet as the preferred – if not only – venue to talk about society. Therefore, it is relevant to take into account both the blogs' content and the broader social context where blogs are created. In order to do so, Nick Couldry (2012) looks at "actions that are *directly oriented* to media, actions that *involve* media without necessary having media as their aim or object; and actions whose possibility is *conditioned* by the prior existence, presence or functioning of the media" (110, emphasis in original). In his theorization of a non-media-centric media studies approach, Couldry considers media as venues for representations of the world, which are defined and conditioned by people's practices. It is methodologically useful to take into account the ways people use media, as well as the ways in which media modify and condition people's everyday actions (Couldry 2010). In looking at people's media practices, it is possible to conceptualize the internet as both an object of study and the platform through which one can understand religious change.

Therefore, I outlined a hybrid methodological approach to analyze blogs and their context of production, in order to understand actions "directly oriented at media" and actions that "involve media." As it is common for researchers to combine different methods, I perform textual analysis, interviews, and, in some cases, observation. The novelty of my approach lies in using methods that are not specific to the study of the internet to understand various aspects of blogs: the content of the posts, the ways bloggers create and circulate the posts, the motivations behind their engagement with blogging, the offline activities that are connected to the blogs. In this way, I qualitatively explore different elements that the analysis of blog content alone would probably not reveal.

As for the textual analysis, I explore blogs as texts that contain indications of people's religious practices and beliefs. In the field of Religious Study, the analysis of sacred texts is usually paired with the study of written accounts of everyday life and comments about religious practices. The internet is no exception in representing a form of textuality that is relevant to understand people's religious lives. I familiarized myself with the blogs I was studying by extensively reading them and selecting entries that are relevant to understand religious change, taking into account the timeframe between 2011 and 2016. In certain cases, blogs started after 2011, while others ended before 2016, so the timeframe can vary in relation to specific case studies, as will be discussed in the next chapters. Then, inspired by the principles of Critical Discourse Analysis (CDA), I performed an ideological and textual analysis of blogs content.

Considering the complex and interactive nature of blogging, I took into account comments to posts (when blogs allow commenting) as well as connections with social network platforms and other websites. I considered blog's discourses as the product of social relationships heavily informed by groups' identities (Wodak and Bush 2004; Bliuc et al. 2012). I looked at recurrent expressions by keeping in mind that language is never neutral, but reflects power structures within social groups (Bakhtin 2010). Indeed, groups that consider themselves as not belonging to the dominant culture, for example, those that wish to criticize the concept of Catholic secularism, may use blogs to negotiate their social positions in relation to other groups and communities. They may employ highly emotional language to invite readers to empathize with their ideas, use sarcasm and irony to belittle other claims, or suggest certain metaphors to describe how they would modify society.

This approach to textual analysis involves an active participant reading that negotiates the meaning of the text (Souto-Manning 2014) and can be successfully paired with qualitative interviews. In interviewing bloggers, I could understand why and how they decide to engage with blogging and under which circumstances they write. Because the blogs I analyze are written by multiple authors, I was able to collect different experiences within each group. I often met with bloggers in person, sometimes visiting groups and associations' headquarters; when geographical distances prevented face-to-face conversations, I conducted my interviews on Skype, facilitated by the interviewees' familiarity with technology-mediated interactions. As blogs tend to attract a high number of readers and have a public role, some of the bloggers had already been interviewed by academics or media practitioners. I intentionally asked general questions that allowed my interviewees to freely express their opinions. In this way, the interviews assumed the form of long and spontaneous conversations about different religious groups and their position in the media sphere and in society.

I was able to perform interviews with bloggers from Muslim, atheist, and Catholic organizations based in Italy and France. Members of Muslim and atheist groups generally responded positively to my initial inquiries and agreed to be part of the project, sometimes actively collaborating by providing additional sources and contacts for my work. However, I encountered challenges in interviewing members of the Catholic-inspired group *Sentinelle in Piedi* because they either ignored my messages or explicitly explained that they avoid talking with journalists and researchers. As will be analyzed in the next chapters, this constitutes an interesting data: in some cases, groups avoid certain forms of publicity to express an open media critique. I was nonetheless able to interview members of *La Manif pour Tous*, another Catholic-inspired group, and I observed a public protest of the group *Sentinelle in Piedi*. On this occasion, I had informal conversations with a spokesperson and some of the group's members.

Questions of gender, ethnicity, and race cannot be ignored when it comes to religion. In relation to gender, it is important to notice that almost all of my interviewees were men. This was not intentional, as I contacted the main spokesperson of each group regardless of their gender and asked them to suggest bloggers to interview. The fact that I was mostly suggested to approach men constitutes a surprising and interesting data, considering that women generally write blogs more than men (Lövheim 2011). In the case of atheist blogs, this might be partially explained by the fact that organized atheism seems to be more appealing to men (Taira 2015); the atheist blogs I analyze, indeed, are mostly male-dominated. However, this is not the case for Muslims and Catholics: as will be explained in the following chapters, the Muslim blog *Yalla*, while founded by two men, has more female bloggers than male, and the Catholic groups *La Manif Pour Tous* and *Sentinelle in Piedi* rely on formal or informal female leadership. Despite this, the people who emerged as more likely to answer interview inquiries were men. I thus consider that my interview dataset might lack an accurate gender perspective, especially given that the blogs often discuss gender-related questions: reproductive rights, gender equality, Muslim garments for women.

Ethnicity and race mostly emerged in interviews with Muslims. In my case studies, atheist and Catholic groups tend to be prominently white, and both interviews and blog analysis suggest that they do not often discuss the question of race. I considered the fact that only Muslims talk about ethnicity and race as an interesting data to understand power relationships between these groups and society at large. I gave particular attention to the implicit and explicit mentioning of gender, race, and ethnicity while performing textual analysis on blog posts, in order to better understand motivations and backgrounds of all the bloggers and acquire insights that the interviewees might not have provided.

When approaching interviewees, I often had the feeling that I was perceived as an "outsider." While a researcher with an "insider" position in relation to the studied groups can gain better access to their subjects (Echchaibi 2011), I tried to approach all groups by intentionally positioning myself as an "outsider." I choose this positionality to gain a better understanding of the groups' antithetical and sometimes conflicting claims. At times, during the interviews, I shared my opinions about secularism and multiculturalism to establish a constructive dialogue, but I also disclosed my book's aims of describing competing religious identities. Aware that there is an inevitable degree of subjectivity in social research, I tried to give opposite claims and ideologies the same importance and to describe social phenomena regardless of my personal opinions.

My knowledge of languages and cultures of the bloggers facilitates my approach to both textual analysis and interviews, partially compensating for my "outsider" position. Born and raised in Italy, I lived in France and Belgium as an adult. When working in Brussels for European-level NGOs, I occupied a privileged position to observe institutional and cultural negotiations of European identity, also in terms of religious identity. Living outside Europe – for few months in Japan and for a number of years in the US doing my Ph.D. – also helped me to understand from a distance the peculiarities of European culture and religiosity. Therefore, I was able to situate my analysis in a social and cultural context with which I am familiar and to approach the bloggers in their own language. My fluency in Italian and French allowed for the understanding of the linguistic nuances of various discourses. In translating quotes from Italian and French to English, I privileged meaning over form: I did not strictly follow the original sentence structure, but adapted it to obtain the same meaning in the English translation. I tried to convey the sense of anger, sarcasm, fear, or satisfaction that emerges from texts and interviews, sometimes (especially in the case of neologism) also employing words in the original language. This book, therefore, aims at giving relevance to the linguistic and cultural context of blog production and in combining various methodological approaches in order to understand blogs as hypermediated religious spaces.

About this book

This book analyzes religious change in Catholic Europe through the study of blogs. Catholic Europe is an interesting area to study the relationship between religion and digital media because religious groups often create discourses alongside – and, sometimes, against – the strong mediated presence of the Vatican and the concept of Catholic secularism. Blogs represent relevant case studies to understand religious change because they can offer venues for the discussion of religious practices and identities outside religious institutions. They are hypermediated religious spaces that have connections with physical spaces and discuss the role of religion and the secular in Europe. Three case studies – Muslim, atheist, and Catholic blogs – illustrate this theory in practice and help to reflect on religious change in Europe.

Chapter 1 critically analyzes the growing body of academic research in the field of religion and media, situating the study of religious blogs within the existing literature. The chapter offers a definition of "religion" by exploring its relationship with the secular and the post-secular, and a definition of "media" by means of a review of the existing theories of mediation, mediatization, and religious-social shaping of technology. Building on these theoretical frameworks, the theory of hypermediation is applied to the study of religion in order to capture the social changes created by digital media, including the accelerated pace of contemporary life and the emotional character of participatory culture.

Chapter 2 builds on the analysis in Chapter 1 in order to apply a spatial perspective to the theory of hypermediation. Blogs are understood as "hypermediated religious spaces" that connect activities in online and offline environments. The chapter discusses spatial theories in relation to the internet by defining hypermediated religious spaces through three dialectical pairings: as for the work of Antonio Gramsci and the Cultural Studies tradition on hegemony, space can be mainstream or alternative; drawing from critical reflections of the Habermasian public sphere, space is described in public and private terms; and, following the concepts of "myth" and "heterotopia," space can be considered as real and imaginary. These dichotomies help to understand how the concept of space completes the theory of hypermediation by putting emphasis on the connections between media and physical spaces, as well as between various media platforms. The concept of hypermediated religious spaces is empirically discussed in Chapter 3, 4, and 5, which are organized thematically around religious phenomena: Muslim, atheist, and Catholic blogs.

Chapter 3 presents the case of Muslim bloggers who use digital spaces to show the compatibility of Islam with European values, for example, commenting and condemning terrorist attacks claimed by Islamic fundamentalists. The chapter describe the website of EMF (*Etudiantes Musulmans de France*, French Muslim Students, www.emf-asso.com), and the blog *Yalla Italia* (www.yallaitalia.it), written by youth born in Italy from immigrant parents; these two digital spaces go against stereotypes that describe Muslims as "other" to Western identities, and offer narratives of everyday activities that normalize the presence of Islam in Europe. These internet spaces often describe the presence of Muslims in public spaces by discussing the concept of *laïcité* and the female veil. In elaborating strategies to adapt Islam to the European culture, negotiate religious authorities, and discuss the terms of European citizenship, these blogs seek to articulate hybrid Muslim European identities that may contribute creating a more multicultural and multifaith society.

Chapter 4 describes blogging practices of atheist organizations that show how religious re-publicization coincides also with an increasing visibility of atheist ideas. It talks about the blog of the Italian association UAAR (*Unione degli Atei e degli Agnostici Razionalisti*, Union of Atheists and Rationalist Agnostics, www.blog.uaar.it) and the blog of the French association UFAL (*Union des Familles Laïques*, Union of Secular Families www.ufal.org), which are engaged in a variety of activities and campaigns that help to articulate atheist identities based on shared values, such as freedom of speech. In relation to specific national contexts, atheist associations are concerned with the prominent role that the Catholic Church occupies at physical and symbolic level in public spaces. In addition, atheists often see the growing presence of Muslims wearing religious garments as incompatible with *laïcité*. Blogs, therefore, discuss expressions of material religion and criticize religious institutions to establish atheism both as an alternative that should exist alongside religious identities and as a principle that should occupy a more prominent social role than religion.

Chapter 5 presents the digital activities of groups that are against gender ideology and organize protests against same-sex unions to protect traditional Catholic values. It analyzes the Catholic-inspired association *La Manif Pour Tous* (Demo for Everybody, www.lamanifpourtous.fr), which has been created in France, and the group *Sentinelle in Piedi* (Standing Watchmen, www.sentinelleinpiedi.it/category/blog), particularly prominent in Italy. They represent a form of religious change within the Catholic Church as they mainly involve lay Catholics engaged in public militancy. These movements consider so-called "gender theory" as threatening to religious identities. They indirectly advocate for a re-appropriation in religious terms of the public sphere and for a more prominent role of the Catholic Church in civil society. Such protests often symbolically charge a public and secular space with religious meanings, with participants either marching through public streets or remaining still and reading books. Blogs are used also to negotiate religious authority and to respond to anxieties for the progressive secularization of late modernity.

The book concludes by offering remarks on how the study of hypermediated religious spaces can enrich the understanding of religious change in Europe. The chapter argues that the theory of hypermediation can be used both to study alternative forms of religion in contemporary Europe and to enhance the researcher's role as public scholar. In this way, researchers may decide to create hypermediated religious spaces to amplify the voices of certain religious groups. The aim of the chapter is to provide some reflections about future processes of religious change in Europe, which at the present moment seem difficult to foresee. In an episode of Sorrentino's *The Young Pope*, Pius XIII says that he would like the Catholic Church to go back to being "inaccessible and mysterious." He says,

> What I want is absolute love and total devotion to God. Could that mean a Church only for the few? . . . I say: better to have a few that are reliable than to have a great many that are distractible and indifferent.

The fictional Pius XIII seems to be interested in true faith rather than popularity. On the contrary, real Pope Francis engages with believers in a friendly way, probably trying to maintain the popularity of the Catholic Church. However, it is not clear what the future of Catholic Europe will be. Will it become more multicultural, allowing Muslims to be more visible in the public sphere? Will it become more secular, drastically decreasing the public role of the Vatican and its relationships with politics? Will a Catholic Church "only for the few" emerge, facilitated by the active militancy of certain groups? Or none of these possibilities? This book cannot give a definitive answer to these questions. But it can suggest that the future of Catholic Europe might depend also on religious changes that occur in non-traditional spaces, such as the internet.

References

Allievi, Stefano. 2003. *Islam italiano. Viaggio nella seconda religione del paese.* Torino: Einaudi.

Ardizzoni, Michela. 2004. "Unveiling the Veil: Gendered Discourses and the (In)Visibility of the Female Body in France." *Women's Studies* 33 (5): 629–49. doi:10.1080/00497870490464440.

Ardizzoni, Michela. 2007. *North/South, East/West: Mapping Italianness on Television*. Lanham, MD: Lexington Books.

Asad, Talal. 2003. *Formations of the Secular: Christianity, Islam, Modernity*. 1st edition. Stanford, CA: Stanford University Press.

Bakhtin, M. M. 2010. *The Dialogic Imagination: Four Essays*. Austin, TX: University of Texas Press.

Beyer, Peter. 2016. "Sensing Religion, Observing Religion, Reconstructing Religion: Contingency and Pluralization in Post-Westphalian Context." *Social Compass* 63 (2): 234–50. doi:10.1177/0037768616628794.

Bliuc, Ana-Maria, Craig McGarty, Lisa Hartley, and Daniela Muntele Hendres. 2012. "Manipulating National Identity: The Strategic Use of Rhetoric by Supporters and Opponents of the 'Cronulla Riots' in Australia." *Ethnic and Racial Studies* 35 (12): 2174–94. doi:10.1080/01419870.2011.600768.

Bowen, John R. 2010. "Religious Discrimination and Religious Governance Across Secular and Islamic Countries: France and Indonesia as Limiting Cases." *American Behavioral Scientist* 53 (12): 1749–62. doi:10.1177/0002764210368095.

boyd, danah. 2006. "A Blogger's Blog: Exploring the Definition of a Medium." *Reconstruction* 6 (4).

Campbell, Heidi A. 2010. "Religious Authority and the Blogosphere." *Journal of Computer-Mediated Communication* 15 (2): 251–76. doi:10.1111/j.1083-6101.2010.01519.x.

Campbell, Heidi A. 2012a. "Understanding the Relationship Between Religion Online and Offline in a Networked Society." *Journal of the American Academy of Religion* 80 (1): 64–93. doi:10.1093/jaarel/lfr074.

Casanova, José. 1996. "Global Catholicism and the Politics of Civil Society." *Sociological Inquiry* 66 (3): 356–73. doi:10.1111/j.1475-682X.1996.tb00225.x.

Cheong, Pauline Hope, Alexander Halavais, and Kyounghee Kwon. 2008. "The Chronicles of Me: Understanding Blogging as a Religious Practice." *Journal of Media and Religion* 7 (3): 107–31. doi:10.1080/15348420802223015.

Couldry, Nick. 2010. *Why Voice Matters: Culture and Politics After Neoliberalism*. Los Angeles; London: Sage Publications, Incorporated.

Couldry, Nick. 2012. *Media, Society, World: Social Theory and Digital Media Practice*. 1st edition. Cambridge; Malden, MA: Polity.

Couldry, Nick. 2013. *Media Interventions: Afterword by Nick Couldry*. Edited by Kevin Howley. 1st edition. New York, NY: Peter Lang Publishing Inc.

Davie, Grace. 2002. *Europe: The Exceptional Case: Parameters of Faith in the Modern World*. London: Darton, Longman & Todd Ltd.

Davies, Peter. 2010. "The Front National and Catholicism: From Intégrisme to Joan of Arc and Clovis." *Religion Compass* 4 (9): 576–87. doi:10.1111/j.1749-8171.2010.00237.x.

Dayan, Daniel, and Elihu Katz. 1994. *Media Events: The Live Broadcasting of History*. Reprint edizione. Cambridge, MA: The Belknap Press of Harvard University Press.

Echchaibi, Nabil. 2011. *Voicing Diasporas: Ethnic Radio in Paris and Berlin Between Cultural Renewal and Retention*. Lanham, MD: Lexington Books.

Echchaibi, Nabil. 2013. "Muslimah Media Watch: Media Activism and Muslim Choreographies of Social Change." *Journalism*. doi:10.1177/1464884913478360.

Foret, François. 2009. "Religion: A Solution or a Problem for the Legitimisation of the European Union?" *Religion, State and Society* 37 (1–2): 37–50. doi:10.1080/09637490802693213.

Frisina, Annalisa. 2011. "The Making of Religious Pluralism in Italy: Discussing Religious Education from a New Generational Perspective." *Social Compass* 58 (2): 271–84. doi:10.1177/0037768611402611.

Garelli, Franco. 2007. "The Public Relevance of the Church and Catholicism in Italy." *Journal of Modern Italian Studies* 12 (1): 8–36. doi:10.1080/13545710601132722.

Giorgi, Alberta, and Xabier Itçaina. 2016. "Religion and Local Politics in Southern Europe: A Research Agenda." *Religion, State and Society* 44 (3): 276–95. doi:10.1080/09637494.2016.1212588.

Graves, Lucas. 2007. "The Affordances of Blogging: A Case Study in Culture and Technological Effects." *Journal of Communication Inquiry* 31 (4): 331–46. doi:10.1177/0196859907305446.

Green, Todd. 2010. "Religious Decline or Religious Change? Making Sense of Secularization in Europe." *Religion Compass* 4 (5): 300–11. doi:10.1111/j.1749-8171.2010.00216.x.

Herbert, David E. J. 2011. "Theorizing Religion and Media in Contemporary Societies: An Account of Religious 'publicization'." *European Journal of Cultural Studies* 14 (6): 626–48. doi:10.1177/1367549411419981.

Hjarvard, Stig, and Mia Lovheim, eds. 2012. *Mediatization and Religion: Nordic Perspectives*. Göteborg: Nordicom.

Hoover, Stewart, and Nabil Echchaibi. 2014. "Media Theory and the Third Spaces of Digital Religion." Working Paper Center for Media, Religion, and Culture.

Horsfield, Peter. 2015. *From Jesus to the Internet: A History of Christianity and Media*. 1st edition. Chichester, West Sussex; Malden, MA: Wiley-Blackwell.

Kavakci, Elif, and Camille R. Kraeplin. November 2016. "Religious Beings in Fashionable Bodies: The Online Identity Construction of Hijabi Social Media Personalities." *Media, Culture & Society*. doi:10.1177/0163443716679031.

Keller, Jessalynn. 2015. *Girls' Feminist Blogging in a Postfeminist Age*. New York, NY: Routledge.

Kelly, Michael. 2017. "Introduction Religion in France: Belief, Identity and Laïcité." *French Cultural Studies* 28 (1): 3–4. doi:10.1177/0957155816678596.

Leigh, Ian, and Rex Ahdar. 2012. "Post-Secularism and the European Court of Human Rights: Or How God Never Really Went Away." *The Modern Law Review* 75 (6): 1064–98. doi:10.1111/j.1468-2230.2012.00933.x.

Lövheim, Mia. 2011. "Young Women's Blogs as Ethical Spaces." *Information, Communication & Society* 14 (3): 338–54. doi:10.1080/1369118X.2010.542822.

Maeder, Evelyn, Julie Dempsey, and Joanna Pozzulo. 2012. "Behind the Veil of Juror Decision Making: Testing the Effects of Muslim Veils and Defendant Race in the Courtroom." *Criminal Justice and Behavior* 39 (5): 666–78. doi:10.1177/0093854812436478.

Masci, David. 2015. "Europe Projected to Retain Its Christian Majority, but Religious Minorities Will Grow." *Pew Research Center*. Accessed April 15. www.pewresearch.org/fact-tank/2015/04/15/europe-projected-to-retain-its-christian-majority-but-religious-minorities-will-grow/.

McCullagh, Karen. 2008. "Blogging: Self Presentation and Privacy." *Information & Communications Technology Law* 17 (1): 3–23. doi:10.1080/13600830801886984.

Menéndez, Agustín José. 2005. "A Christian or a Laïc Europe? Christian Values and European Identity." *Ratio Juris* 18 (2): 179–205. doi:10.1111/j.1467-9337.2005.00294.x.

Napolitano, Valentina. Forthcoming. "Francis, a Criollo Pope." *Journal of Royal Anthropological Institute*.

Ozzano, Luca, and Alberta Giorgi. 2013. "The Debate on the Crucifix in Public Spaces in Twenty-First Century Italy." *Mediterranean Politics* 18 (2): 259–75. doi :10.1080/13629395.2013.799344.

Paternotte, David. 2015. "Blessing the Crowds: Catholic Mobilisations against Gender in Europe." In *Anti-Genderismus: Sexualität und Geschlecht als Schauplätze aktueller politischer Auseinandersetzungen.* Edited by Sabine Hark, and Paula-Irene Villa. 1st edition. Bielefeld: Transcript.

Pew-Templeton: Global Religious Futures Project. 2017. Accessed June 27. www.globalreligiousfutures.org/.

Rogers, Richard. 2015. *Digital Methods.* Cambridge, MA: The MIT Press.

Roy, Olivier. 2013. "Secularism and Islam: The Theological Predicament." *The International Spectator* 48 (1): 5–19. doi:10.1080/03932729.2013.759365.

Russell, Adrienne, and Nabil Echchaibi. 2009. *International Blogging: Identity, Politics and Networked Publics.* 1st printing edition. New York, NY: Peter Lang International Academic Publishers.

Sandberg, Russell, and Norman Doe. 2007. "Church – State Relations in Europe." *Religion Compass* 1 (5): 561–78. doi:10.1111/j.1749-8171.2007.00040.x.

Schmidt, Jan. 2007. "Blogging Practices: An Analytical Framework." *Journal of Computer-Mediated Communication* 12 (4): 1409–27. doi:10.1111/j.1083-6101.2007.00379.x.

Scolari, Carlos A. 2015. "From (New)Media to (Hyper)Mediations. Recovering Jesús Martín-Barbero's Mediation Theory in the Age of Digital Communication and Cultural Convergence." *Information, Communication & Society* 18 (9): 1092–107. https://doi.org/10.1080/1369118X.2015.1018299.

Schnabel, Annette, and Mikael Hjerm. 2014. "How the Religious Cleavages of Civil Society Shape National Identity." *SAGE Open* 4 (1): 2158244014525417. doi:10.1177/2158244014525417.

Souto-Manning, Mariana. 2014. "Critical Narrative Analysis: The Interplay of Critical Discourse and Narrative Analyses." *International Journal of Qualitative Studies in Education* 27 (2): 159–80. https://doi.org/10.1080/09518398.2012.73 7046.

Taira, Temu Patrik. 2015. "Media and the Nonreligious." In *Religion, Media, and Social Change.* Edited by Kennet Granholm, Marcus Moberg, and Sofia Sjö. London: Routledge.

Taira, Teemu Patrik, and Ruth Illman. 2012. "The New Visibility of Atheism in Europe." https://helda.helsinki.fi/handle/10138/162153.

Taylor, Charles. 2007. *A Secular Age.* 1st edition. Cambridge, MA: The Belknap Press of Harvard University Press.

Torfs, Rik. 2010. "The Religion – State Relationship in Europe." *The Review of Faith & International Affairs* 8 (2): 15–20. doi:10.1080/15570274.2010.487987.

Toronto, James A. 2008. "Islam Italiano: Prospects for Integration of Muslims in Italy's Religious Landscape." *Journal of Muslim Minority Affairs* 28 (1): 61–82. doi:10.1080/13602000802011069.

Torpey, John. 2010. "A (Post-) Secular Age? Religion and the Two Exceptionalisms." *Social Research: An International Quarterly* 77 (1): 269–96.

Tremayne, Mark, ed. 2006. *Blogging, Citizenship, and the Future of Media.* New edition. London; New York, NY: Routledge.

Vilaça, Helena, Enzo Pace, Inger Furseth, and Per Pettersson, eds. 2014. *The Changing Soul of Europe: Religions and Migrations in Northern and Southern Europe.* 1st edition. Surrey, England; Burlington, VT: Routledge.

Wakefor, Nina, and Kris Cohen. 2008. "Fieldnotes in Public: Using Blogs for Research." In *The Sage Handbook of Online Research Methods*. Edited by Nigel Fielding. Los Angeles: Sage Publications, Incorporated.

Willaime, Jean-Paul. 2009. "European Integration, Laïcité and Religion." *Religion, State and Society* 37 (1–2): 23–35. doi:10.1080/09637490802693262.

Wodak, Ruth, and Brigitta Bush. 2004. "Approaches to Media Texts." In *The Sage Handbook of Media Studies*. Edited by John D. H. Downing, Ellen Wartella, Denis McQuail, and Philip Schlesinger. Thousand Oaks, CA: Sage Publications, Incorporated.

Web sources

Etudiantes Musulmanes de France: www.emf-asso.com
La Manif Pour Tous: www.lamanifpourtous.fr
Sentinelle in Piedi: www.sentinelleinpiedi.it/category/blog
Union des Familles Laïques: www.ufal.org
Unione degli Atei e degli Agnostici Razionalisti: www.blog.uaar.it
Yalla Italia: www.yallaitalia.it

1 The hypermediation of religion

Situating religion in a media-saturated world

The previous chapter has described various instances of mediated religion. Broadcast of Pope Francis' visit to Lampedusa, his pictures on magazines' covers, and his Twitter account show how various media platforms contribute in communicating religious messages to the audience. Many religious-inspired events – such as young Muslims making viral videos, atheists challenging the presence of religious symbols, Catholics organizing public protests – also exist in mediated forms. It is for this reason that Stewart Hoover (2006) suggests thinking of religion and media as intertwined elements that contribute to their mutual evolution. He writes, "They occupy the same spaces, serve many of the same purposes, and invigorate the same practices in late modernity. Today, is probably better to think of them as related than to think of them as separate" (9). Indeed, in contemporary Europe, media offer representations of religion and believers use media to negotiate their religious identities and practices. In relation to religious change, thinking about religion and media as related helps to understand the ways in which people approach religion in their everyday lives.

The marriage between religion and media is far from being a recent phenomenon or from being connected exclusively to digital technologies. From oral communication to printing, from religious icons to movies, from embodied practices to social networks, religion has always been mediated, asserts Peter Horsfield (2015). While he focuses on Christianity, Horsfield's remarks can be applied to other religious traditions, as well. Religious authority is often legitimated not only by religious knowledge, but also by the ability to communicate through media. The diffusion of media technologies – mass printing of sacred texts, religious sermons on television, religious leaders' social network accounts, just to mention some – is an example of how religion continuously adapts to new and available media. The communication strategy of the Vatican today does not represent an entirely new phenomenon, but rather a continuum with the past. For example, the Vatican's Twitter account diffuses messages that do not substantially differ from what Pope Francis says from the balcony of St Peter's Square in Rome, except for the fact that he addresses a virtual public instead of a physical one. In establishing himself as a "digital leader," the Pope transfers his religious role in the digital platform (Narbona 2016).

It is, however, important to consider that the pace of technological changes in Europe during the last century has been increasing faster, thus altering the perception of space and time. While religion has always been mediated, it now exists in a context where media are ubiquitous within society. The proliferation of media technologies leads to changes in terms of religious practices and meanings. This often results in an unconventional type of religion that exists outside institutions and that is defined also by media practices. As for the case studies of this book, Muslim groups frame themselves in terms of multiculturalism or youth action rather than religion; atheists form communities based on the very refusal of religion; Catholics eschew a direct connection with the Vatican and negotiate its authority. In addition, the blogs I analyze represent complex spaces that embed material forms, enter in conversation with media institutions, and refer to various digital technologies. Such connections are not always unproblematic, as there could be tensions with mainstream media or difficulties in emerging in non-media spaces. Therefore, they need to be analyzed in relation to the networks of actions and actors involved in their creation.

This chapter aims at providing working definitions of "religion" and "media" that go beyond traditional institutions and that are specific to phenomena of religious change occurring in Catholic Europe – definitions that could apply not only to the media strategy of the Vatican, but also to the mediated negotiations of religion that occur outside the Vatican. The chapter employs these definitions to outline the theory of hypermediation of religion, which seeks to capture religious change in a media-saturated world. The rest of the chapter is divided into three sections: the first section theorizes religion as being dependent on people's definitions and practices, and including seemingly non-religious phenomena; the second section discusses definitions of media in relation to the theoretical frameworks of mediation, mediatization, and religious-social shaping of technology; the third section builds on these existing frameworks to introduce the theory of hypermediation, which takes into account intensified speed and emotions of the contemporary media moment. Hypermediation considers religion as being entangled with secular and post-secular spaces and defines media as materiality, institutions, and technologies.

Defining "religion"

Scholars in the 1970s and 1980s, notably Brian Wilson, Peter Berger, and Karel Dobbelaere, predicted that religion would soon disappear in Europe (Smith 2003). They were influenced by social theories that tended to ignore religion and likely had in mind the famous Karl Marx' definition of religion having a consolatory role for the proletariat as "opium of the people" (Callinicos 2009, 83). According to this perspective, religion was an irrational legacy of the past and secularism a necessary byproduct of modernity (Taylor 2007).

These predictions were not correct. The examples discussed in the introduction and those that will be discussed in the next chapters show that religion is still present in the European public sphere and often intertwined with secular values in a model of Catholic secularism. According to José Casanova (1994), religious changes in late modernity sparkle also from the increasing – and unexpected – visibility that religion gained in the public sphere starting from the 1980s. Casanova considers the theory of secularization as made by the three propositions of religious differentiation, decline, and privatization. These three elements are historical options that may occur in different ways in different geographical contexts. The greater visibility of European contemporary religion suggests that it is resisting privatization and de-politicization. Contrarily to what Thomas Luckmann (1967) theorized, religion is not necessarily becoming "invisible," but undergoes instances of deprivatization that makes it more public, rather than confining it to the private sphere of individual practice.

While public religion persists in contemporary Europe, it is also true that some forms of institutional religion are declining. Grace Davie (2002) analyzes religion in Europe through the theory of "believing without belonging." The concept of "believing without belonging" indicates the phenomenon of people believing in religion but, at the same time, not subscribing to a religious institution. "Believing without belonging" is paired with the idea of "vicarious religion," churches and churchgoers performing religious functions on behalf of the population at large, which turns to religious institutions only in exceptional times. This suggests that Europe is an "exception" not because Europeans are necessarily less religious than inhabitants of other parts of the world, but "differently so" (19). Religious institutions continue existing and people might still consider them as socially relevant, but their importance decrease as alternative models of religious beliefs and authority emerge.

Therefore, the type of religion that exists in Europe tends to be more public and, at the same time, less tied to traditional religious institutions than it was before. This suggests that religion is not fixed in time, but continuously engages in the redefinition of its own terms, both in traditional religious spaces and in non-traditional venues. Peter Beyer (2016), assuming a lived religion approach, stresses the increasing plural character of contemporary religion:

> Religion can be and increasingly is multi-formed, multi-modelled, and multi-present: it takes more forms that are lived, institutionalized, *and recognized* than before; it comes in different strengths in those different forms; it can be clearly institutionalized or less clearly institutionalized and still be lived and recognized as religion; it can be sensate, cognitive, performative, or any combination of these in different proportions; it can be clearly bounded and exclusive, or not.
>
> (248, emphasis in original)

According to Beyer, religion needs to be found within and outside religious institutions, also in spaces that used to not be considered religious before and embedded within other social elements. This reflection is relevant for this book as it explores a type of religion often not featured in traditional media and involving informal groups that do not belong to religious institutions. The question this chapter tries to answer is: How can we define this type of religion?

While offering a comprehensive and universal definition of religion is beyond the scope of this book, it aims at elaborating a working definition of religion that captures the entanglements of religious, secular, and post-secular spaces in contemporary Europe. Following Stewart Hoover (2006) and Heidi Campbell (2007), who draw from the work of Clifford Geertz in their reflections on religion and media, the inquiry starts from the following definition of religion:

> [Religion is] (1) a system of symbols which acts to (2) establish powerful, persuasive, and long-lasting moods and motivations in men by (3) formulating conceptions of general order of existence and (4) clothing these conceptions with such an aura of factuality that (5) the moods and motivations seems uniquely realistic.
>
> (Geertz, quoted in Campbell 2007, 7)

In other words, Geertz considers that religious believers employ religion as a symbolic and authentic source of meaning for their lives. This definition of religion has the advantage of encompassing a wide range of beliefs and practices, including those that are not tight to traditional understandings of religion. While Geertz' conceptualization might seem at times too broad, this book tries to avoid definitions that narrow religion to pre-defined practices and experiences only. On the contrary, looking at religion as a "system of symbols" and at religious "mood and motivations" is a starting point to understand how people experience, define, and communicate religious meanings in their own terms, even outside religious institutions.

This approach is found also in Birgit Meyer's definition of religion as "the ways in which people link up with, or even feel touched by, a meta-empirical sphere that may be glossed as supernatural, sacred, divine, or transcendental" (2014, 6). According to Meyer, religion is found in people's practices and beliefs and in the ways they define their own religious experience. This definition applies to the spaces explored in this book. Atheist identities created in opposition to religious values, Muslim youth groups involved in social actions, and Catholic-inspired protests are forms of religion because they elaborate on religious meanings. In so doing, they define what religion (and the secular) means for them and how they differentiate between religious and non-religious elements. While these definitions do not pertain to religious institutions and do not draw from official sources, they are authentic in helping a given group to articulate their religious-related meanings and values.

This does not mean that religion is undifferentiated from other social elements; on the contrary, religion is found precisely in the differentiation between ordinary and extraordinary elements. As Volkhard Krech (2012) asserts, the historical formation of the religious field is dependent on internal and external demarcations. Methodologically, these demarcations can be found in "specific semantic differences pointing to a specific religious meaning" (201). This means that a given religious group relates to other religious communities and with non-religious elements in a way that produces a distinct understanding of religion. This understanding is often the result of negotiations between how the group members categorize themselves and how they are categorized by non-members. It is for this reason that the definition of religion is often dependent on processes of religious contact and communication.

Another strength of Geertz' definition is that it includes phenomena that are not strictly religious. According to Ann Taves (2016), formally non-religious groups can find inspiration in religious experiences – such as those she defines as "revelatory events" – whose meanings they contribute determining. For example, Alcoholics Anonymous and the networks associated with "A Course in Miracle" are not religious groups *stricto sensu*, but embed religious-like feelings. It is for this reason that definitions of religion should include what Knut Lundby and Stewart Hoover define as "seemingly non-religious phenomena" (1997, 7). Groups are religious in virtue of the intentions of their actions and the meanings they attach to their practices. In addition, religious-like behaviors that develop in the digital space can be considered as religious because they mirror authorities, symbols, and rituals that characterize religious institutions. Blogs, for example, perform cultural work in articulating the bloggers' understanding of religion and in negotiating alternative religious authorities. They produce "seemingly non-religious phenomena" that are religious in defining – consciously or unconsciously – the space religion should occupy in society and its role in relation to culture and politics.

Because religion can be defined by people's practices and beliefs and includes also phenomena that are seemingly non-religious, it increasingly interacts with secular elements. This does not mean that religion loses its specific character, but rather that it increasingly intersects with spaces that, in the past, were not considered as religious. It is for this reason that the definition of what religion *is* needs to be put in relation to what religion *is not*, meaning the secular. The term "secular" – coming from the Latin *saeculum*, "century" – was first used in Europe during the Middle Age to indicate the realm of worldly affairs, as opposed to the religious sphere (Calhoun, Juergensmeyer, and VanAntwerpen 2011). Therefore, the religious and the secular originally occupied sharply separate spaces within society. They were mutually exclusive, the former pointing to transcendence, and the latter finding life fulfillment in immanence and in rationality (Taylor 2007).

The secular does not only designate the absence of religion, but it can become a meaning-charged concept that defines the ways in which religion exists in society. It is for this reason that Talal Asad (2003) differentiates between "secular" as an epistemological category and a set of behaviors, and "secularism" as a political ideology. Secularism may entail meanings that preclude the presence of religion in certain social and cultural spaces. For example, the French *laïcité*, the doctrine of church–state separation, is not only an abstract secular principle, but has precise legal and social consequences and a specific role in the articulation of national identities, as will be explored in the next chapters. In addition, state secularism can be used politically to marginalize certain groups, such as Muslims, supposedly not able to embrace European secular values. The three groups analyzed in this book not only discuss the secular as a neutral concept, but they also face secularist ideologies, either supporting or challenging them. Therefore, their understanding – and, as a consequence, definition – of religion cannot be separated from their understanding of the secular.

Religion in contemporary Europe does not exist as a completely separated domain from the secular, as was initially the case during the Middle Age. As for Casanova's (1994) analysis, the differentiation thesis of the secularization theory considers that the separation of religious and secular spheres creates new spatial structures. Religious spaces become secular following the decline of certain types of institutional religion, and they might become religious again because of the increasing re-publicization of religion. For example, Pope Francis gave a speech at the European Parliament in Strasbourg, France, on 25 November 2014. The speech addressed the need for Europe to recognize its religious roots, implicitly commending a friendly relationship between the Vatican and the secular institutions of the European Union. In this case, the European Parliament in Strasbourg, a secular institutional space, was symbolically charged with religious meanings through the Pope's presence and speech; therefore, it is possible to consider that it temporally became a religious space. After the Pope left the Parliament, it symbolically returned to being a secular space. From this perspective, space is not fixed, but charged with meanings depending on people's actions and interpretations. Therefore, " 'religion' and 'secular' " are better analyzed as "mutually constituted terms," and "in virtue of their relation" (Calhoun 2010, 1), rather than as separated elements.

Religious change is arguably caused by processes in which religion starts to occupy former secular spaces, and vice versa. Therefore, this book conceptualizes the relationship between religion and the secular in spatial terms. Kim Knott's (2014) spatial methodology individuates religion in apparently secular spaces and secular in formally religious spaces. Knott considers space as not only being a container for cultural and social manifestations, but also directly shaped and invested by people's actions, as will be further explored in the next chapter. In assuming this perspective, Knott avoids specific definitions of religion, looking instead at "how the 'religious' and the 'secular' are used, and how they are formed practically and discursively in the various spaces" (81). Similarly to Birgit Meyer, Knott looks at ways in which religion and the secular are defined in the context of the case study she analyzes.

According to this model, the term "post-secular" completes the relationship between religion and the secular. The concept of post-secular seeks to explain the phenomena of religious persistence currently occurring in Europe and elsewhere and addresses questions about the public role that religion still holds in formally secular contexts (Gorski et al. 2012). Knott takes into account religious confessions, secular confessions, and post-secular confessions as being in a triangular dialectic – or "trialectic," as I will refer to it in this book – with each other. She considers that the religious and the secular do not stand in opposition to each other, and that the post-secular is a consequence rather than a negation of secularism. The camp of the post-secular, indeed, completes the religious and the secular by capturing the tensions in these two fields' mutual relationship.

By drawing from Knott's spatial methodology, religion, secular, and post-secular are considered as distinctions that are in a fluid relationship with each other, rather than separated concepts. The terms of religion and the secular indicate spaces that are either charged with religious meanings or purposefully voided from religious values. This model does not consider secular spaces as invested with rationality and religious spaces as being characterized by irrationality, but they are spaces that hold different symbolic meanings and coexist in modern societies. At the same time, the distinction between the religious and the secular does not coincide with demarcations of sacred and profane: this book does not define how spaces are made religious, but rather reflects on the ways religion is present (or absent) from social spaces. The post-secular, in this context, indicates the spatial transformations and the religious deprivatization that occur when there is a shift between religious and secular spaces. If a given space goes from being secular to religious, or vice versa, it undergoes post-secular transformations. Therefore, I propose to represent religion as standing in a trialectic with the secular and the post-secular (Figure 1.1).

Groups that negotiate the space religion should or should not occupy within society help to understand the relationship between religion, secular, and post-secular: Muslim women wearing hijab in formally secular venues subtly charge them with religious meanings; atheists protesting against religious symbols in public spaces indirectly claim that institutions should be invested with secular meanings; Catholics finding ways to become visible in public spaces implicitly state that the Catholic Church should aspire to re-create a religious public sphere. These groups help to understand religious change in Europe because they shift the perception of religious identities by creating spaces of tension between the religious, the secular, and the post-secular. They also partially explain the phenomenon of "believing without belonging": people are not necessarily less religious, but rather navigate a society where religious and non-religious domains continuously evolve and intersect with each other.

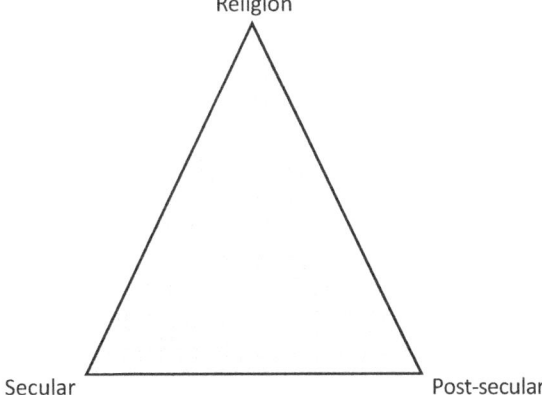

Figure 1.1 Religion, secular, and post-secular

By looking at these examples, this book explores the ways religion does not disappear, but becomes more private, or seeks greater publicity, or discusses traditional authorities, or creates alternative communities of practice, or negotiates its meanings, or occupies spaces that used to be secular. Religion is defined as a system of symbols depending on people's experiences of the transcendence, which is increasingly present in non-traditional venues and entangled with secular and post-secular spaces. These spatial entanglements need to be mediated. It is, indeed, through processes of communication that religion becomes more visible and religious spaces are discussed, negotiated, and given meaning. Media saturate contemporary European society so pervasively that they influence the understandings of religious symbols, authorities, practices, and beliefs. It is for this reason that the definition of religion employed in this book depends also on definitions of media.

Defining "media"

Media help to determine the position religion occupies in contemporary Europe. According to David Herbert (2011), recent developments in media institutions and media practices are directly responsible for new relationships between religion, politics, and popular culture. Media contribute to the phenomenon of religious re-publicization, a term that Herbert employs in relation to Casanova's idea of deprivatization. In addition, media allow for the creation of alternative counterpublics that emerge in opposition to traditional authorities and symbols, allowing for believers' negotiation of religious meanings.

Because media influence people's everyday life, they need to be defined not only in terms of their technological characteristics, but also in relation to the social and cultural work they perform. While this book distinguishes between "national," or "mainstream" media, and "new," or "digital" media, it does not look at definitions that are tight to specific media platforms. On the contrary, following Nick Couldry (2013) social theory, this book looks at media practices rather than media platforms. In so doing, it aims at going beyond the dichotomy between media texts and institutions and focuses on how people make sense of media in ways that are meaningful for the negotiation of religious spaces within society. Therefore, media are defined in a broad perspective, considering them both tools that people use to communicate religious messages, and objects that help people to experience transcendence and define their religious practice. They are multilevel means of communication, which include embodied practices and sensorial experience. In order to provide more specific definitions, dominant theoretical frameworks in the field of religion and media are explored: the theory of mediation helps to understand media in virtue of their materiality; the theory of mediatization allows conceptualizing media as institutions; and the religious-social shaping of technology thinks of media as technologies.

The theory of mediation helps to understand the role of media within society. Through the concept of mediation, Jesus Martin-Barbero (1993) looks at ways in which the audience receives media messages and culturally negotiates them in a local and transnational perspective. Martin-Barbero defines "mediations" as the "articulations between communicative practices and social movements and the articulation of different tempos of development with the plurality of cultural matrices." (Martin-Barbero, quoted in Hoover and Lundby 1997, 300). In other words, mediation considers media as tools that provide communication in a way that produces cultural effects. This perspective allows for a focus on media practices that are meaningful in relation to a number of different social processes.

This definition of media lends itself to theories of religious mediation. According to Birgit Meyer (2010), mediation is the process that allows the experience of the transcendence and makes it tangible. In considering religion as belonging to the realm of the sensorium rather than solely confined to the domain of ideas, Meyer focuses on what she defines as "sensational forms." These forms are "relatively fixed, authorized modes of invoking and organizing access to the transcendental, thereby creating and sustaining links between believers in the context of particular religious regimes" (2014, 27). As for this definition, objects charged with religious meanings serve the purpose of connecting religious practice with what is beyond the realm of the physical. The embeddedness of religion in the domain of the physical creates what Birgit Meyer calls "aesthetic formations." Meyer defines "aesthetic" in the Aristotelian sense, thus considering it as connected with the sensuous knowledge of the world; "formation" indicates communities that form around shared beliefs. Therefore, in processes of mediation, media are those material objects functioning as transmitters between the ordinary and the extraordinary.

Processes of religious mediation, therefore, interest various media forms that allow embodied practices and multisensorial experiences. This compels attention to material culture, which David Morgan (2016) defines as "the registers of sensation that apprehend the object, the techniques of the body that object activates, and the value or salience that is generated by the use of the object in religious practice" (14–15). Such conceptualization of mediation as embedded in material qualities compels a broad definition of "media," intended as objects charged with meanings that allow religious experiences. Borrowing Morgan's definition, media are "images, sensations, spaces, food, dress, or the material practices of putting the body to work" (*ibidem*). Therefore, an object becomes a religious medium when it allows certain sensations and practices that, in a certain context, are religiously charged. That does not mean that objects involved in religious practices automatically become religious media. Their religious relevance is often dependent on how they are produced, circulated, and classified; what poses the basis for the formation of a religious medium are the intentions behind its creation, the ways it is remediated, and the uses people make of it.

These material-dependent processes of religious mediation include various forms of media technologies. Believers can, indeed, experience the divine through technologies, as in the case of television sermons that may awake a sense of religious transcendence among viewers (Meyer 2014). Similarly, religious practices on the internet, far from being detached from the physical, help the formation of communities because they are complementary to physical objects in defining religious experiences (Hutchings 2016). For example, clothing – such as the Muslim hijab – are religious material forms because they are "physical, tangible or embodied indication of lived religion" (Arweck 2016, 185). The internet provides a venue to show, discuss, and define religious garments, allowing religious groups to take control of their visibility and negotiate meanings through internet-mediated displays of materiality. Hijab-wearing women may use the internet to counteract existing stereotypes about their religious garments, decide in which ways they want to show their veiled bodies, and create virtual groups where they discuss the stylistic and religious implications of their clothing (Evolvi 2018). From this perspective, the computer also becomes a material form that, allowing for connections with other believers and the negotiation of religious practices, establishes new forms of community. It is for this reason that blogs, intended both as internet spaces and venues of discussion of religious material practices, are involved in processes of mediation that embed the use of sensational forms. Thinking about blogs in these terms helps to remind that communication processes rely on aesthetic and tangible practices connected with offline spaces.

While the concept of mediation describes the ways in which religion relies – and has always historically relied – on media, it is impossible to ignore how the recent proliferation of media technologies has substantially changed the experience of religion in contemporary societies. Because of the diffusion of media – defined by Nick Couldry as "media supersaturation" (2012) – social relationships are often defined by mediated interactions. It is for this reason that media are producing both large- and small-scale changes in various spheres of human existence, including religion. Media institutions, indeed, help to experience religion differently from material objects.

The theory of mediatization implies that media influence extends to all domains of social life (Couldry 2012). Mediatization, according to Nick Couldry and Andreas Hepp (2013), refers to the "processes of a communicative construction of socio cultural reality." They describe mediatization as follows:

> The term "mediatization" here is designed to capture both how the communicative construction of reality is manifested within certain media processes and how, in turn, specific features of certain media has a contextualized "consequence" for the overall process whereby socio-cultural reality is constructed in and through communication.
>
> (196)

Therefore, mediatization posits that media have a central role in shaping the ways people perceive and act upon reality. Media have effects in influencing people's behaviors and in conditioning their interactions. While mediatization does not exclusively refer to recent media technologies – as it may include, for example, printed texts – it intensifies with modern communication processes and mainly understands media in terms of institutions (Lundby 2014).

This theory describes the role of media in relation to cultural and social institutions, including religious institutions. Mediatization can create new social conditions for the experience of religion because it "concerns the ways that religious organizations, practices and beliefs are altered through the increasing presence of media both inside and outside the institution of religion" (Hjarvard 2012, 26). When religious groups are situated in contexts where media are highly diffused, they need to adapt to media logics in order to communicate their messages and establish their position in society. Mediatization lends itself to David Herbert's (2011) idea of religious re-publicization as it entails an enhanced presence of religion in public spaces. It helps to contextualize how the decline of certain types of religion in Western Europe is paradoxically paired with an increasing interest in religion within media discourses (Hjarvard and Lövheim 2012). As Mia Lövheim (2014) writes with respect to the theory of mediatization, media contribute to religious change in three main ways. First, people tend to gain knowledge about religion primarily through media. Second, media diffuse forms of religious-inspired pop culture that create new perceptions of religious practices, symbols, and beliefs. Third, media take over functions that beforehand belonged to religious institutions. As a consequence, traditional religious authorities become weaker, religious practice more individualized, and religious institutions less able to control their representations. These three interrelated phenomena help to understand also European exceptionalism because they partially explain the decline of traditional authorities and the tendency of people to personalize their beliefs outside institutions.

The mediatization approach looks at forms of mass-mediated communication that are heavily dependent on recent technological developments and that are particularly relevant in highly modernized areas, also because the theory emerged in North European settings. However, as Knut Lundby (2014) asserts, mediatization is found relevant in other parts of the world, too. Catholic European countries arguably sustain processes of mediatization as they are characterized by strong religious institutions and by media infrastructures able to shape dominant discourses. Moreover, while the theory of mediatization mostly focuses on media institutions, it can also help to understand digital media practice, provided that it is complemented "with a focus on agency and the dynamics of religious values and identities" (Lovheim 2012, 133). Therefore, a mediatization approach to digital media looks at the context of production and people's practices in creating media discourses, and takes into account the ways various media platforms intersect in creating religious narratives.

Mediatization helps to situate religious blogs within the context where they are produced. The way secular European media report, frame, and diffuse actions and speeches of Pope Francis constitutes an example of how media become a source of religious knowledge, but also of how religion enters popular media discourses. The Pope's leadership expands beyond religious institutions as media audiences tend to view him as a "celebrity" (Brown 2009). The television series *The Young Pope* shows how the Pope is not only a religious authority for the believers, but an international character who inspires pop culture products; arguably, the series also contributes to shaping people's perceptions and knowledge of Catholicism. Vatican-organized events often follow the logic of media institutions, thus holding a "hybrid" religious and secular character (Hepp and Krönert 2009). Blogs that address Catholic secularism and religious change are written alongside – and, sometimes, in contrast – with media institutions that create and circulate these narratives.

The two theories of mediation and mediatization, even if sometimes used as synonyms, represent different approaches to the question of religion and media. While mediation, intended as communication through a medium, does not necessarily imply a change in social institutions, mediatization entails a new social condition in the long-term structural change of religious practice. Drawing from these two theories helps to go beyond the technology-agency dichotomy and to regard "media" both in relation to their material characteristics and their institutional dimensions. There is no sharp distinction between "traditional" and "new" media. Rather, media representations influence people's realities and identity narratives and, as a consequence, create venues for religious practices. However, this book does not ignore the ways in which the internet is unique and the peculiar characteristics of new media technologies. While the internet is a media form that builds on previous technologies, it does determine important changes in terms of users' agency. Digital media technologies, indeed, intensify people's practices by increasing the pace of communication, facilitating interconnectivity, and creating new environments for media consumption and production.

The theory of religious-social shaping of technology focuses on new media. Heidi Campbell (2007) analyzes the ways religious communities negotiate media practices in relation to digital – or networked – technologies. Drawing from the social shaping of technology theory, this approach focuses on religion and offers a framework that "acknowledges how a religious community's historical life practice, interpretative tradition, and the contemporary outworking of their values inform their choices about the adoption and the adaptation of technology" (41). In other words, religious groups might decide to use – or to avoid – new media technologies depending on how they can negotiate them within their practices. Campbell, indeed, focuses on history and traditions of a given religious group, its core beliefs and patterns, its negotiations of new media, and its religious discourses. As a result, this approach allows exploring how religious individuals and communities become active and empowered users of digital technologies. For example, in creating a "kosher cell phone," Jewish communities negotiate their internet use and connote the telephone as a material object whose characteristics need to be adapted to the religious lifestyle (2007).

Religious-social shaping of technology looks at media as interplays between technical and social factors. "New media" are conceptualized both as networked and digital technologies, but also as devices that are "new" in relation to older communication tools. All media technologies – including writing and printing – have been "new" at a certain point in history. Therefore, this perspective allows theorizing the emergence of digital technologies in society by providing a sense of continuity with the past. Such approach could account for the ways people use digital venues to negotiate religious beliefs and practices. Indeed, while this book does not look at institutional religions, it does analyze the ways in which religion becomes a cultural system in informing people's lives, including communities' negotiation of technology and media use. The blogs under analysis do not explicitly reject or criticize technology, as the communities in Campbell's research do, but they nonetheless reflect on digital practices. In specific, blogs seek to create narrative spaces that are counter-hegemonic in respect to other media platforms and define the relations a specific group sustains with media in terms of consumption, representations, and embedded meanings.

Furthermore, the religious discourses produced in digital spaces can be described through Campbell's concept of "networked religion" (2012). In defining five key aspects – networked community, stories identities, shifting authority, convergent practices, and multisite reality – Campbell accounts for how religion is articulated in between online and offline spaces. According to Campbell's argument, blogging practices may not only define religion on the internet, but also give insights on larger processes of religious change in an increasingly networked society. From this perspective, the internet both mirrors and enhances general processes of sociocultural change. Therefore, looking in specific at digital media technologies can help to analyze some contemporary religious trends and to understand certain groups' negotiation of religious values and media use.

So far, theoretical traditions that offer various definitions of media have been addressed: media as *materiality*, media as *institutions*, media as *technologies* – including *digital* technologies. These definitions represent various modes to conceptualize the relationship between religion and media. Blogs embed these aspects on different levels: they allow sensorial experiences and discuss forms of material religion; they are created in a media-saturated environment which shapes people's perception of reality and knowledge of religion; and they are digital media platforms whose functions are negotiated by various religious groups in between online and offline activities. Therefore, these three definitions of media – materiality, institutions, and technologies – can be considered as interconnected with each other and defining the spaces religion, secular, and post-secular occupy within society. I propose to represent visually the relationship between religion and media as follows:

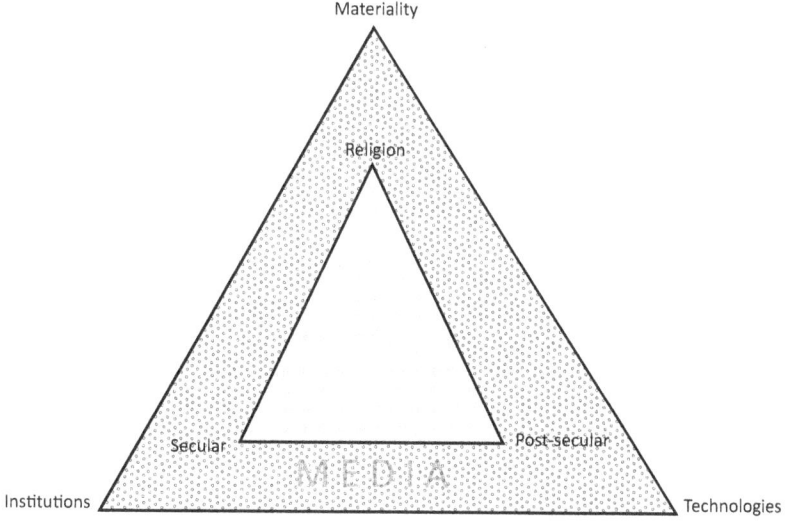

Figure 1.2 Media as materiality, institutions, and technology

This visual representation considers each aspect of media – materiality, institutions, and technology – as relating simultaneously to religious, secular, and post-secular spaces. Each of the larger triangle's angles corresponds to the three angles of the smallest triangle. For example, material media regard religious, secular, and post-secular spaces at the same time. The trialectic aims at showing that digital media do not represent a sharp rupture with the past, but sustain processes of mediation and mediatization that interest other media platforms, as well. The novelty of the internet lies in the intensification of existing media processes and the increasing ubiquity of media practices. Therefore, this triad can be a starting point for a further theoretical effort that aims at understanding contemporary religion in a society where digital media create new ways of approaching communicative spaces. Building on these definitions, I here adopt the perspective of "hypermediation" to bring together relevant aspects of existing theories on religion and media.

The hypermediation of religion

The theory of hypermediation aims at capturing the relationship between media and religion in media-saturated environments, such as Catholic Europe. Drawing from Jesus Martin-Barbero's theory of mediation, Carlos Scolari (2015) coins the term hypermediation to account for networks of practices enacted by multiple users. The term "hypermediation" is formed by adding to the word "mediation" the Greek prefix *hyper-*, which means "beyond" and can also be translated as "excess." The concept of hypermediation seeks to analyze the facilitated character of information reproduction, as well as complex textual structures and hybridization of different languages. While the theory of hypermediation naturally builds on mediation, it happens in a context of media saturation that characterizes processes of mediatization, and it holds a focus on new media technologies. In particular, hypermediation interests the fluidity of media practices where traditional and new media are embedded in everyday experiences, creating what Henry Jenkins (2008) defines as "convergence" or "participatory" culture.

According to Jenkins, the so-called "old" and "new" media converge in creating new modes of expression. Users, consumers, and audiences are all involved in the articulation and the circulation of content across various media platforms. Therefore, convergence is a multidimensional process characterized by increasing audience participation. Scolari finds a set of commonalities between Jenkins and Martin-Barbero's theories. In going beyond technological determinism, they both focus on processes of meaning-making which put emphasis on people's agency. While there are some differences between the two scholars – especially given the focus of Martin-Barbero on 1980s telenovela viewers and that of Jenkins' on fandom culture in relation to digital media – Scolari proposes that the theory of mediation can enrich the idea of convergence culture, and vice versa. By putting emphasis on the dialectic between media users and institutions, the theory of hypermediation focuses on the environment of media production, the mutual interactions between media users, and the interplay of media institutions and digital media practices.

In addition, the comparisons between Martin-Barbero and Jenkins emphasize how the current media moment does not represent a rupture from the past, but rather builds on practices that existed in the pre-internet era. The theory of hypermediation is mostly limited to technologically saturated societies, especially in Western contexts. When talking about hypermediation, this book focuses on Catholic Europe and understands the theory as applying prevalently to similar environments. However, stressing the connections between digital and pre-digital media practices partially addresses the geo-cultural limitations of the theory. Therefore, this perspective helps to understand how the intersections between materiality, institutions, and technologies allow for human actors to shape media processes and blur the boundaries between media platforms.

Scolari's approach does not address religion specifically, but describes the general character of media practices in late modernity. However, the theory of hypermediation could successfully draw from the aforementioned theories of religious mediation and mediatization, and religious-social shaping of technology. In so doing, hypermediation does not aim at overlooking their conceptual differences; on the contrary, it tries to account for the multiple layers of media complexity and to capture the shifting character of contemporary religion. The theory of hypermediation could be put in conversation with Arjun Appadurai's (2015) analysis of materiality. Building on theories of religion – including Birgit Meyer's work on mediation – Appadurai expands from the study of religion to other sociocultural processes. In his exploration of material life, Appadurai focuses on both human and non-human mediants and analyzes the interplay between human bodies, technological devices, physical spaces, and nature. While he does not refer to the term "hypermediation," he proposes to create a more robust theory of mediation that could focus on the shifting character of contemporary relations. Employing Appadurai's idea of mediants, the scholars of the Center for Media, Religion, and Culture at the University of Colorado Boulder have been exploring hypermediation in order to analyze religion in digital spaces. Hypermediation is conceptualized as follows:

> We foreground the condition of a hyper-ization of mediation first to capture how the current social interface is sustained by an impressive network of ubiquitous communication technologies, practices, and experiences that arguably promise immediacy, visibility, and interconnectivity. A dynamic ecology of mediation in which a broad spectrum of users participates in a fragmented culture of media production and consumption.
> (Echchaibi 2017, 1)

The quotation shows how the prefix *hyper-* can be used to describe the accelerated character of modern communication, as well as the role of digital media users as both consumers and producers. This perspective is useful to understand how contemporary religion increasingly holds characteristics of "immediacy, visibility, and interconnectivity," becoming what Campbell defines as "networked religion." People frequently experience social elements, including religion, in an intensified way – as the prefix *hyper-* suggests – for two main reasons.

First, contemporary life is characterized by increased speed. As for Hartmut Rosa's (2003) and Steve Redhead's (2004) works, which engage with Paul Virilio's "dromological" approach to history, contemporary life could be defined in terms of, respectively, "social acceleration" and "accelerated modernity." This type of acceleration regards technology, social change, as well as the pace of life. The logic of acceleration lends itself to processes of modernization, because it changes the temporal structures of economic, cultural, and social dynamics. Media, and digital media in particular, decisively contribute to this acceleration of social structures because they shorten time and spatial distances and intensify human relationships. For example, blogs and social networks help to diffuse news almost at the same moment they happen, and people can comment on them in real time. This logic does not only lead to positive outcomes. Indeed, the accelerated pace of modernity, especially in capitalist societies, can also result in crisis, alienation, and instability: speed might become a condition that needs to be satisfied at the expense of people and the environment (Costa 2017). Therefore, social acceleration may encounter instances of resistance. People who feel anxious for the emergence of digital culture may try to decelerate the pace of life or to disconnect from intensified social relations. For example, media users might refrain from reading news on the internet because they consider it too superficial or not trustworthy. Hypermediation, by looking at fast media connections that shrink the perception of time and space, aims at capturing both the ways in which media technologies substantially contribute to change the speed of society and the modes of media critique against acceleration and media saturation.

Second, the accelerated interactions created through digital media are emotional in character. Zizi Papacharissi (2014) considers that digital media help the creation of affective networks. Internet platforms, and the increasing participation of convergence culture, allow for collective storytelling. Papacharissi thus considers digital platforms as creating "networked publics that are mobilized and connected, identified, and potentially disconnected through expressions of sentiment" (2016, 5). From this perspective, emotions are social and cultural practices that are often determined by questions of power, for example, regarding liminal actors that belong to non-mainstream groups. Emotions can be embodied and connected to material objects in temporal or long-lasting manifestations of affects. According to Sara Ahmed (2014), emotions can be found in texts – including online texts, such as blogs – that, through figures of speech, point to objects of emotions. In addition, modes of affective expression exist in new languages, such as pictures, sound, or video, often used in digital venues. This creates what has been defined as "digital affect culture" (Döveling, Harju, and Sommer 2018). Hypermediation seeks to capture how, in a context of media saturation and media convergence, users continue to negotiate and enhance interpersonal relationships. Instead of becoming emotionally disconnected, they intensify personal exchanges that are not only characterized by increased speed, but also by emotional engagement. By focusing on media practices and human actors, hypermediation points to the emotional structures created by digital media.

The theory of hypermediation can be applied to a number of digital spaces, but this book focuses on religion. The two elements of hypermediation, speed and emotions, can indeed apply to religious-related practices and to processes of religious change. As will be analyzed in the following chapters, religious groups discuss media use in terms of intensifying either their engagement with society at large or resistance to the speed of modernity, thus creating practices that are aimed at accelerating or slowing the pace of life. Because emotions tend to be embedded in religious practices and beliefs – Pope Francis, for example, has been described as holding "affective charisma" (Napolitano, Forthcoming) – the use of digital media to negotiate religious identities and meanings often involve the creation of affective networks. This does not mean that religion is emotional because it rejects rationality; rather, it is connected with people's intimate feelings and sensations. Hypermediation is based on the aforementioned definitions of religion and media: processes of religious change result from the shifting relationship between religious, secular, and post-secular spaces; theories of religion and media conceptualize media as materiality, institutions, and technologies. Trying to capture these multilayered definitions of religion and media, the theory of hypermediation focuses on the acceleration and deceleration of contemporary life and the articulation of emotions embedded in people's participation in digital media.

This chapter has explored definitions and theories that help to understand the relationship between religion and media. It talked about processes that often embed material and symbolic spaces, such as the spaces religion occupies in society and the ways media interact with physical spaces. Therefore, the theory of hypermediation of religion is better understood in spatial terms. The term "hypermediated religious spaces" indicates those spaces that contribute to religious change by offering venues for people to discuss religious identities and practices. Blogs are an example of hypermediated religious spaces as they both provide venues to facilitate fast and emotional interactions and discuss the position of religion in contemporary society. The next chapter theoretically situates hypermediated religious spaces through the dichotomies of mainstream and alternative, public and private, real and imaginary. By so doing, it shows how the question of space is central in understanding religious change in contemporary Europe.

References

Ahmed, Sara. 2014. *The Cultural Politics of Emotion*. Revised edition. New York, NY: Routledge Chapman Hall.

Appadurai, Arjun. 2015. "Mediants, Materiality, Normativity." *Public Culture* 27 (2 76): 221–37. doi:10.1215/08992363-2841832.

Arweck, Elisabeth. 2016. "Religion Materialised in the Everyday: Young People's Attitudes Towards Material Expressions of Religion." In *Materiality and the Study of Religion: The Stuff of the Sacred*. Edited by Tim Hutchings and Joanne McKenzie. New York, NY: Theology and Religion in Interdisciplinary Perspective Series in Association with the Bsa Sociology of Religion Study Group.

Asad, Talal. 2003. *Formations of the Secular: Christianity, Islam, Modernity*. 1st edition. Stanford, CA: Stanford University Press.

Beyer, Peter. 2016. "Sensing Religion, Observing Religion, Reconstructing Religion: Contingency and Pluralization in Post-Westphalian Context." *Social Compass* 63 (2): 234–50. doi:10.1177/0037768616628794.

Brown, William J. 2009. "Mediated Influence of Pope John Paul II." *Journal of Communication & Religion* 32 (1): 33–61.

Calhoun, Craig. 2010. "Rethinking Secularism." *The Hedgehog Review* 12 (3): 35–48. ISSN 1527-9677.

Calhoun, Craig, Mark Juergensmeyer, and Jonathan VanAntwerpen, eds. 2011. *Rethinking Secularism*. Oxford: Oxford University Press.

Callinicos, Alex. 2009. *Making History: Agency, Structure, and Change in Social Theory*: Historical Materialism. Chicago, IL: Haymarket Books.

Campbell, Heidi A. 2007a. *When Religion Meets New Media: Media, Religion and Culture*. 1st edition. London; New York, NY: Media, Religion and Culture.

Campbell, Heidi A. June 1, 2007b. " 'What Hath God Wrought?' Considering How Religious Communities Culture (or Kosher) the Cell Phone," *Continuum* 21 (2): 191–203. https://doi.org/10.1080/10304310701269040.

Campbell, Heidi A. 2012. "Understanding the Relationship Between Religion Online and Offline in a Networked Society." *Journal of the American Academy of Religion* 80 (1): 64–93. doi:10.1093/jaarel/lfr074.

Casanova, Jose. 1994. *Public Religions in the Modern World*. Chicago: University of Chicago Press.

Costa, P. 2017. "Se il nostro problema è l'accelerazione, la "risonanza" può essere la soluzione? La crisi della stabilizzazione dinamica e le prospettive di una critica del presente." *Annali di Sudi Religiosi* 18: 7–36.

Couldry, Nick. 2012. *Media, Society, World: Social Theory and Digital Media Practice*. 1st edition. Cambridge; Malden, MA: Polity.

Couldry, Nick. 2013. *Media Interventions: Afterword by Nick Couldry*. Edited by Kevin Howley. 1st edition. New York, NY: Peter Lang Publishing Inc.

Couldry, Nick, and Andreas Hepp. 2013. "Conceptualizing Mediatization: Contexts, Traditions, Arguments." *Communication Theory* 23 (3): 191–202. doi:10.1111/comt.12019.

Davie, Grace. 2002. *Europe: The Exceptional Case. Parameters of Faith in the Modern World*. London: Darton, Longman & Todd Ltd.

Döveling, Katrin, Anu A. Harju, and Denise Sommer. 2018. "From Mediatized Emotion to Digital Affect Cultures: New Technologies and Global Flows of Emotion." *Social Media + Society* 4 (1): 2056305117743141. https://doi.org/10.1177/2056305117743141.

Echchaibi, Nabil. 2017. "Hypermediation as an Argument." Center for Media, Religion, and Culture, University of Colorado Boulder. Unpublished essay.

Evolvi, Giulia. 2018. "The Veil and Its Materiality: Muslim Women's Digital Narratives About the Burkini Ban." *Journal of Contemporary Religion*. Forthcoming

Gorski, Philip S., David Kyuman Kim, John Torpey, and Jonathan Vanantwerpen. 2012. *The Post-Secular in Question: Religion in Contemporary Society*. Brooklyn, New York, NY: New York University Press.

Hepp, Andreas, and Veronica Krönert. 2009. "Religious Media Events. The 'Catholic Youth Day' as an Example of Mediatization and Individualization of Religion." In *Media Events in a Global Age*. Edited by Nick Couldry, Andreas Hepp, and Friedrich Krotz. 1st edition. London; New York, NY: Routledge.

Herbert, David E. J. 2011. "Theorizing Religion and Media in Contemporary Societies: An Account of Religious 'publicization'." *European Journal of Cultural Studies* 14 (6): 626–48. doi:10.1177/1367549411419981.

Hjarvard, Stig, and Mia Lovheim, eds. 2012. *Mediatization and Religion: Nordic Perspectives*. Göteborg: Nordicom.

Hoover, Knut, and Stewart M. Lundby. 1997. *Rethinking Media, Religion, and Culture*. Thousand Oaks, CA: Sage Publications, Incorporated.

Hoover, Stewart M. 2006. *Religion in the Media Age*. 1st edition. London; New York, NY: Routledge.

Horsfield, Peter. 2015. *From Jesus to the Internet: A History of Christianity and Media*. 1st edition. Chichester, West Sussex; Malden, MA: Wiley-Blackwell.

Hutchings, Tim. 2016. "Augmented Graves and Virtual Bibles. Digital Media and Material Religion." In *Materiality and the Study of Religion: The Stuff of the Sacred*. Edited by Tim Hutchings, and Joanne McKenzie. New York, NY: Theology and Religion in Interdisciplinary Perspective Series in Association with the Bsa Sociology of Religion Study Group.

Jenkins, Henry. 2008. *Convergence Culture: Where Old and New Media Collide*. Revised edition. New York, NY: New York University Press.

Knott, Kimm. 2014. *The Location of Religion: A Spatial Analysis*. 1st edition. Routledge.

Krech, Volkhard. 2012. "Religious Contacts in Past and Present Times: Aspects of a Research Programme." *Religion* 42 (2): 191–213. https://doi.org/10.1080/0048 721X.2012.642572.

Lovheim, Mia. 2012. "A Voice of Their Own: Young Muslim Women, Blogs and Religion." In *Mediatization And Religion: Nordic Perspectives*. Edited by Stig Hjarvard, and Mia Lovheim. Göteborg: Nordicom.

Lovheim, Mia. 2014. "Mediatization and Religion." In *Mediatization of Communication*. Edited by Knut Lundby. Berlin: De Gruyter Mouton.

Luckmann, Thomas. 1967. *The Invisible Religion: The Problem of Religion in Modern Society*. 1st Printing edition. Palgrave Macmillan.

Lundby, Knut. 2014. *Mediatization of Communication*. Berlin: De Gruyter Mouton.

Martin- Martin-Barbero, Jesus. 1993. *Communication, Culture and Hegemony: From the Media to Mediations*. London; Newbury Park: SAGE Publications Ltd.

Meyer, Birgit, ed. 2010. *Aesthetic Formations: Media, Religion, and the Senses*. 2009 edition. New York, NY: Palgrave Macmillan.

Meyer, Birgit. 2014. "Mediation and the Genesis of Presence: Toward a Material Approach to Religion." *Religion and Society: Advances in Research 5*.

Morgan, David. 2016. "Material Analysis and the Study of Religion." In *Materiality and the Study of Religion: The Stuff of the Sacred*. Edited by Tim Hutchings, and Joanne McKenzie. New York, NY: Theology and Religion in Interdisciplinary Perspective Series in Association with the Bsa Sociology of Religion Study Group.

Napolitano, Valentina. Forthcoming. "Francis, a Criollo Pope." *Journal of Royal Anthropological Institute.*

Narbona, Juan. 2016. "Digital Leadership, Twitter and Pope Francis." *Church, Communication and Culture* 1 (1): 90–109. doi:10.1080/23753234.2016.1181 307.

Papacharissi, Zizi. 2014. *Affective Publics: Sentiment, Technology, and Politics.* Oxford; New York, NY: Oxford University Press.

Papacharissi, Zizi. 2016. "Affective Publics and Structures of Storytelling: Sentiment, Events and Mediality." *Information, Communication & Society* 19 (3): 307–24. doi:10.1080/1369118X.2015.1109697.

Redhead, Steve. 2004. *Paul Virilio: Theorist for an Accelerated Culture.* 2nd ed. Edition. Toronto: University of Toronto Press, Scholarly Publishing Division.

Rosa, Hartmut. 2003. "Social Acceleration: Ethical and Political Consequences of a Desynchronized High – Speed Society." *Constellations* 10 (1): 3–33. doi:10.1111/1467-8675.00309.

Scolari, Carlos A. 2015. "From (New)Media to (Hyper)Mediations: Recovering Jesús Martín-Barbero's Mediation Theory in the Age of Digital Communication and Cultural Convergence." *Information, Communication & Society* 18 (9): 1092–107. doi:10.1080/1369118X.2015.1018299.

Smith, Christian, ed. 2003. *The Secular Revolution: Power, Interests, and Conflict in the Secularization of American Public Life.* 1st Printing edition. Berkeley: University of California Press.

Taves, Ann. 2016. *Revelatory Events: Three Case Studies of the Emergence of New Spiritual Paths.* Reprint edition. Princeton, NJ: Princeton University Press.

Taylor, Charles. 2007. *A Secular Age.* 1st edition. Cambridge, MA: The Belknap Press of Harvard University Press.

2 Hypermediated religious spaces
Conceptualizing religion in digital spaces

"Thank you for following @Pontifex which turns five years old today. May social media always be spaces that are rich in humanity!," says Pope Francis in a tweet written on 12 December 2017. The choice of the word "space" to describe social media is interesting. Is the internet a space? The internet might indeed give the perception of being spaceless: users can transcend distances and communicate in real time, messages are rarely printed or made available in physical venues, and images and videos that reproduce places behind the screen are generally described as "virtual." However, Pope Francis is right in talking about "spaces rich in humanity." Social networks and other digital venues, allowing the exchange of conversations, pictures, and messages, are not dissimilar from physical spaces in helping people to discuss and experience various aspects of their lives, including religion.

The previous chapter outlined the theory of hypermediation to account for digital religion in the contemporary media moment and for internet-mediated changes in terms of speed and emotions. This chapter will explain that the hypermediation of religion can be better understood in spatial terms. The concept of "hypermediated religious spaces" designates those internet-based venues that exist in between online and offline activities and discuss the presence of religion in various spaces. Space is considered as plural: there is no single space of religion within society, but multiple spaces with different meanings that may intersect with each other. These spaces are physical and virtual venues that function as containers of actions and discourses. This book talks about blogs as examples of hypermediated religious spaces where people exchange ideas about religious change in Catholic Europe, negotiate religious identities, and discuss the concept of Catholic secularism. A spatial perspective is useful for two main reasons: space helps to conceptualize religion, and space helps to conceptualize media. I will here briefly explore why I make these two claims.

Religion is a system of values that creates spatial structures through practices that provide meanings. This book defines religion through the trialectic of religious, secular, and post-secular spaces. As for Kim Knott's work, religious spaces are the product of contestations between these three categories, which are embedded in locations (Hopkins, Kong, and Olson 2013). Knott

(2014) offers a spatial methodology to locate religion in everyday spaces and to understand how religion exists and develops within society. She considers space as "a *medium*, a *methodology* and an *outcome*" (3, emphasis in original) as she explores venues where religion is situated, looks at the relationship between religious and secular contexts, and analyzes spaces produced by religion. In describing space as dynamic and embodied, Knott writes,

> Speaking generally, all places (. . .) are gathered, produced and reproduced by spatial practice, configured and also openly extended by social relations, constrained by the dominant order, but the living expression of everyday practices and dynamic local interpretations (local knowledge) of that place. They are repeatedly bounded and settled in common discourse only to be punched through and unsettled by alternative accounts. The particularity of a place arises from the complexity of its social relations and the sum of the stories told about it.
>
> (33)

In other words, spaces are culturally and socially negotiated. Spaces are constructed by people's action and enacted through their discursive production. This definition of space draws from Henri Lefebvre's (1992) spatial triad, which Knott applies to the study of religion. According to Lefebvre, space can be "conceived," "perceived," or "lived." Conceived spaces (representations of space) are hegemonically designed for a specific function. Perceived spaces (spaces of representation) are places where people's everyday actions occur. Finally, lived spaces (spatial practices) are the result of the imaginary activity of changing the pre-planned functions of spaces. Therefore, lived spaces can potentially disrupt the hegemonic design of conceived spaces. Assuming this perspective, Knott takes into account space as holding both material and metaphorical qualities, and as existing at physical, mental, and social levels. Such conceptualization of space proves itself apt in case of religious blogs, where tangible spaces are discursively negotiated and intangible spaces are produced through religious imaginaries.

In approaching the question of religious geographies, Knott draws from the work of Lily Kong. According to Kong (2001), politics and poetics of religious places, identities, and communities are deeply entangled with each other. Kong explores religious spaces beyond the "officially sacred," thus taking into account public and private places that are not traditionally framed as religious. By considering processes of ritualization that "make" the space sacred, Kong looks at religious spaces in virtue of the power and hierarchical relationships that condition their existence. Following this approach, religious spaces are not considered through the dichotomy of sacred and profane – which does not exist in the same terms for every religious tradition – but as venues that contain religious expressions, at physical or symbolical levels.

There are many examples of how spaces frame religion in contemporary Europe. The project Iconic Religion explores some of these spaces, such as church buildings that are closed down and eventually converted to other functions. These reconversions include a Jesuit church becoming a Turkish mosque, and a Roman Catholic church becoming a dance school (Beekers 2016). This shows how space can assume different meanings depending on how it is used and conceptualized. Religious change, from this perspective, is the ways in which religion negotiates its boundaries by carving spaces of existence in secular and post-secular venues, and vice versa.

Media also participate in processes of space creation. In the previous chapter, I defined media in terms of materiality, institutions, and technologies. By taking into account this trialectic, it is possible to explore media practices that create, define, and give meaning to spaces. According to Nick Couldry (2000), the media process is "inherently also a *spatial* process" (23, emphasis in original) and "*the media themselves are a social process organized in space*" (25, emphasis in original). This happens because media have a direct impact on territories and their representations, thus affecting the spatial organization of social life.

According to economist Harold Innis, media devices can be space- or time-bounded. That means that certain modes of communication are suited for creating messages that resist in time, while others for diffusion in space (Blondheim 2007). Innis employs the time-space distinction as a criterion to classify media practices, even if time and space are not necessarily two mutually exclusive categories. While the aspect of time has important implications in relation to internet practices, this book focuses solely on the question of space. In particular, it follows Nick Couldry (2012) who, commenting upon Innis' idea of "time-biased media," writes,

> The Internet is certainly *space-biased* because it changes communications' movement across space not just by extension, but in term of complexity: the folding of the Internet information-space into everyday action-space requires a different understanding of what can be done where and by whom.
>
> (3, emphasis added)

This means that the internet enhances people's potential in terms of communication in space, connecting them to remote locations. It also has an impact on behaviors that occur in everyday spaces. By drawing from Pierre Bourdieu's field theory, Couldry conceptualizes media capital as a meta-capital that has a symbolic power in relation to other fields, such as religion. Because of the pervasive character of contemporary media, they can legitimate people's actions and discourses. As a result media, and the internet in particular, validate, condition, and ultimately create physical spaces characterized by media-related actions.

Therefore, the internet is not a merely metaphorical space, but it is deeply embedded in physical spaces because it holds material qualities and is entangled with actions that happen outside media platforms. A number of scholars explore the internet from a spatial perspective. Richard Rogers (2015), for example, talks about "engine-demarcated spaces," which he defines as "spheres" (8). Such web spheres, including the so-called "blogosphere," are ways in which sources are organized within engines and create spatial hierarchies of information and hyperlink-based relations. In addition, engines are geographically situated as they are connected to locations through domains that follow national regulations. While the idea of sphere can account for the ways different media platforms intersect with each other, this book employs the term "space" to conceptualize both the interactions between websites and hyperlinks, and the internet's influence on people's actions in specific locations.

According to danah boyd (2006), the definition of blogging as a medium is connected to the question of space, because "spatiality dominates the social structure of computer-mediated communication" (16). Boyd takes into account various layers of complexity: blogs are places to access other venues, spaces of conversation delineated by the computer, venues of bloggers' performances. From this perspective, space is not strictly physical, but rather performatively enacted by the discursive production of the bloggers, as well as by the ways readers approach blogs as if they are personal spaces. Blogs address the question of space within society and, at the same time, can be considered a corporeal extension of the blogger's personality.

In analyzing young women's blogs, Mia Lövheim (2011) employs the concept of "ethical spaces" to describe how blogs allow for the expression of meanings and identities. Blogs are considered as "spaces" because they are the result of interactions between media producers, texts, and users; they embed public and private negotiations of identities, relationships, opinions, and emotions. By reflecting on their position within society, young women's blogs become "ethical" because they are "spaces to expand, differentiate and negotiate social norms and cultural values" (350). Therefore, blogs constitute performative spaces that do not only exist on the internet, but whose discourses are deeply embedded within society.

Stewart Hoover and Nabil Echchaibi (2014) conceptualize digital venues as "third spaces" where people negotiate religion. The theory of third space helps to understand how the internet allows for the articulation of religious narratives, hybrid religious identities, and shared religious aesthetics. The idea of "thirdness" has been previously explored in relation to social spaces, for example, to describe how architecture creates spaces in between public and private venues, as for the works of Edward Soja (1996) and Ray Oldenburg (1999). Building on these theories, Hoover and Echchaibi consider internet spaces as holding qualities of thirdness that allow the articulation of religious narratives. Elaborating on Homi Bhabha's (2004) concept of third space in relation to post-colonialism, which accounts for the creation of hybridized subjectivities in between the colonizer and the colonized culture, Hoover and Echchaibi look at digital spaces as potentially enabling hybrid religious identities.

This book follows Hoover and Echchaibi in talking about "space" – rather than "place" – to point away from physical venues only and include fluid and conceptual locations (3). In addition, internet-based third spaces have two aspects that are particularly relevant to theorize hypermediated religious spaces. First, they hold characteristics of "in-between-nes," being situated at the intersection of different physical and mental spaces. As Hoover and Echchaibi (2014) write, third spaces

> Exist between private and public, between institution and individual, between authority and individual autonomy, between large media framings and individual "pro-sumption," between local and translocal, etc. Digital third spaces of religion are fluidly bounded. Boundaries are important, but they are subject to a constant process of negotiation.
>
> (26)

Therefore, these spaces hold characteristics of "thirdness" because they are created by the encounter – and, sometimes, the tensions – between the other two spaces. They may exist between religious and secular spaces, and between various types of media practices. The "in-between-nes" of third spaces is closely related to a second element, the "as if-ness." While they are not necessarily institutional religious spaces, third spaces can enable practices and discourses that, for the users, hold religious authenticity. Hence,

> People act "as if" these were bounded contexts of discourse and interaction. They act "as if" they were communities of shared experience and sentiment. They act "as if" they were contexts of public discourse and public deliberation. They act "as if" these were powerful media for the communication of ideas and "as if" there are relatively broad audiences of listeners out there. They act "as if" the various expressions they craft in these spaces represent grounded, received truth claims for known communities of shared experience and value.
>
> (13)

As for this quote, people often consider spaces as charged by meanings. In so doing, they are able to define and negotiate actions that happen in these spaces. This perspective is useful to account for how informal groups create structures that can impact social change by acting "as if" they are an institutional group and have an established voice in the public sphere.

Because of their "in-between-ness" and "as if-ness," third spaces allow for the creation of internet-based religious communities and practices. Similarly to the theory of third space, hypermediation takes into account spaces that are situated between media and non-media venues, and are approached as if they sustain authentic religious experiences. Echchaibi (2017) considers that the theory of hypermediation deepens the concept of third space by offering a focus on the networked complexity and speed of the contemporary media moment, as well as attention to emotional and affective uses of the internet. However, while the internet enhances interconnectivity and allows for the creation of spaces charged with religious meanings, it does not have an inherently hypermediated character. Hypermediated religious spaces are those digital venues that are unique in negotiating social and cultural meanings. They are spaces that, without the internet, would not exist or would not produce the same discourses. At the same time, they distinguish themselves from other internet spaces because they enable actions and narratives that aim at having an impact offline. Therefore, a digital space – such as a blog – is a hypermediated space when it creates a new set of networked relations and meanings that would not exist in other venues.

In addition, hypermediated religion holds spatial characteristics that are found in three dialectical pairings: it is situated at the intersection of mainstream and alternative spaces; it is concerned with both public and private spaces; it reflects on the implications of real and imaginary spaces. These three pairings are lenses through which it is possible to explore religious change. They allow analyzing how an internet space can be unique in terms of meaning creation while being connected with other media platforms and society at large. By using these pairings as criteria for spatial differentiation, this chapter aims at explaining why a spatial perspective can help to define the relationship between religion and media in a media-saturated environment.

Mainstream and alternative spaces

This book explores hypermediated spaces created by groups that often criticize what they perceive as mainstream culture and society. The term "mainstream" – as well as the term "alternative," here used as its counterpart – is broad and nuanced. What does it mean that a group is "mainstream"? Are hypermediated spaces "mainstream" or "alternative"? What is "alternative" and what is "mainstream" in relation to internet-based religion? In this book, I use the concept of "mainstream" to designate something that belongs to the domain of hegemony, and therefore occupies a socially, culturally, or politically dominant space within society. The term "alternative" indicates something that is excluded from, rejects, or aspires to hegemony. This section will define hegemony through the work of Antonio Gramsci and of the Cultural Studies tradition. It proceeds by presenting Mouffe's concept of agonistic spaces and briefly addressing literature on alternative media, which are spaces that can potentially transcend hegemonic structures.

Antonio Gramsci (2014) conceptualizes hegemony as built through popular agreement, and not solely based on domination. Gramsci's definition of hegemony encompasses both top-down enforced decisions and bottom-up processes of values and norms negotiations. Therefore, coercion and consensus both concur in the creation of hegemony: people are not only forced into a hegemonic system, but they are lead to believe in it. People's "half-conscious complicity in their own victimization" (Lears 1985, 573) indicates how they actively participate in and accept the hegemonic status quo. The theory of hegemony regards structures – including churches, schools, and the mass media – that legitimize the existing political and social order, as well as the modes people relate to these social structures (Carragee 1993). People's complicity in their own victimization often leads to what Gramsci calls "contradictory consciousness," which is the tendency to act in contradiction with their own beliefs. As a consequence, people may consider conflicting meanings as equally acceptable.

This book's introduction mentioned Pope Francis' visits to the island of Lampedusa. The Pope's interactions with political (and secular) characters may be understood as a display of hegemony in the Gramscian sense: the Pope represents a mainstream form of religiosity that finds legitimation – and, in return, provides legitimization – to institutional and secular spaces. Pope Francis' ability to interact with institutional and political leaders, as well as the ways he is represented by national and international media, symbolically reinforces the influence of Vatican on the apparatus of state institutions. It also further legitimizes Catholicism's hegemonic position in respect to other religions, which are often prevented from approaching certain spaces and rarely have their voices heard within – or against – mainstream media platforms. Because of the Catholic Church's hegemony, many people, including non-Catholics, do not find the words and the presence of Pope Francis at odds with secular values, as it would probably happen for other religious leaders.

This hegemony is not only symbolic, but also materially and spatially displayed: in Catholic Europe, Christian buildings are often visible in the urban landscape, "as a result of their social power, material resources as well as the architectural sophistication that emerged from the close relationships between churches, architects and political authorities" (Becci, Burchardt, and Giorda 2017, 79). The presence of church buildings in Europe, indeed, may be described as a visual memento of the hegemonic position of the Catholic Church. Even if countries in Catholic Europe formally embrace secularism, Catholicism remains socially and culturally hegemonic in many spaces, as churches are often protected and celebrated also by non-religious institutions and citizens. This contributes to reinforcing the concept of Catholic secularism.

Gramsci's idea of hegemony influences several theoretical approaches. Notably, the Cultural Studies tradition draws on the Gramscian hegemony to explore people's cultural production. In incorporating Gramsci into his theorization of culture, prominent Cultural Studies exponent Raymond Williams (1973) sees culture as the product of a "selective tradition," defined as "the way in which from a whole possible area of past and present, certain meanings and practices are chosen for emphasis, certain other meanings and practices are neglected and excluded" (9). From this perspective, hegemony assumes the character of a set of culturally dominant meanings that coexists with non-dominant elements. In specific, non-dominant meanings can be residual, if inherited from the past, or emergent, if in the process of coming into being.

According to Williams, both residual and emergent elements can be incorporated into mainstream values. In case they fail to be incorporated, they can become alternative elements, which do not necessarily imply social transformations, or oppositional elements, which aim at resisting the dominant system. This classification of cultural elements accounts for hegemony's embeddedness in social structures and counter-hegemonic resistance. The history of religion is characterized by instances of religious contact that result in the incorporation or rejection of alien elements within a religious tradition (Krech 2012). The hegemonic position of the Catholic Church in Europe exists alongside alternative and oppositional elements. For example, the cult of saints and healing rituals in certain regions pacifically coexist with mainstream Catholicism, and they may even be incorporated in the Catholic doctrine (Pace 2007). At the same time, Catholic groups may enter in competition with the Vatican and undermine its power (Ballardini 2011).

The groups that will be described in the following chapters not only exist alongside mainstream Catholicism, but they also sometimes criticize its hegemonic position. I define these groups as "alternative" because they create non-hegemonic discourses and propose non-mainstream religious and cultural values. In this context, the term "alternative" does not exactly coincide with Williams' definition, but rather encompasses also "oppositional" elements. Chapter 4, for example, talks about atheist organizations that promote secularism in Europe. These associations include people that do not believe in religion and actively seek to diffuse secular values. In this case, these groups are alternative because they situate themselves outside cultural values that they perceive as mainstream, such as the concept of Catholic secularism; they are oppositional because they articulate narratives and actions against the Catholic Church.

Groups that are counter-hegemonic in criticizing the existing status quo often occupy "antagonistic" or "agonistic" positions. Chantal Mouffe's (2013) concept of antagonistic and agonistic politics in relation to hegemony can inform the position of non-mainstream (or alternative) groups. By applying Gramsci to contemporary social movements, Mouffe looks at the construction of certain subjects in society as subordinate to others in power relationships. These subjectivities, which exist alongside social and cultural categories such as religious belonging, often stand in conflicting relation with each other. From this perspective, counter-hegemonic resistance can take two possible forms: on the one hand, it can produce antagonistic spaces, where certain groups are prevented from participation, or agonistic spaces, where a plurality of different actors interacts as equals. According to Mouffe, democracy needs to be based on "consensual conflict," where agonistic spaces allow competing groups to express their claims. Groups, according to this model, are turned from "enemies" into "adversaries" in virtue of their engagement in constructive conflicts.

Mouffe's model usefully accounts for how alternative groups can, or should, interact with mainstream society and with each other. In specific, the tension between agonistic and antagonistic participation helps to understand the struggles certain individuals and communities experience in finding their place in society. When trying to have their claim recognized, alternative groups do not always manage to enter in agonistic conversations, and they are sometimes framed as "other" to mainstream culture. As will be analyzed in Chapter 3, this is frequently the case of Muslims in contemporary Europe: they are often prevented from dialogic participation in virtue of their religion, deemed as incompatible with the mainstream idea of Christian secularism. In this case, Muslims tend to occupy an antagonistic space in society because they are considered as scapegoats for social problems and cannot establish a dialogue with other groups as equals.

When it comes to tensions between different groups, media can offer spaces to negotiate mainstream and non-mainstream values. For example, media can frame or resist religious authority. On the one hand, media are repositories of symbolic power that legitimize religious leaders. By employing media technologies, traditional religious authorities can enhance their communication potential and gain validation, as in the case of Christian priests or the Pope on Twitter (Cheong 2015). On the other hand, media may disrupt traditional and institutional religious authority, because they help people to gain agency to determine their own religious meanings. Stewart Hoover (2009) argues that media hold "horizontalizing" or "homogenizing" effects on religion, as they challenge the traditional power hierarchies between who holds power claims and who does not. This happens as religious leaders tend to lose control on symbols and no longer hold the exclusivity of religious interpretation.

Media, when used by non-mainstream groups and individuals to challenge hegemonic structures of authority, are defined as "alternative." As for literature on alternative media practices, these media "employ the communication artifact, practices and social arrangements to challenge dominant aspects of the society" (Lievrouw 2011, 19). This means that they are counterhegemonic in resisting certain dominant social elements through communicative practices. Alternative media hold heterogeneous characteristics, usually including the creation of collective identities, articulation of participatory and interactive culture, and "unconventional" repertoires of actions.

The term alternative media designates all kinds of media that are counter-hegemonic in producing cultural, social, and religious change through different strategies. While existing literature on alternative media mainly focuses on left-wing social justice movements (Della Porta and Marchetti 2011), religious groups often engage in different kinds of media activism. The Catholic blogs analyzed in Chapter 5, for example, promote a conservative view of family and protest against certain types of civil rights, such as same-sex unions. While these Catholic groups are not explicitly political, they mostly appeal to a right-wing public, which is usually not explored in the literature about alternative media. Nonetheless, their blogs are an instance of alternative media because they express an ideology that is non-mainstream within society and negotiate Catholic authority.

This understanding of alternative media is informed by Rita Raley's (2009) work on "tactical media." According to Raley, "tactical media" are alternative media that are concerned with negotiating social and cultural values rather than producing abrupt social changes. In enforcing micropolitics of disruption, intervention, and education, tactical media form "strategical openings" that subvert hegemonic systems through the creation of non-mainstream identities and meanings. In the analysis of Michela Ardizzoni (2013), the Italian alternative television channel *Insu^TV* is an example of tactical media because, by telling stories of migrants often overlooked by other media platforms, it articulates alternative perspectives on society and redefines the concept of citizenship even without engaging in open political activism.

The concept of tactical media can account for media practices of religious groups that articulate non-mainstream religious identities and challenge established authorities. For example, Nabil Echchaibi (2013) describes the Muslim blog *Muslimah Media Watch* as a tactical media platform because it discusses the position of religion in contemporary society. While the blog does not elicit direct social action, it allows for a thickening of religious experience through what Echchaibi defines as "disruptive flows of dissent." By creating narratives against common stereotypes of Islam and gender in Western contexts, the blog produces dissent in form of counter-hegemonic discourses. Similarly, the following chapters will analyze the ways in which religious blogs help in addressing hegemonic meanings in a way that has the potential to produce long-term changes, even if not connected to social justice movements or "conventional" activism.

This perspective is useful to avoid thinking that the internet alone can produce direct and measurable social change, or that it is always alternative in helping non-mainstream voices emerge. Even if the internet allows fast connections that facilitate alternative practices, I do not wish to conceptualize "new" media as inherently counter-hegemonic and "old" media as tight to hegemonic structures. There are several limiting factors to social media's potential for resistance, as for example, issues of access and skills due to political economy and technical infrastructures; not all people have the technical means, or the critical ability, to inform themselves and to intervene in public debates through the internet. Indeed, internet spaces are often subject to power relations that influence the production, distribution, and use of information on various platforms (Fuchs 2017). Social media can reproduce social inequalities and promote verbal violence against minority groups, thus creating antagonistic spaces instead of promoting the constructive agonism described by Chantal Mouffe (Evolvi 2017). A tactical media perspective stresses how digital discourses are not "alternative" because they create drastic and short-term social change, but because they help to address the general perception of religion in the long-term.

The dialectical pairings of alternative and mainstream, therefore, aims at showing how hegemonic and non-hegemonic spaces can interact with each other creating both resistance and change. This section described mainstream religious spaces in Catholic Europe – addressing the presence of church buildings in the urban landscape, and the discourses of the Pope in certain secular spaces – and about alternative spaces – such as digital media that have a "tactical" function in trying to challenge mainstream culture. Physical and media spaces are mainstream or alternative when they are symbolically charged with certain hegemonic or counter-hegemonic meanings. The theory of hypermediation can help to describe the ways hegemonic and non-hegemonic spaces interact with each other.

Mainstream and alternative spaces may be hypermediated as they are intensified by internet practices. It is important here to notice that if, on the one hand, people use the speed of digital venues to create alternative and resistive spaces, on the other hand, they can also resist internet use. For example, people might react to social acceleration by advocating for a slowing down of practices instead of fast connections, and for silence instead of visibility (Bassett 2013). Paradoxically, this type of resistance – which is also alternative in going against dominant communicative patterns and in expressing anxieties for digital culture – needs to take into account the contemporary media ubiquity. As will be analyzed in the next chapters, the willingness to disconnect from the speed of internet communications as an alternative practice is often expressed through digital spaces, which are critically employed in selective ways.

Negotiations of mainstream and alternative spaces may be hypermediated also because they are often invested with the articulation of emotions. Social movements have been explored in relation to emotions because counter-hegemony can overcome the dichotomy between feelings and knowledge, and embed together popular and intellectual elements. A Gramscian perspective on social movements may help to understand the entanglement between ideology and affectivity, as well as the importance of subalterns' passions to challenge existing social and political conditions (Zembylas 2013). In this respect, Zizi Papacharissi (2014, 2016) connects the emotional character of social movements to alternative media platforms. She describes internet spaces, such as Twitter, as bringing liminal publics to express underrepresented viewpoints through affective storytelling.

Hypermediated religious spaces are created by the tensions between mainstream and alternative elements. Processes of religious change concern the ways in which the alternative acknowledges and engages with the mainstream, and vice versa. This book focuses on groups that are counter-hegemonic in criticizing, directly or indirectly, the dominant position of the Catholic Church in Europe, as well as the concept of Catholic secularism. It analyzes blogs that talk about religion in physical spaces, for example, discussing the presence of Catholic crucifix in public spaces as a display of hegemony. These discourses serve also the purpose of negotiating religious authorities by offering new interpretations of religious symbols and their material characteristics. At the same time, blogs target media spaces that enforce mainstream discourses. This can result either in a refusal to engage with mainstream media, thus privileging blogging as the primary mean of communication, or in efforts to gain visibility within such media, for example, trying to have blog posts quoted in national newspapers. Spatial perspectives help to understand digital venues as porous spaces of resistance that engage with physical and symbolical forms of hegemony, and that have the potential of becoming themselves hegemonic. This engagement is often embedded in relationships between the private sphere of the individual and the public dimension of communities, which also characterize hypermediated religious spaces.

Public and private spaces

Hypermediated spaces aim at reaching members of a specific group as well as connecting with society at large. Blogs, for example, collect both private narratives for a small audience and public reflections that target more people. However, the pervasive character of media within contemporary society complicates the definition of public and private. Religion simultaneously becomes more public and sustains processes of privatization. In this context, how is it possible to distinguish between "public" and "private" narratives? Is hypermediated religion "public" or "private"? What does "private" mean in the "public" internet space? The concepts of public and private are addressed through Jürgen Habermas' work on the public sphere, and the critical readings that other scholars – notably, Chantal Mouffe, Nancy Fraser, and Michael Warner – did of it. Then, the concepts of private and public will be discussed in relation to religion in Catholic Europe.

When defining the concept of "public" and "private," it is certainly helpful to acknowledge the paramount work on the public sphere of Jürgen Habermas (1991). According to Habermas, the separation of public and private occurs in social life in eighteenth-century Europe. This historical moment coincides with the formation of public opinion, which is the result of private individuals coming together and debating. Therefore, the Habermasian notion of "public" lies in the idea of individuals – which are defined as "private" – reaching consensus. This historical process leads to the creation of the public sphere, which "mediates between society and state, in which the public organizes itself as the bearer of public opinion" (Habermas, Lennox, and Lennox 1974, 50). First created in literary contexts and further developed in political environments, the public sphere is sustained by discussion and debates and based on rationality. Therefore, spaces that allow for opinion exchanges – such as theaters and cafés – become public as they help private citizens to constitute themselves into civil society. Alongside physical spaces, media participate in the formation of civil society by offering an additional space to articulate and exchange opinions and by facilitating communication between individuals.

The Habermasian public sphere is the result of a specific historical process. Indeed, the transition to mass democracy of the welfare state leads to a so-called "re-feudalization" of public authority, with a progressive re-intertwinement of public and private. In this transition, mass media take up the role of public debate, further blurring the distinction between public and private spaces. Despite the historical and geographical specificity of Habermas' public sphere, the notion of civil society is useful to understand how groups may situate themselves between the domestic sphere and state authority. As will be analyzed in the following chapters, blogs can assume the function of narrative platforms that have a role – or aspire to have a role – within the public sphere. Habermas does not equal publicness with hegemony, but considers the public sphere as potentially generating alternative meanings against public authority (1974, 5).

However, the distinction between public and private theorized by Habermas struggles to account for how certain groups interact with each other and with society. This is true also in the case of religious groups. While, according to Habermas, the public sphere is based on equal participation of privates in collective discourses and is characterized by general accessibility, it fails to be fully inclusive in practice, especially because of its focus on consensus and rationality. In elaborating the aforementioned theory of agonistic politics, Chantal Mouffe (2005) criticizes the issue of public participation in Habermas. In focusing on ideological minorities, Mouffe contests Habermas' notion of consensus arguing that it is not only "conceptually mistaken," but also "fraught for political danger" in Western modernity (2). Indeed, consensus inevitably entails a certain degree of exclusion, as the creation of a collective "we" is based on the distinction with "they" (Carpentier and Cammaerts 2006). The Habermasian public sphere, according to Mouffe, would inevitably lead to antagonism because of the power relations it involves. The refusal to acknowledge differences within democracies does not result in a society beyond antagonism, but rather in lack of plurality that perpetuates the oppression of certain groups, often prevented from entering the public sphere.

Nancy Fraser (1990) also criticizes the Habermasian notion of the public sphere. She focuses on gender and racial minorities, pointing out that in the Habermasian public sphere groups can be "weak" or "strong" according to their capacity of influencing public opinion and state decisions. Because Habermas' public sphere is constituted by white men, women and racial minorities inevitably experience substantial inequality in participation. Through a feminist reading of Habermas and a focus on identity, Fraser calls for greater inclusivity and the creation of non-liberal, non-bourgeois, and competing public spheres. According to Fraser, there is a need to establish multiple publics that benefit from real equality and therefore can influence public decisions.

In Fraser's analysis, the interplay between public and private informs minority groups' actions and behaviors: through a feminist approach, she conceptualizes the body as the center of the creation of alternative public spheres and becomes of interest for public debates. This is arguably the case of European Muslim women wearing a hijab, whose body is often policed as the bearer of certain values and meanings within the public sphere. As will be analyzed in the following chapters, the veiled body is no longer only private, but it becomes of public interest as it materially symbolizes the public presence of religion. In this case, Muslim women tend to be viewed as "other" and struggle to participate in mainstream debates, having at the same time their veiled bodies displayed and talked about in public media venues.

Michael Warner (2005) critically discusses Habermas' work by describing the concept of "public" as a social entity that is created in virtue of media attention and mass media consumption. Indeed, a public is tight to the reflexive circulation of media texts, which brings together strangers around the same discourses. Publics can be both related to dominant social values or subcultural ones, thus establishing tensions between mainstream and alternative spaces. In specific, Warner conceptualizes "counterpublics" as "defined by their tension with a larger public" (56). Therefore, the creation of counterpublics is often the result of the exclusion of certain groups from the public sphere in terms of participation.

Warner's notion of counterpublics is also based on the distinction between public and private. In the case of queer counterpublics, for example, members of the LGBTQ community look for public spaces where it is possible to enact a private performance of the self. From this perspective, media and society at large are the public dimensions of discussion, while the body incarnates the private sphere (in this case represented by sexuality and gender norms). Such distinction between private and public reveals itself apt to describe certain public religious discourses. As will be analyzed in Chapter 5, some Catholic groups engage in narratives against homosexuality and non-traditional families. By criticizing the rights to marry and procreate of LGBTQ citizens through public protests, these groups force a public rethinking of the private sphere. They also use their own bodies to establish a presence in public spaces during protests, usually amplified through the internet. Therefore, they implicitly state that the lives of members of the LGBTQ community need to be publicly discussed and scrutinized in social and media venues, and they do so through public performances enacted by private citizens.

Fraser and Warner's works may account for the existence of multiple publics that are not monolithic, but rather negotiate their boundaries between private and public spheres. While not explicitly mentioning religion, they associate the notion of private with the dimension of the body, central in religious embodied practices. The body, indeed, is often the focus of identity politics and enables ritual spaces and material practices (Morgan 2016). From this perspective, the body represents both the locus of the private religious experience and the public embodiment of religious feelings within society, as in the case of hijab-wearing Muslim women's bodies. As for the work of Lily Kong (2001), modern geographies of religion are concerned with the body as directly related to global, national, and local scales. Therefore, religion can be considered as existing on various levels, from the private dimension of the body to the global sphere of international exchanges. For Kong, media contribute defining such levels as they help certain groups to gain a more international reach and create communities with no territorial basis. This results in the establishment of a "global" religious civil society and modifies traditional understandings of religious geographies (2001, 222).

These critical engagements with Habermas can be employed to address the position of religious groups within the public sphere because they focus on identity. Habermas' conceptualization of a public sphere based on rationality, indeed, tends to exclude religious groups. The idea that religion is not rational considers religious groups as unable to participate in public debates, even when they engage in the public negotiation of identities. Habermas (2008) himself later recognizes that modernity and rationality are not necessarily secular, and he analyzes contemporary religion in terms of post-secularism. The re-thinking of the public sphere in religious terms sparkles from the increasingly public relevance of religion, as analyzed in the previous chapter. Habermas writes in this regard,

> Religion is gaining influence not only worldwide but also within national public spheres. I am thinking here of the fact that churches and religious organizations are increasingly assuming the role of "communities of interpretation" in the public arena of secular societies. They can attain influence on public opinion and will formation by making relevant contributions to key issues, irrespective of whether their arguments are convincing or objectionable.
>
> (20)

As the quote illustrates, religious institutions at the national and international level assume a public role by expressing opinions about a number of issues that are not necessarily religious-related. While Habermas' recognition of the public role of religion helps to conceptualize the public sphere in more inclusive terms, his account of the post-secular tends to overlook certain aspects of contemporary religion. In specific, it posits secular and religious spaces as separated instead of seeing them as mutually constituted; as analyzed in the previous chapter, the post-secular is considered as a consequence of secularism that allows for the interplay between religious and secular spaces. Furthermore, Habermas tends to consider religion exclusively in its public manifestations, without analyzing the ways private forms of religion shape people's identities.

In this respect, the work of José Casanova (1994) helpfully contextualizes modern religion between private and public spaces. According to Casanova, religion exists on many interrelated levels from individual practice to collective communities. Processes of religious privatization and deprivatization show this complex character of contemporary religion. For instance, modern Catholicism exists both as an element located primarily in the domestic sphere and at the level of political society. As public religion, Catholicism has the potential to influence social change and political decisions, as in the case of ethical matters such as abortion. Therefore, according to Casanova, the public locus of modern Catholicism is not the state or the political society, but rather the civil society. Casanova's perspective is relevant to describe Catholic European countries where religion has a public relevance and connects individual behaviors and feelings with political and social influences. This is the case of Pope Francis when, commenting on matters such as immigration, symbolically places the messages of the Catholic Church in the public arena of society and politics. The notion of Catholic secularism lies in the ability of the Catholic Church to become public but not explicitly political, thus maintaining a hegemonic role even in contexts where there is a formal separation between church and state.

Religion in contemporary Catholic Europe, therefore, can be found in private expressions of practice and in public spaces. The definition of private and public employed in this book takes into account embodied practices and identities. The private is found in the domestic sphere, the dimension of the body, and the individual identity; the public is the domain of society, mass-mediated interactions, the political sphere. This section mentioned some cases – such as the Muslim hijab or the Catholic preoccupation with LGBTQ issues – where the body represents the private dimension that is publicly scrutinized in the public sphere. At the same time, the Catholic Church becomes public by intervening in social and political debates. A spatial approach helps to understand the categories of public and private both in relation to physical social spaces invested by specific practices and to the private or public character of certain narratives. From this perspective, the internet may articulate narratives characterized by the "in-between-ness" – as in Hoover and Echchaibi's (2014) theory of third spaces – of private experiences and public concerns.

Public and private spaces may be hypermediated when they are characterized by intensified speed. The entanglement of private and public is made more fluid by the current "media supersaturation" and the increasing ubiquity of the internet in contemporary society (Couldry 2012). This contributes to shrinking temporal and spatial distances, allowing individuals to experience the global in a more immediate manner and to re-think their local boundaries. Because of the possibilities offered by the internet, people can find multiple venues – such as social networks or blogs – to describe their private experiences and make them public. The public character of the internet is often negotiated by individuals and groups that create secured and intimate digital venues for real time, but private, conversations. The speed that characterizes the internet, therefore, may result in the blurring of boundaries between the public and the private sphere.

At the same time, private and public spaces can be increasingly invested with emotions, as people use the internet to connect their affective religious experiences with society at large. For example, with the expression "emotional economy of the household" Lynn Schofield Clark (2014) indicates how families emotionally negotiate technology in the private sphere of the home. The ways in which the body is frequently mediated in internet discourses concerns the public display of private experiences and emotions. The blogs described in the following chapters use storytelling techniques to describe private religious-related experiences and transpose them on a digital platform that is understood as a public space because of its open accessibility. These experiences often embed emotions, which have a role in delineating the private dimension of religious practice within society, as well as the public character of contemporary religiosity.

Therefore, hypermediated religious spaces are both private and public in character and help to situate religion in Catholic Europe. The internet is not conceptualized as a public sphere because it is not universally inclusive; while it is in theory based on the notion of publicity, it often contributes to keeping certain users from full knowledge of facts and opinions (Dean 2003), also because of the aforementioned issues of access and skills. It is for this reason that, instead of thinking of the internet as a public sphere, it is better to conceptualize it as a space – or, rather, an entanglement of multiple spaces – that negotiates public and private religion without erasing their boundaries, but complicating them. This book mentions the notion of public sphere to describe the efforts of certain groups to seek consensus and connect with society at large through conversations and debates, without referring in specific to the internet.

Hypermediated spaces fluidly move between private and public dimensions. Private and public spaces are entangled with the aforementioned categories of mainstream and alternative: it is in the tension between private and public that resistive, identity-based counterpublics emerge and contest their lack of participation. However, the public does not always correspond with the mainstream, but rather it is the venue where religious feelings and practices are communicated to society at large. It is for this reason that the categories of mainstream and alternative, public and private, are connected with a third pairing: real and imaginary spaces, which involve imaginative negotiations of religion in society.

Real and imaginary spaces

Hypermediated spaces often elicit cultural change and criticize existing social structures. In this respect, people may use the internet as a venue to discuss the place religion should have within society and the tangible articulation of religious practices and beliefs, but also to imagine realities that are different from the one in which they live, both at the aesthetic and conceptual level. Therefore, what can be considered as "real" and "imaginary" in relation to the internet? Is internet-based religion (and hypermediated spaces) "real"? When does "imaginary" become "real," and vice versa? This section will address the question of real and imaginary hypermediated spaces by exploring the notion of imagined communities in relation to religion. It discusses the definitions of myth in Roland Barthes and heterotopia in Michel Foucault; it also briefly addresses concepts of hyperreality and synthetic reality and the question of authenticity of internet-based practices.

The term "imagination" indicates the creative process of negotiating reality by elaborating new meanings and values that can potentially have an impact on society and culture. Such a process is found in Benedict Anderson's (2006) definition of "imagined communities." For Anderson, nationality is a cultural artifact because citizens do not directly know each other, but feel bound by shared meanings. The nation-state, therefore, is the product of collective imaginations. These imaginations are often shaped, enacted, and circulated through media, which diffuse common languages and narratives. In the case of the Pope's visit to the European Parliament in Strasbourg mentioned in the previous chapter, the interplay between Christian and secular values may frame Europe as an "imagined community" where citizens share the same religion. The creation of European identities, indeed, arguably passes through media representations that use religion as a source for imaginative feelings of belonging.

Birgit Meyer (2010) connects Anderson's concept of imagined communities to religion and media. Instead of talking about nationalism, Meyer focuses on religious communities, which can transcend and be embedded within national boundaries. With the term "aesthetic formations," used as an alternative to "imagined communities," Meyer indicates the creation of religious communities around shared sensual practices and knowledge. This process of community making is based on the materialization of religious imaginaries through bodies, senses, and objects. The theory of aesthetic formations puts emphasis on the need for imagined communities to be grounded in reality through processes of mediation. This performative understanding of community, therefore, considers media as producing imaginaries and, at the same time, embedding them in material practices. This perspective is useful to address internet groups that form communities based on common social imaginaries and in the way they experience religion. The groups I talk about in this book, for example, can be considered as imagined communities whose members find commonalities with each other because of their religious beliefs.

Media, therefore, help to create social and cultural imaginations through visual and narrative production. They do not only provide sources for collective identities, but they negotiate reality by articulating metaphors of meaning. In this respect, the relationship between real and imaginary spaces can be understood through Roland Barthes' (1970) concept of mythology. Barthes considers ideologies as created by language: a "myth" is a kind of metalanguage that describes various realities through images. Therefore, a myth's meaning goes beyond its form; for example, the picture of a French black soldier saluting the flag on the cover of a magazine undergoes a process of distortion by which it no longer only represents the soldier as a person, but becomes the "very presence of French imperiality" (10).

In Barthes' theory, media circulate and legitimize images that serve as sources for myths. This is the case of cinema and newsreel production in the Italian post-war period, which helped to frame a national identity that denied connections with Fascism and drew from Catholicism as a moral resource (Evolvi 2016). The way in which post-war media talked about the Catholic Church resonates with the creation of religious-related mythologies in contemporary Catholic Europe. When Pope Francis visited the island of Lampedusa, for example, media tended to report the event through the symbolic narrative of the Vatican welcoming migrants to Europe. The visual presence of the Pope throwing flowers in the sea arguably symbolizes the Catholic Church's ethical concerns with migration and the Catholic attitude to help those in need. As a result, the Pope – as happens for Barthes' French black soldier – does not only represent the leader of the Catholic Church, but becomes the "myth" of religious values displayed in contemporary Europe. It is this mythology that arguably contributes to making the Pope a media event, to employ Sorrentino's expression in *The Young Pope.*

The imaginative effort of depicting reality results also in what Michel Foucault (2004) defines as "heterotopias." According to Foucault, utopias are purely imaginary spaces that do not occupy physical venues but exist at imaginary levels. Differently, heterotopias are real places where utopias are lived and enacted. Therefore, real places, utopias, and heterotopias stand in a triangular relation with each other. Hence,

> There are also, probably in every culture, in every civilization, real places – places that do exist and that are formed in the very founding of society – which are something like counter-sites, a kind of effectively enacted utopia in which the real sites, all the other real sites that can be found within the culture, are simultaneously represented, contested, and inverted. Places of this kind are outside of all places, even though it may be possible to indicate their location in reality.
>
> (3)

In other words, because heterotopias exist within real places but are inspired by utopias, they occupy liminal social positions and are symbolically detached from other venues. These spaces of contestation address space-related anxieties in contemporary society, as they shelter and confine social groups in moments of crisis. Foucault describes psychiatric hospitals as examples of heterotopias because they form spaces of deviation separated from mainstream society. Such spaces are not simply imagined, but lived within the specific venue of the hospital. Heterotopias are not freely accessible and have boundaries that separate certain groups from others.

Media's ability to employ imaginary metaphors in negotiating reality can be analyzed as a form of heterotopia. For example, Foucault's concept of heterotopia can account for how movies represent reality through multiple audiovisual layers embedded in global filming locations (Chung 2018). The ways in which digital media defined real and imaginary spaces also may establish a form of heterotopia. While Foucault focuses on liminal spaces of deviation, the internet does not necessarily create spaces that separate social groups from society at large. Hypermediated spaces can be considered heterotopias when they performatively establish communities that are ideologically and symbolically divided by the rest of society in the tension between mainstream and alternative values.

These digital spaces are not purely utopic, because they do not only create social imaginations; on the contrary, they connect with existing physical spaces where their ideas are enacted. The following chapters will analyze groups that create social and religious heterotopias by trying to make their utopias real: young Muslims employ internet spaces to show how it is possible to create multicultural venues that challenge dominant social stereotypes; atheists imagine through digital spaces a secular society where certain facets of public religion do not exist, trying, for example, to remove religious symbols from public places; and anti-gender Catholics create digitally mediated nostalgic discourses and engage in public protests to advocate for a society where religion has a more pervasive role.

While considering real and imaginary spaces as intertwined, hypermediation is not to be understood as a form of "hyperreal" as defined by Jean Baudrillard (1994). Hyperreality, according to Baudrillard, is the condition of creating a simulation not based on actual reality, a representation that is a pure simulacrum. An example that Baudrillard employs is that of Disneyland: by conceptualizing the amusement park as "imaginary," the rest of the United States are considered as "real" by contrast; however, Disneyland embeds and exalts American values, and embodies its very ideology. The United States, Baudrillard argues, is not more "real" than Disneyland, as they draw from the same symbolic imaginaries.

The current saturation of media images contributes to creating a hyperreal environment, where reality may become impossible to grasp. However, in commenting on the notion of hyperreality, Nick Couldry (2000) points out that Baudrillard's claims about the media tend to be generic. Considering media-reproduced images as inevitably contributing to the suppression of reality would imply that people have no agency on media representations and that they cannot negotiate media meanings through practice. Therefore, while they share the same prefix (*hyper-*), hypermediation is not a form of hyperreality in Baudrillard's sense. On the contrary, hypermediation takes into account the contemporary media ubiquity as providing opportunities to negotiate – and not to negate – reality within different spaces. Hypermediated spaces can rather be considered as examples of "synthetic reality," to employ the terms of Lev Manovich (2002). According to Manovich, the representations of reality enacted by new technologies are not an "inferior representation of our reality" but rather a "realistic representation of a different reality" (183). From this perspective, the narratives, videos, and images featured in internet spaces are not a poor re-making of what exists in the offline space, but rather hold imaginative potential in creating an alternative world. Digital religion is not an inferior form of religion, but an expression of how some people negotiate religious identities, beliefs, and practices.

This book talks about real and imaginary spaces to avoid the dichotomy between the online and the offline. Indeed, it does not imply that the physical space (here used as a synonym for "offline" space) is real – and, therefore, authentic – and the internet is imaginary. On the contrary, the internet and the physical are equally invested with processes of imagining different realities. It is for this reason that this book focuses on heterotopias and not utopias, which would not be embedded in real places. Hypermediated spaces are real because, in offering venues for the imagination of religion, they activate religious feelings and elicit religious practices. They are also imaginary, because they act as if they are venues for the gathering of religious communities that have a direct impact on existing religious structures. And they are authentic, because people arguably approach them as if they contain authentic religious meanings and consider them as legitimate sources of information and discussion. It is because of this "as if-ness" – to employ Hoover and Echchaibi's (2014) definition – that the theory of hypermediation seeks to describe processes that are often imaginary but not unreal: imagination is not to be understood as the antithesis of reality but as its completion.

While not distinguish between online and offline spaces, it is important to analyze the interplay between virtual and physical actions. This section described the media imaginaries and myths of the Pope and the Catholic Church, and internet spaces that seek to establish heterotopias in between the physical space and the utopic dimension. These examples show how media have an impact on the physical, and how the offline world shapes digital media discourses and representations. Online actions, indeed, can create strong networks between users and social impact on the condition that they are able to kindle offline behaviors (Rotman et al. 2011). Spatial perspectives help to underscore that the interplay between the online and the offline dimension, as it is the case for the entanglement between real and imaginary spaces, creates a fluid relationship that is generative of new meanings.

The process of transforming imaginary spaces into real spaces (and vice versa) can be considered hypermediated as it is characterized by the speed of the internet: the increasing acceleration of hypermediated practices, instead of further separating online and offline spaces, can potentially enhance the connections between the digital and the physical dimension. People increasingly use digital technologies such as smartphones in every moment of the day, and they are able to be always – or almost always – connected to the internet. In this way, internet-mediated imaginaries about society (and religion) are often perceived as real because they are embedded in everyday life. At the same time, people can mediate their experiences by transferring them to social networks and other digital platforms almost at the same time they occur.

Intensified emotions also need to be taken into account when talking about authenticity in relation to real and imaginary spaces. According to Benedict Anderson (2006) and Birgit Meyer (2010), imagined communities are fictional but able to invoke strong emotional affects. It is for this reason that in the name of nationalism – and, one may say, religion – people can even kill or die. The affective character of internet practices can engage users through feelings of common belonging that create authentic communities, define identities, and kindle actions. The fact that an internet space – such as a blog – is not based on physical and face-to-face interactions does not mean that it cannot affectively connect people. Exactly as it happens with national identities, the sense of belonging to an ideology, even if created and circulated through digital media, is emotionally relevant to mobilize people for a specific goal.

Hypermediated spaces, therefore, are real (and authentic) in virtue of the imaginative processes that they allow. They regard both online spaces, understood as potentially generative of social imaginations and authentic in virtue of the meanings and feelings they elicit, and offline spaces, which are tangible locations impacted by the creative activity of digital spaces. The next chapters will talk about blogs that use digital venues to imagine a different society and try strategies – both at media and physical level – to turn such imaginaries into real actions. By acting in between online and offline venues, these processes articulate public discourses and private narratives and try to address the mainstream and alternative character of certain types of religiosity.

Hypermediated religious spaces in practice

Space helps to understand hypermediated religious practices. By considering the internet as a form of space that has a direct impact on physical spaces, and analyzing religion through spatial methodologies, it is possible to explore how religion is currently mediated in different venues. In particular, the concept of space grounds media and religious practices in concrete locations: it places a focus on how religion is materially experienced, and how technology helps such experience; it looks at media as embedded in contemporary society and creating venues for action; and it puts emphasis on the uniqueness of certain spaces that articulate narratives that would not exist in other venues. From this perspective, space is performatively produced by people's practices, discourses, and negotiations. Therefore, hypermediated religious spaces are fluid entities whose boundaries shift according to the ways they are lived and enacted.

This chapter described these spaces through three dialectical pairings. First, hypermediated religious spaces exist in between mainstream and alternative spaces. Groups are alternative when they negotiate the perceived social, cultural, and religious hegemony, thus articulating counter-hegemonic actions and discourses. Alternative media practices discuss religious identities and authorities outside – and against – traditional institutions. Second, hypermediated religious spaces negotiate the boundaries of public and private. Instead of being public spheres in the Habermasian sense, these spaces allow for the formation of multiple counterpublics that discuss private and embodied experiences within public platforms and debate the private and public role of contemporary religion. Third, hypermediated religious spaces are invested in imaginative processes of defining reality. Created in between online and offline actions, these spaces are considered authentic by the people that use them. At the same time, they function as heterotopias, real places where utopias – in this case, the imaginary of a society where religion has a different role – are lived and enacted.

The three pairings are not mutually exclusive, but rather insist on the fluid exchanges between mainstream and alternative, public and private, imaginary and real spaces. To borrow Hoover and Echchaibi's (2014) language, hypermediated religious spaces are characterized by the "in-between-nes" of these various elements. They are also entangled with each other: the concept of hegemony informs the ways in which counterpublics exist in between public and private platforms and helps to articulate imaginary practices to negotiate reality. They can be combined in different ways. As will be analyzed in the next chapters, blogs may generate narratives that employ private experiences to create alternative discourses and enact an internet-based heterotopia; or they may try to establish a public role through actions that aspire to reach mainstream culture and have an impact on reality, just to mention some possibilities. The three pairings' mutual interactions and their ability to define space can be represented as follows:

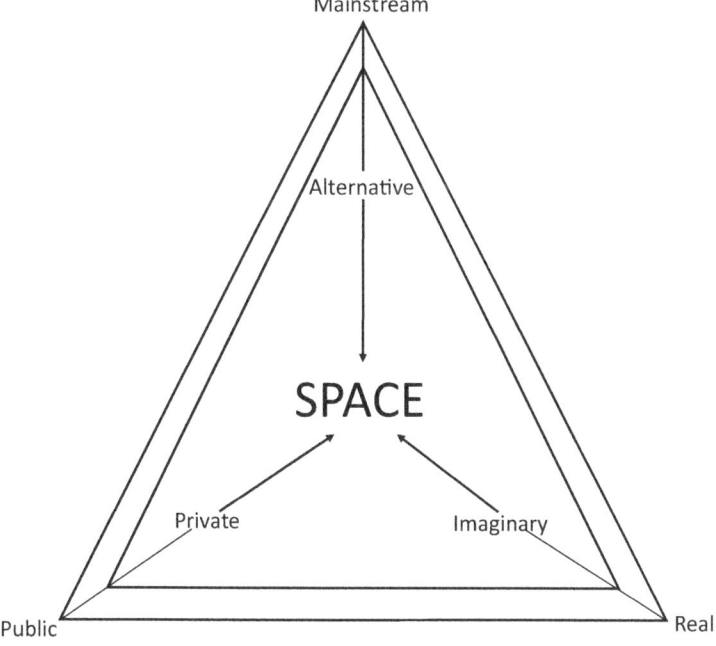

Figure 2.1 The three dialectical pairings

The entanglement of these three dialectical pairings takes into account the current media supersaturation and the intensification of mediated practices it creates. In particular, hypermediation accounts for the increasing speed (and consequent resistance to speed) of contemporary media use, and the emotional character of mediated interactions. Because of their pervasive presence in contemporary Europe, media are defined as material objects, institutions, and technologies. Religion, a system of symbols whose characteristics depend on people's practices and discourses, is also defined by the trialectic of the secular and the post-secular.

The theory of hypermediation does not exclusively apply to religion, but rather describes the ways media operate in certain contexts. The three dialectical pairings, indeed, do not explicitly refer to religious elements, but describe the ways in which religion can exist in contemporary Catholic Europe. From this perspective, hypermediated religious spaces are not *religious spaces* that are invested by sacred meanings, but *spaces of religion* where people discuss the ways in which religious discourses, practices, and beliefs exist and change in contemporary Europe. At the same time, they define various modes in which people's practices establish media spaces and give meanings to social reality through mediated discourses. Therefore, the three pairings described in this chapter can be combined with the graphical representation of religion and media elaborated in the previous chapter:

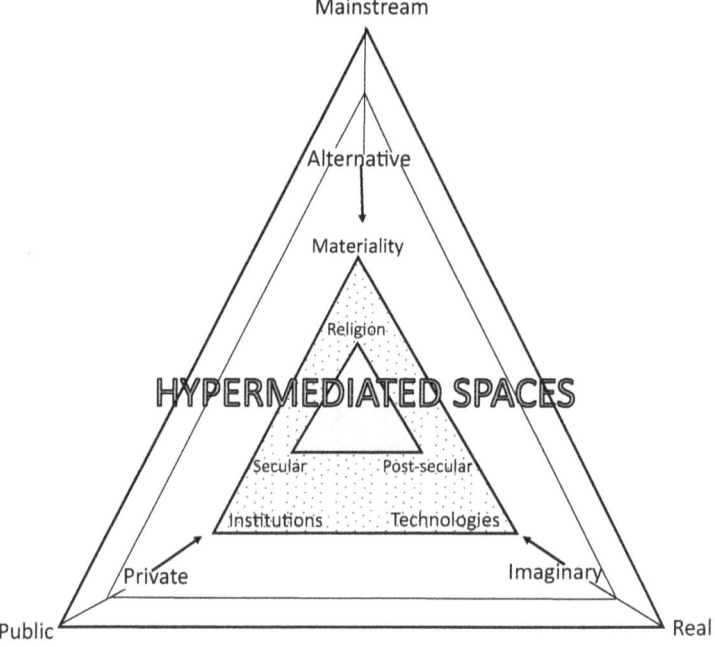

Figure 2.2 Hypermediated religious spaces

This graphic representation of hypermediated religious spaces shows how contemporary religion is entangled with the three pairings of alternative and mainstream, private and public, real and imaginary. Intensified speed and emotions blur the boundaries between various media platforms and contribute to the shifting character of religious and secular spaces in Catholic Europe. The rest of this book applies the concept of hypermediated religious spaces to three case studies. The next chapters will describe Muslim blogs as resistive spaces that seek to overcome stigma and find a place of participation in public debates; atheist blogs as examples of hypermediated religious spaces that aim at diffusing secularism and going against the hegemonic influence of the Catholic Church; Catholic blogs that criticize secularism through activities situated outside the influence of the Vatican. Blogs are examples of hypermediated religious spaces because they are digital venues of discursive production that can lead to alternative journalism as well as describe personal experiences, thus creating imagined, transnational, religious-like communities. These examples will ground the concept of hypermediated religious spaces in practice, thus showing how the internet helps the negotiation of religious identities and meanings in a way that can potentially produce new ways of approaching religion.

References

Anderson, Benedict. 2006. *Imagined Communities: Reflections on the Origin and Spread of Nationalism*. Revised edition. London; New York, NY: Verso.

Ardizzoni, Michela. 2013. "Tactical Media Practices in Italy: The Case of Insu^tv." *Journalism* 14 (7): 868–84. doi:10.1177/1464884913478362.

Ballardini, Bruno. 2011. *Gesù e i saldi di fine stagione. Perché la Chiesa non "vende" più*. Milano: Piemme.

Barthes, Roland. 1970. *Mythologies*. Paris: POINTS.

Bassett, Caroline. 2013. "Silence, Delirium, Lies?" *First Monday* 18 (3). http://firstmonday.org/ojs/index.php/fm/article/view/4617.

Baudrillard, Jean. 1994. *Simulacra and Simulation*. Translated by Sheila Glaser. Ann Arbor: The Body in Theory, Histories of Cultural Materialism.

Becci, Irene, Marian Burchardt, and Mariachiara Giorda. 2017. "Religious Super-Diversity and Spatial Strategies in Two European Cities." *Current Sociology* 65 (1): 73–91. https://doi.org/10.1177/0011392116632030.

Beekers, Daan. 2016. "The Urban Sacred Has Left Amsterdam." https://iconicreligion.wordpress.com/2016/07/11/the-urban-sacred-has-left-amsterdam/.

Bhabha, Homi K. 2004. *The Location of Culture*. 2nd edition. London; New York, NY: Routledge.

Blondheim, Menahem. 2007. " 'The Significance of Communication' According to Harold Adams Innis." In *The Toronto School of Communication Theory: Interpretations, Extensions, Applications*. Edited by Rita Watson, and Menahem Blondheim. Toronto: University of Toronto Press.

boyd, danah. 2006. "A Blogger's Blog: Exploring the Definition of a Medium." *Reconstruction* 6 (4).

Carragee, Kevin M. 1993. "A Critical Evaluation of Debates Examining the Media Hegemony Thesis." *Western Journal of Communication* 57 (3): 330–48. https://doi.org/10.1080/10570319309374457.

Carpentier, Nico, and Bart Cammaerts. 2006. "Hegemony, Democracy, Agonism and Journalism: An Interview with Chantal Mouffe." *Journalism Studies* 7 (6): 964–75.

Casanova, Jose. 1994. *Public Religions in the Modern World.* Chicago: University of Chicago Press.

Cheong, Pauline. 2015. "Tweet the Message? Religious Authority and Social Media Innovation." *The Journal of Religion, Media and Digital Culture* 3 (3): 1–19.

Chung, Hye Jean. 2018. *Media Heterotopias: Digital Effects and Material Labor in Global Film Production.* Durham: Duke University Press Books.

Clark, Lynn Schofield. 2014. "Mobile Media in the Emotional and Moral Economies of the Household." In *The Routledge Companion to Mobile Media.* Edited by Gerard Goggin, and Larissa Hjorth. New York, NY: Routledge.

Couldry, Nick. 2000. *The Place of Media Power: Pilgrims and Witnesses of the Media Age.* 1st edition. London; New York, NY: Routledge.

Couldry, Nick. 2012. *Media, Society, World: Social Theory and Digital Media Practice.* 1st edition. Cambridge; Malden, MA: Polity.

Dean, Jodi. 2003. "Why the Net Is Not a Public Sphere." *Constellations* 10 (1): 95–112. doi:10.1111/1467-8675.00315.

Della Porta, Donatella, and Raffaele Marchetti. 2011. *Transnational Activism and the Global Justice Movement.* http://cadmus.eui.eu//handle/1814/19866.

Echchaibi, Nabil. March 2013. "Muslimah Media Watch: Media Activism and Muslim Choreographies of Social Change." *Journalism.* doi:10.1177/1464884913478360.

Echchaibi, Nabil. 2017. "Hypermediation as an Argument." Center for Media, Religion, and Culture, University of Colorado Boulder. Unpublished essay.

Evolvi, Giulia. July, 2016. "The Myth of Catholic Italy in Post-Fascist Newsreels [5]." *Media History*, 1–15. doi:10.1080/13688804.2016.1207510.

Evolvi, Giulia. 2017. "#Islamexit: Inter-Group Antagonism on Twitter." *Information, Communication & Society*: 1–16. https://doi.org/10.1080/1369118X.2017.1388427.

Foucault, Michel. 2004. "Des espaces autres." *Empan* 54 (2): 12–19.

Fraser, Nancy. 1990. "Rethinking the Public Sphere: A Contribution to the Critique of Actually Existing Democracy." *Social Text* 25/26: 56–80. doi:10.2307/466240.

Fuchs, Christian. 2017. *Social Media: A Critical Introduction.* 2nd revised edition. Thousand Oaks, CA: Sage Publications, Incorporated.

Gramsci, Antonio, and V. Gerratana. 2014. *Quaderni del carcere.* Torino: Einaudi.

Habermas, Jürgen. 1991. *The Structural Transformation of the Public Sphere: An Inquiry into a Category of Bourgeois Society.* Cambridge, MA: The MIT Press.

Habermas, Jürgen. 2008. "Notes on Post-Secular Society." *New Perspectives Quarterly* 25 (4): 17–29. doi:10.1111/j.1540-5842.2008.01017.x.

Habermas, Jürgen, Sara Lennox, and Frank Lennox. 1974. "The Public Sphere: An Encyclopedia Article (1964)." *New German Critique* 3: 49–55. doi:10.2307/487737.

Hoover, Stewart M. 2009. "Transformations: The Case of Religious Cultures." In *Mediatization: Concept, Changes, Consequences.* Edited by Knut Lundby. London: Peter Lang Publishing Inc.

Hoover, Stewart M., and Echchaibi, Nabil. 2014. "Media Theory and the Third Spaces of Digital Religion." Working Paper Center for Media, Religion, and Culture.

Hopkins, Peter, Lily Kong, and Elizabeth Olson, eds. 2013. *Religion and Place: Landscape, Politics and Piety*. New York: Springer.

Knott, Kim. 2014. *The Location of Religion: A Spatial Analysis*. 1st edition. New York, NY: Routledge.

Kong, Lily. 2001. "Mapping 'new' Geographies of Religion: Politics and Poetics in Modernity." *Progress in Human Geography* 25 (2): 211–33. doi:10.1191/030913201678580485.

Krech, Volkhard. 2012. "Religious Contacts in Past and Present Times: Aspects of a Research Programme." *Religion* 42 (2): 191–213. https://doi.org/10.1080/0048 721X.2012.642572.

Lears, T. J. Jackson. 1985. "The Concept of Cultural Hegemony: Problems and Possibilities." *The American Historical Review* 90 (3): 567–93. doi:10.2307/1860957.

Lefebvre, Henri. 1992. *The Production of Space*. 1st edition. Malden, MA: Wiley-Blackwell.

Lievrouw, Leah. 2011. *Alternative and Activist New Media*. 1st edition. Cambridge; Malden, MA: Polity.

Lövheim, Mia. 2011. "Young Women's Blogs as Ethical Spaces." *Information, Communication & Society* 14 (3): 338–54. doi:10.1080/1369118X.2010.542822.

Manovich, Lev. 2002. *The Language of New Media*. Revised edition. Cambridge, MA: The MIT Press.

Meyer, Birgit, ed. 2010. *Aesthetic Formations: Media, Religion, and the Senses*. 2009 edition. New York, NY: Palgrave Macmillan.

Morgan, David. 2016. "Material Analysis and the Study of Religion." In *Materiality and the Study of Religion: The Stuff of the Sacred*. Edited by Tim Hutchings, and Joanne McKenzie. New York, NY: Theology and Religion in Interdisciplinary Perspective Series in Association with the Bsa Sociology of Religion Study Group.

Mouffe, Chantal. 2005. *On the Political*. New Ed edition. London, New York: Routledge.

Mouffe, Chantal. 2013. *Agonistics: Thinking the World Politically*. 1st edition. London; New York, NY: Verso.

Oldenburg, Ray. 1999. *The Great Good Place: Cafes, Coffee Shops, Bookstores, Bars, Hair Salons, and Other Hangouts at the Heart of a Community*. 3rd edition. New York, NY: Berkeley, CA: Marlowe & Company.

Pace, Enzo. 2007. "A Peculiar Pluralism." *Journal of Modern Italian Studies* 12 (1): 86–100. doi:10.1080/13545710601132979.

Papacharissi, Zizi. 2014. *Affective Publics: Sentiment, Technology, and Politics*. 1st edition. Oxford; New York, NY: Oxford University Press.

Papacharissi, Zizi. 2016. "Affective Publics and Structures of Storytelling: Sentiment, Events and Mediality." *Information, Communication & Society* 19 (3): 307–24. doi:10.1080/1369118X.2015.1109697.

Raley, Rita. 2009. *Tactical Media*. Minneapolis: University of Minnesota Press.

Rogers, Richard. 2015. *Digital Methods*. Cambridge, MA: The MIT Press.

Rotman, Dana, Sarah Vieweg, Sarita Yardi, Ed Chi, Jenny Preece, Ben Shneiderman, Peter Pirolli, and Tom Glaisyer. 2011. "From slacktivism to activism: participatory culture in the age of social media." *CHI '11 Extended Abstracts on Human Factors in Computing Systems* (CHI EA '11). ACM, New York, NY, USA, 819

Soja, Edward W. 1996. *Thirdspace: Journeys to Los Angeles and Other Real-and-Imagined Places*. 1st edition. Cambridge, MA: Wiley-Blackwell.

Warner, Michael. 2005. *Publics and Counterpublics*. New York, NY; Cambridge, MA: Zone Books.

Williams, Raymond. 1973. "Base and Superstructure in Marxist Cultural Theory." *New Left Review: London* 1 (82): 3–16.

Zembylas, Michalinos. 2013. "Revisiting the Gramscian Legacy on Counter-Hegemony, the Subaltern and Affectivity: Toward an Emotional Pedagogy of Activism in Higher Education." *Critical Studies in Teaching and Learning* 1 (1). doi:10.14426/cristal.v1i1.2.

3 Muslim and European

Spaces to defeat stereotypes and articulate hybrid identities

On 13 November 2015, suicide bombers committed coordinated terrorist attacks in Paris. They targeted people at a football match and a concert, in restaurants and bars. The attacks, which are considered among the deadliest in the European Union after the Second World War, killed 130 people and injured more than 400. The Islamic State (ISIS) claimed responsibility for the attacks. Paris had already witnessed terrorism in January 2015, when 17 people were killed in an attack against the editorial staff of *Charlie Hebdo*, a satirical magazine accused of ridiculing the Prophet Mohammed. Following the Paris attacks, other terrorist incidents claimed by ISIS occurred in Europe: three bombs were placed in Brussels, trucks were driven into people in Berlin, London, Nice, and Barcelona, and a bombing occurred at a concert in Manchester, to name but a few.

The hashtag *#NousSommesUnis* (We Are United) was created in France in response to the November 2015 Paris attacks. Muslims and non-Muslims alike use the hashtag not only to mourn the victims of the attacks and condemn terrorism, but also to refuse ethnic, racial, and religious divisions within society. *Nous Sommes Unis* became a collective organization that groups Muslim, secular, Christian, as well as multifaith associations. The organization promotes various campaigns and demonstrations for tolerance and social cohesion. *Nous Sommes Unis* explains its aims on its website (www.noussommesunis.com) as follows:

> Terrorists sent us a clear message. They are willing to bring France to her knees. Let's assert them that we will remain together and standing up for the other! Upright and together, side by side, hand in hand and never against each other. Our unity is our most precious wealth.
>
> (Nous Sommes Unis)

After November 2015, the *#NousSommesUnis* hashtag has been used also in relation to other terrorist attacks. While people belonging to different religions employ the hashtag, it assumes a specific relevance for Muslims who wish to dissociate themselves from Islamic terrorism. The attacks in France and Europe, indeed, resulted in increased anti-Muslim attitudes

Figure 3.1 A screenshot from the *#NousSommesUnis* video. Retrieved from www. youtube.com/watch?v=WVUCMBuAQNs on the 25 February 2018

and stigmatization of Islam as a violent religion. Some European Muslims employ the hashtag in order to establish a voice in the larger public debate, stressing their acceptance of Western values and their willingness to work together for a more peaceful society.

The association *Etudiants Musulman de France* (EMF, French Muslim Students), which is also member of the organization *Nous Sommes Unis*, created a video in response to the November 2015 Paris Attacks (EMF Asso, You Tube, 15 November 2015). The video alternates footages of the attacks with images of EMF members; they hold a black sign with the hashtag *#NousSommesUnis* and the logo of the association written on, as shown in Figure 3.1. They appear to be from different ethnic backgrounds, with the majority of the women wearing a Muslim veil. The students do not speak, but the images are accompanied by a dramatic music and a poem in French about the attacks. The poem explains that French Muslims "have no voice" and their hearts are "wounded" because of the terrorist attacks. The video refuses the connection between Islam and terrorism, with a paragraph of the poem saying,

> They think they're conducting a war against crusaders. / And they invoke the Quran and rely on its verses. / But there is no law that allows spilling the blood of an innocent / If they didn't understand it, I don't understand them.
>
> (EMF Asso, YouTube, 15 November 2015)

The video reiterates the need for remaining united and explains that the French principle of *fraternité* (fraternity) is stronger than violence. It ends with a written quote from the Quran, which states, "If anyone slays a person, it would be as if he slew the whole people." The video reached 200,000 views in 24 hours and became viral because of its simple but highly emotional message. According to EMF President Iaad Ben Dhia, who is also in charge of the association's communication and public relations, the EMF got positive media attention after the video and was soon contacted by French, European, and international media outlets for interviews (personal communication, 22 June 2017).

The French channel CNEWS, for example, interviewed some members of EMF, including Nadjib Bedani, the student from Toulouse who conceived of and created the video (CNEWS, YouTube, 16 November 2015). Bedani explains that he is "relieved to be heard" because "after *Charlie Hebdo* and other attacks that shocked the world, we needed to express ourselves, but we did not necessarily have the occasion to be heard." The internet, in this case, helps Muslim students to be heard when talking about their emotions and to reiterate their beliefs in French values.

Besides the #*NousSommesUnis* campaign and video, European Muslims expressed their feelings and opinions about terrorist attacks in various ways. The Forum of European Muslim Youth and Student Organization (FEMYSO, www.femyso.org), of which the EMF is a member, explains that terroristic attacks result in counter-terrorism measures that are often discriminatory against all Muslims; for example, many Muslim women are searched in airports and train stations only because they wear a hijab. According to Brussels-based FEMYSO, therefore, Muslims do not only need to condemn terrorism, but also to actively fight growing Islamophobia in Europe, for example, by lobbying European institutions for policies against religious-based discrimination (FEMYSO, 21 September 2016).

Alongside anti-Islamophobia campaigns and actions, some European Muslims criticize the anti-Islam attitude after terrorist attacks. The Italian blog *Yalla Italia*, for example, offered a space for young Muslims to write about their feelings after the *Charlie Hebdo* attack. A blogger denounces how "everybody brutally condemns Islam and nobody condemns the fact that Islam is used as a scapegoat," and that "one cannot criticize *laïcité*, freedom, a non-believer, or a gay person, but Muslims are all [considered as] terrorists and everybody despises them!" (*Yalla*, 9 January 2015). The post argues that, because many Europeans consider Islam and terrorism as intrinsically connected, Muslims are continuously expected to somehow prove the peaceful character of their beliefs.

While not directly linked to the #*NousSommesUnis* campaign and video, these reactions can be seen as young Muslims' efforts to maintain their religious identities in a society that increasingly accuses them of not accepting its values. ISIS-claimed terrorist attacks, indeed, seem to confirm the idea that Islam is not compatible with European values. This idea is connected with the concept of Catholic secularism, analyzed in the previous chapters. Even if secularism is meant to transcend religious differences, in Europe it tends to privilege Christianity and shows anxieties about what is perceived as non-European religions, notably Islam (Asad 2003). This may result in regulations that Muslims consider discriminatory and in negative media representations of Islam (Roy 2013).

In addition, videos and digital discourses created by young European Muslims often show the heterogeneous character of European Islam. As analyzed in this book's introduction, Pope Francis visited the island of Lampedusa and met some Muslim migrants. While the media coverage of the event may suggest that the growth of Islam in Europe is mainly due to these recent Muslim migrations, social reality is more nuanced. Indeed, many Muslims have already been living in Europe for generations and are neither fundamentalists nor recent migrants. I would argue that the strategies these Muslims employ to practice Islam in Europe also represent a type of religious change because it negotiates and adapts religious and cultural values.

The creation of digital narratives, such as the aforementioned video and blog posts, helps these European Muslims to become more visible. In counteracting violence and pledging a symbolic alliance to European values, they show their faith's compatibility with democracy and secularism. These voices create hypermediated religious spaces because they mostly find a venue of expression on the internet, especially through circulation of videos, hashtags, and personal stories. In particular, they address the tension with mainstream culture by talking about Islamophobia and negative stereotypes and by discussing the question of the female Muslim veil in public spaces. Emotional discourses, as in the *#NousSommesUnis* video, help to connect with non-Muslims and to imagine a more multicultural society.

This chapter analyzes how European Islam is discursively articulated in digital spaces by young Muslims. After addressing academic literature about Muslims in Europe, the chapter will explore the discourses created by the French association *Etudiants Musulman de France* and the Italian blog *Yalla Italia*. In particular, it discusses narratives aimed at negotiating the principle of *laïcité* in France in relation to Islamophobia and anti-hijab laws. The chapter will then address strategies to adapt Islam to European culture and society, and talk about the issue of citizenship in Italy. The chapter concludes by explaining why these spaces are hypermediated in challenging dominant stereotypes, normalizing the presence of Islam in Europe, and articulating hybrid Muslim identities that are compatible with European culture.

Islam in Europe: a short summary

Islam existed in Europe since the seventh century, and in certain cases it actively contributed shaping European culture, architecture, and society (Allievi 2003). The number of Muslims in Europe has been recently growing, going from 4 percent of the population in 1990 to 6 percent in 2010, and it is projected to reach 8 percent in 2030 (Hackett 2016). The Muslim presence is usually higher in those countries, like France, whose colonial past provides a bond with predominantly Muslim areas. Migrations are a contributing factor to the growth of Islam in Europe, especially following the Arab Spring in 2011.

Media and political discourses in Europe tend to portray Muslims in a negative way. Muslim migrants are often described as "invaders" that can threaten European values (Vaccari 2009). The aforementioned terrorist attacks seem to confirm the idea that Muslims are violently opposed to Western democracies. As a result, media representations of European Islam tend to either frame Muslims as impoverished migrants or potential terrorists, without leaving substantial space for self-representation (el-Aswad 2013).

The negative portrayal of Muslims in Europe is often paired with national laws aimed at regulating the public visibility of Islam, often considered more problematic than that of Christianity (Gatti 2016). For example, Switzerland restricted the building of Muslim minarets with a referendum in 2009 (Awad 2013). In France, a series of laws address the presence of hijab-wearing students in public schools. Following the expulsion of veiled schoolgirls starting in 1989 (Ferrara et al. 2010), the French parliament approved in 2004 a law that prohibits wearing "ostensible" symbols of religious beliefs in educational establishments (Maeder, Dempsey, and Pozzulo 2012), extended in 2007 to all governmental employees (Kavakci and Kraeplin 2016). Furthermore, in 2010, full-covering veils were also banned for security reasons (Fredette 2015). Prohibitions of the face-covering *niqab* have been frequently discussed in various European countries, such as Germany, Belgium, and the UK.

These examples show how various polities may have a problem with the increasing visibility of Islam in public spaces. Grace Davie (2013) discusses the visibility of Muslim communities in Europe by writing that, even if not particularly numerous, they pose issues for secularism because

> They are challenging the deeply held conviction among the great majority of Europeans that belief is a private matter. The reason is simple enough. Islam forms part of a very different cultural heritage in which religion is not a discrete activity as it has become in the West, but a way of life. In the ummah, the religious and the secular are inseparable from each other and both, it follows, are present in the public sphere.
>
> (5)

Therefore, according to Davie, the presence of Muslims is considered problematic in virtue of their alleged inability to separate private and public forms of religiosity. Their embodied presence in secular spaces is often perceived as a challenge for secularism. This idea that Islam and its symbols are somehow incompatible – or even threatening – to European culture can lead to instances of Islamophobia. The Runnymede Trust (1997) defines Islamophobia as "unfounded hostility towards Islam" (4). Islamophobia usually targets Muslims in virtue of their cultural belonging to Islam (Linehan

2012). Therefore, Islamophobia is often the product of a "racialization" of Islam, a term that indicates the tendency to focus on religion more than color and race, thus considering Islam as a racial category. This "racialization" often compels Muslims to articulate their identity in terms of religious – rather than ethnic – belonging (Ahmad and Evergeti 2010). While this phenomenon is particularly prominent in the UK (Werbner 2009), it can arguably inform Islam-related discourses throughout Europe.

Anti-Muslim feelings are increasingly employed by European populist political parties. From Italian *Lega Nord*, to French *Front National*, to *British National Party* (Wood and Finlay 2008; Davies 2010), xenophobic political formations contribute connecting migrations with terrorism and frame Islam as "other" to European culture. In addition, anti-Muslim protest groups, such as the German *Pegida*, promote explicit Islamophobic discourses in the public sphere (Dostal 2015). These groups often use the internet as preferred venue to spread their ideas and organize their activities (Allen 2015). Social networks, such as Twitter, have indeed been recognized as a fertile venue for anti-Islam discourses (Evolvi 2017b).

However, the internet can also help Muslims articulate narratives that counteract dominant stereotypes and address existing media representations (Echchaibi 2011a). Examples of Muslim digitals spaces are hijab tutorials that discuss Islamic fashion and garments (Akou 2010; Peterson 2016), blogs that help the articulation of identities and hybrid subjectivities in the West (Echchaibi 2013), and YouTube videos that counteract Islamophobic claims (Zoonen, Vis, and Mihelj 2011). These examples show how the internet can potentially become a "safe space" where Muslims create religious-based counterpublics and promote a tactical media use to change dominant perceptions of Islam.

Therefore, the analysis of internet discourses may help to understand European Islam in its heterogeneity. While Davie (2013) asserts that the issue of Islam in Europe is largely dependent on its inability to separate private and public forms of religiosity, European Muslims' discursive production can frame the relationship between Islam and *laïcité* in more nuanced terms. This chapter takes into account two hypermediated spaces that, while not connected to each other, contribute to religious change in Europe by showing how young Muslims make sense of their religion in Western contexts: the French EMF and the Italian *Yalla*.

The association *Etudiants Musulman de France* (EMF, www.emf-asso. com) was founded in 1989 with the name UISEF (*Union islamique des étudiants de France*, Islamic Union of French Students), changing to the current name in 1996. The aim of the association is to support both French Muslim students and exchange students from abroad and is also open to non-Muslim members. According to current president Iaad Ben Dhia (personal communication, 22 June 2017), it counts thousands of members and sympathizers. While inspired by Islamic principles and values, EMF is not formally a religious association, and it is not connected with any religious institution. It counts more than 20 local chapters that are involved in educational, cultural, and charity activities. EMF is engaged at European level as a member of The Forum of European Muslim Youth and Student Organization (FEMYSO). The EMF website functions as a platform to offer opinions about student life in France and to present the associations' initiatives. Even if it may not be technically considered a blog – articles are not chronologically organized, often anonymous, and without comments – the EMF website is a digital presence, written by EMF members, which helps French Muslims students to express themselves. It embeds various media platforms, as in the case of the aforementioned #*NousSommesUnis* video. EMF also has various social media accounts, such as a YouTube channel and Facebook pages, which are managed at a national and local level by EMF members.

Yalla Italia (hereinafter *Yalla*, www.yallaitalia.it) is a blog written in Italian by second-generations. The term "second-generation" indicates people that are born or raised in Italy from immigrant parents. *Yalla* was founded in 2006 as a printed magazine within the third-sector publication *Vita* by journalist Martino Pillitteri and Arabic Studies Professor Paolo Branca. While not Muslims and second-generations themselves, Pillitteri and Branca felt that young Italians who live between two cultures and religions needed a venue to express their ideas. In 2011 *Yalla* became a blog written by more than 40 contributors from different backgrounds and religions. The blog discusses issues of multiculturalism and integration and constitutes an interesting platform to understand Islam in Italy because it often describes experiences and feelings of young Muslim Italians. Even if it is not an association, *Yalla* engages in different activities beyond the digital space, such as volunteer campaigns and public talks. According to Pillitteri (personal communication 29 May 2015), the blog reached up to 2,000 visits per day, also because of the bloggers' efforts to circulate posts on social media, and was updated several times a week. However, the blog closed in 2015 and was put offline in 2017, because of bloggers' lack of time to conciliate writing with work and family activities, as well as their willingness to engage in other projects.

EMF and *Yalla* are two different projects in two different national contexts, the former being an association focused on education, and the latter a blog about multiculturalism. They are hypermediated religious spaces that directly or indirectly discuss the practice of Islam in Europe through narratives about issues which include migration, ethnicity, and gender. They are written by young Muslims usually born and raised in Europe, who are not professionals in digital communication but part of a generation that is familiar with digital technologies. Because they do not depend on religious institutions, they can negotiate religious authority more freely. They do not represent all European Muslims, but rather those that are engaged in certain strategies of religious adaptation in both public and private spaces. This chapter will discuss how these groups, by promoting a greater religious integration and challenging the idea that Christian symbols and ideologies alone should be allowed in the European public space, seek to carve multi-culturalist spaces. In particular, the chapter will address the EMF discourses about Islam and *laïcité* in France, and *Yalla* narratives about Islam in Italy, and how they create descriptions, often narratively enabled by the dynamic character of hypermediated spaces, of a type of Islam that is not connected to migrations or terrorism, but coexists with European values.

EMF: I have pain in my France

By creating the #*NousSommesUnis* video described above, Muslim students from the association *Etudiants Musulman de France* did not only condemn terrorism, but also pledged a symbolic alliance to French culture and values. They talk about the attacks not as Muslims, but as French citizens. The concept of *Nous Sommes Unis*, indeed, describes all French citizens as belonging to the same culture, despite their religion. In the poem read during the video, a line recites, *"J'ai mal a ma France"* (I have pain in my France) to describe the distress of young Muslims in seeing their country targeted by terrorist attacks.

However, while the concept of *Nous Sommes Unis* tries to create social cohesion, the position of Muslims in the French public sphere is far from being unproblematic. Muslims in France are among the largest minorities in Western Europe, accounting for around 7.5 percent of the population (Hackett 2016). The presence of Muslims in France is often tied to colonialism. The atrocities of the Algerian independence war and a tendency to consider people from former colonies as "other" to French culture complicate the assimilation process of Muslims. France still suffers from large economic and social inequalities mostly at the expense of citizens originally from Africa and the Middle East, even when they have been in the country for multiple generations. Therefore, these Muslim citizens – sometimes called *Beurs*, a slang for Arabs – often face discriminations because of both their ethnicity and religion (Echchaibi 2011b).

In addition, Islam may find itself at odds with the French principle of *laïcité*. As will be explored in the next chapter, *laïcité* is the doctrine of church–state separation that characterizes in specific the French context. Bans against religious symbols in public spaces exemplify how French *laïcité* aims at regulating the visible and embodied presence of religion between private, public, and institutional spaces. While these bans do not formally target Islam only, they may result in restrictions for hijab-wearing Muslim women, who often have to choose between their religious garments and educational and employment opportunities.

In this context, the EMF provides a voice for young French Muslims by focusing on higher education. In offering support to university students, the association shows how young Muslims adapt to everyday life and society in France and navigate the different nuances of the French *laïcité*. In her ethnography of French Muslims, Jennifer Fredette (2014) interviews members of the EMF, alongside other Muslim associations, in order to explore how elite discourses address the heterogeneity of French Islam in relation to national citizenship. Fredette describes the EMF as trying to normalize the presence of Muslims in France (2011, 61). The EMF website functions as space where young Muslims' activities and feelings are presented in an implicit and explicit fight against Islamophobia, creating, for example, online and offline activities in support of the female veil. The acceptance of French values, as expressed in the #NousSommesUnis video, is arguably a strategy Muslim students employ to counteract existing stereotypes and be an active part of the French society.

Muslims and French Islamophobia

The EMF promotes a number of activities that often do not have a direct connection with Islam, but that may indirectly address anti-Muslim attitudes and stereotypes. For example, it offers kits with dishes, stationaries, and notebooks for the symbolic price of five euros in order to help students to start their university life. Its local sections also provide meals and food baskets through *banques alimentaire* (food banks) to students that do not have means to support themselves. These activities are part of a general effort of the association to both engage students in volunteering and to help students in need.

Alongside charity activities, the EMF also organizes sport and leisure events. This is the case of sports tournaments between different local sections for both men and women, as well as gala dinners whose pictures and videos are usually circulated through social networks. The project *Plumes d'Étudiants* (Students' Feathers), which ran for three editions, is aimed at collecting short novels written by students. While the students who participate are usually not professional writers, the project gives them the possibility of expressing themselves and talking about their ideas and experiences in a creative way. The novels that are judged more interesting are published in a paperback, as well as discussed on the association's social networks and YouTube channel.

These activities are part of a larger EMF's effort to help students with their private and professional life, which often also addresses discrimination and Islamophobia. For example, the EMF denounces the anti-Muslim episodes that spike in the aftermath of terrorist attacks. The EMF website lists some of the episodes occurred after the *Charlie Hebdo* attack in 2015, including Muslim women attacked and their veils ripped off, and Islamophobic slogans and pig's heads left on mosque doors. These acts are commented as follows:

> Some individuals appropriate Islam to act alone in the name of this beautiful religion with actions that are against the very religion they claim. . . . The millions of French Muslims that live their faith in complete

harmony with their society are now mixed up, targeted, aggressed and insulted because of the actions of three individuals [the attackers].

(EMF, 10 January 2015)

With these words, the EMF condemns Islamophobia and reiterates the un-Islamic character of terror attacks. By stating that "millions of French Muslims live their faith in harmony with their society," they oppose the claim that Muslims cannot conform to French values. This attitude might have symbolic connections with the association's charity and leisure activities. Indeed, EMF members both show their commitment creating a better educational and social environment, and describe their unthreatening everyday lives through projects such as *Plumes d'Étudiants*. In so doing, they indirectly situate themselves among the "millions of French Muslims" that are productive members of society and unjustly suffer Islamophobic discrimination because of the actions of isolated terrorists.

Islamophobia in France is expressed through aggression against Muslims, but it can also take more subtle forms of discrimination. Indeed, the EMF writes on its website,

It should also be remembered that Islamophobia negatively impacts many students when they are looking for internships and, after, for jobs. Indeed, many of them every year are denied internship opportunities for this reason (this mainly regards students who wear a veil, but not only).

(EMF, 17 November 2014)

The article explains that Muslim students – especially those that "visibly" belong to Islam because of their garments and ethnicity – are often marginalized in the job market. Such discriminations may target also certain religious practices, such as fasting during Ramadan. This type of Islamophobia heavily impacts EMF members, who are university students trying to find a place in the job market and develop a career. Indeed, the EMF denounces that a practicing Muslim has 50 percent less probability of being invited to a job interview than a Catholic (EMF, 1 November 2015). It is a subtle form of discrimination that arguably echoes a "racialization" of Islam because it uses both religion and ethnicity as marks to marginalize a part of the population.

In order to fight Islamophobia, the EMF created a student guide in collaboration with the aforementioned European-level association FEMYSO and the French *Collectif Contre l'Islamophobie en France* (CCIF, Collective against Islamophobia in France). The guide, available online on the EMF website and distributed in various local sections, aims at giving students practical tools to oppose Islamophobia. For example, it explains in which circumstances the French legislation allows wearing religious garments and how to react if institutional authorities unfairly prohibit them.

Through the guide, information campaigns, and articles, the EMF aims at giving students practical knowledge of *laïcité*. The issue of Islamophobia, indeed, is closely connected to different understandings of the French *laïcité*: anti-Muslim discriminations, when not directly Islamophobic, are usually caused by a "misguided reading of the principle of *laïcité*." (EMF, 17 November 2014). This means that *laïcité* can sometimes be used not only to regulate religious manifestations in public and institutional spaces, but also to openly discriminate Muslims in school environments and in the workplace. This might be an indirect critique of certain atheist groups that, as will be demonstrated in the next chapter, challenge the presence of Muslim symbols in given spaces.

The EMF does not openly oppose *laïcité*, but finds strategies to conciliate the visibility of Muslim beliefs and practices with state secularism. While the EMF is inspired by Muslim ethics and values, as the word *Musulmans* in its name indicates, it presents itself as a cultural association rather than a religious organization precisely to comply with the norms of French *laïcité*. According to Ben Dhia (personal communication, 22 June 2017), indeed, the association deliberately chooses not to focus on religion to avoid conflicts with the principle of *laïcité* in the public education system. From this perspective, the different charity and leisure activities organized by the association assume a double meaning: on the one hand, they engage Muslim students with society at large and they normalize their everyday lives, situating them among the majority of Muslims that are not terrorists; on the other hand, they ensure that the primary aim of the association remains cultural, therefore not at odds with the French principle of *laïcité*.

Therefore, the EMF creates safe spaces where Muslim students can socialize and express themselves, as well as address Islamophobia. Through their website and various activities, Muslim students arguably seek strategies to engage with French mainstream culture. This engagement is not uncritical: by challenging Islamophobia, for example, the EMF also criticizes certain facets of *laïcité*. In this way, it tries to secure physical spaces – for example, within public universities – where Muslims can safely manifest their faith. Negotiating the meaning of French *laïcité* helps to articulate Muslim identities in relation to French values. In particular, personal stories of French Muslims may challenge Islamophobia in an emotional way. This is often the case with stories of hijab-wearing women, who are the main targets of Islamophobic attacks.

Muslims and the veil in France

The EMF often discusses Islamophobia from a gendered perspective because of the greater marginalization of Muslim women in French and European society. In so doing, they talk about gender equality and find strategies, both online and offline, to normalize the visible presence of Islam in public spaces. Indeed, Muslim women not only endure discriminations and harassments because of their gender, but, when they wear a hijab, they are also clearly recognizable as Muslims in the public space. Quoting data collected

by the CCIF, the EMF explains that 74 percent of victims of Islamophobia are women. An article written for the International Women's day on
the EMF website reminds that celebrating women means also addressing
Islamophobia. It articulates the issue with the following words:

> The EMF demands that the rights of all women (included Muslim
> women) are recognized and protected, in particular the right to receive
> an education (threatened every year by a new law proposal against the
> veil in Universities). [This right] is indeed the basis for emancipation of
> spirit and freedom.
>
> (EMF, 8 March 2016)

As the quote suggests, the EMF employs the International Women's Day as
an occasion to talk about discriminations against Muslim women, mentioning in specific laws that prevent veiled women from attending public schools.
In connecting Islamophobia with lack of gender equality and human rights,
EMF challenges the idea that Islam does not subscribe to Western values.
It presents the issue from a perspective that goes against many common
assumptions: it is not Islam that prevents women from going to school and
forces them to cover, but they are anti-Islam norms that, in certain circumstances, take away the right of veiled women to receive an education.

The post is accompanied by a picture and quote of Nobel Prize winner
Malala Yousafzai, saying, "One child, one teacher, one book & one pen
can change the world." The picture of Malala Yousafzai, who advocates for
women's education in predominantly Muslim Pakistan and was attacked by
Muslim fundamentalists, suggests the association's symbolic distance from
a radical version of Islam. The veil – as also worn by Malala Yousafzai in
the picture – is therefore not framed as incompatible with education. The
EMF, in describing education as the "basis for emancipation of spirit and
freedom," makes efforts to allow everybody attending university, including
hijab-wearing women.

The position of veiled women in higher education is somehow ambiguous
in France: law 2004 on religious symbols only affects students until they
graduate high school, allowing women to wear the hijab in public universities. However, in practice, university professors or other students might
discriminate against Muslim women, for example, asking them to remove
the hijab in case of certain public examinations. In addition, as for the quote
above, the EMF fears that the hijab will be eventually banned from French
universities, as well.

In 2014, ten years after the bans against hijabs in educational establishments, the EMF discusses the law by asserting that it goes against a woman's rights to "freely dispose of her own body" and "manifest her religion"
(EMF, 16 March 2014). In the article, the female veil is considered as a part
of women's identity and compared to the Alsace-Moselle region in France.
The Alsace-Moselle has been annexed to France after the First World War

and conquered by Germany during the Second World War. In saying that a veil is for a woman what the Alsace-Moselle is for France, the article frames the hijab in terms of an identity mark that can be removed only in a forced and traumatizing way. At the same time, the Alsace-Moselle is one of the few French regions where there are special agreements with the Catholic Church. The metaphor, therefore, could also be read as an implicit critique of *laïcité*, which is not evenly applied throughout the French territory and tends to privilege Christian symbols rather than Muslim ones.

In occasion of the tenth anniversary of the law 2004 on religious symbols, the EMF also organized a number of public events, described and amplified through the internet. For example, the local section of the city of Toulouse, together with CCIF, distributed roses to passersby in order to raise awareness about Islamophobia and the female veil. A YouTube video (EMF Asso, YouTube, 17 March 2014) shows some Muslim students – prevalently women wearing a hijab but also non-veiled women and men – approaching people in the streets and offering each of them a rose with a letter. The video does not feature any sound, except for the background song "Salaam" by British Muslim artist Sami Yusuf. The letter distributed alongside the roses is written by two veiled Muslim students who remain anonymous. At the end of the video, the text of the letter appears on the screen. The letter starts with a plea to listen to a Muslim woman's story, explaining her choice to wear a veil. She continues by asserting, "You might not understand my choice," but asks nonetheless to be allowed in public schools for "what she is," or better, "what she chose to be." The letter concludes as follows:

Freedom . . . this word seems to remind me of a sweet illusion, the illusion that I am not, in your eyes, only what they want you to believe I am. I am sure that you, who read this letter, will listen to my call, the call of a woman who hopes for herself and for you only three things: LIBERTÉ, ÉGALITÉ, FRATERNITÉ.
(EMF Asso, YouTube, 17 March 2014, emphasis in original)

Concluding the letter with the three words *liberté, égalité, fraternité* – freedom, equality, fraternity, the motto of the French revolution and national motto of France – is a powerful way to frame Muslim identities as part of French identities. The video described at the beginning of the chapter also mentioned the concept of *fraternité*. Indeed, without openly talking about Islamophobia, the letter suggests that wearing a veil is a facet of France culture that should be allowed in public spaces. Having women writing the letter and distributing the roses probably aims at putting emphasis on the veil as a free choice, as opposed to coercion. Therefore, Muslim women likely used this campaign to gain agency on their representations and to show that their choice of wearing a veil should be accepted also within secular spaces.

The video employs an emotional language to frame its message. Roses and letters are probably chosen as a poetic way to bring attention to the unthreatening character of Muslim women and their veils, as well as a symbol of friendship and mutual understanding. As was also the case for the #*NousSommesUnis* video, music and images suggest an affective engagement of EMF members with French society and a desire of being integrated despite – or even through – their religious identities. First-person narratives and videos showing students' faces and veiled bodies likely describe an aspect of French culture that exists and is increasingly visible in a way that is not necessarily threatening. They embed in digital spaces the materiality of the veil in representations of the female body. As for Nancy Fraser's (1990) criticism of the public sphere, mentioned in Chapter 2, the body can represent the private dimension that leads to the formation of alternative public spheres. Because Muslim women's bodies are often publicly scrutinized, these digital narratives are probably strategies to establish the hijab as belonging to the private religious sphere, despite the public attention it attracts.

Even if EMF members seem to be aware that their visibility may exclude them from French mainstream culture, they claim that their diversity should be accepted rather than hidden or opposed. I mentioned activities and discourses aimed at normalizing the presence of Muslims in France and contrasting Islamophobia, supporting the public display of the Muslims veil as connected to gender equality. These strategies may unveil a willingness to modify the existing understanding of *laïcité* in France in a more inclusive way, a position that, as next chapter will demonstrate, is not necessarily shared by other groups. From this perspective, the aforementioned sentence "*J'ai mal a ma France*" can be interpreted in different ways: EMF members suffer because, as French citizens, they feel targeted by terrorist attacks; at the same time, they also might have a complicated relationship with France, because they are torn between the willingness to adhere to its values – *laïcité*, as well as the *liberté, égalité, fraternité* motto – and the difficulties in maintaining certain parts of their identities, such as the veil.

President Ben Dhia explained that he would like the EMF to "evolve the mentality" of French people about Islam (personal communication, 22 June 2017). Because EMF members are educated and active citizens, they may establish a Muslim voice that successfully contrasts existing misgivings and stereotypes. For example, a female Muslim student with a master's degree can clearly explain why the veil she wears is compatible with French culture, while a recently immigrated Imam who is not fluent in French might articulate religious norms in a way that is too conservative and detached from social reality. The EMF could therefore "evolve the mentality" by eliciting debates about *laïcité* and showing that young Muslims do not have problems in conciliating their faith with French identity.

The internet assumes an important role in discussing the visibility of Muslim identities in France. As for Ben Dhia's explanation, EMF members mainly use social networks, such as Facebook, to get in touch with each other and discuss the associations' activities, including charity, gala dinners, and sports events. In this way, they create digital safe spaces where they can connect with like-minded people and talk about their everyday lives without being discriminated because of their religious faith. The website, differently from social networks, targets society at large rather than members of EMF only. Though press releases, opinions, and videos, the association aims at reaching visibility and becoming a public interlocutor for Muslim issues, as happened when national and international media outlets contacted EMF members for interviews after the #*NousSommesUnis* video. Members employ different media platforms to share their emotions and quickly circulate their viewpoints in order to produce alternative narratives about Islam. In so doing, they show their acceptance of French values, but also their willingness to have their voices taken into consideration in larger debates about religion and *laïcité*.

Yalla: Muslim in my own way

The blog *Yalla* aims at offering a voice to second-generation Italians. In the homepage, *Yalla* is described as follows:

> We will tell what we think. Not as Italians, as Arabs or Europeans: we are simply new citizens that belong to two worlds at the same time and that want to understand the most interesting, contradictory, ambiguous, problematic and also provocative aspects of them.
>
> (*Yalla*, homepage)

The idea of "belonging to two worlds" informs the majority of *Yalla* posts. In Italy, where migrations are more recent in comparison to France and other European countries, the population tends to be predominantly white and Catholic. Young second-generation Italians often feel that they represent an "invisible category" overlooked by Italian society, and seek strategies to have their voices heard, for example, through the internet (Zinn 2011).

In responding to the need of making second-generation Italians more visible, *Yalla* constitutes an interesting platform to study Islam in Italy. While it is not a religious blog, *Yalla*'s aim of focusing on "interesting, contradictory, ambiguous, problematic and provocative" aspects of society often leads to discussions about Islam, which represents around 2 percent of the Italian population (CESNUR 2014) and is the fastest-growing religion in Italy (Pace 2013). A natural bridge between Europe and North Africa, Italy has recently experienced increasing migrations from predominantly Muslim countries, as mentioned in this book's introduction in relation to Pope Francis' visit to Lampedusa. Despite this, Islam is still not formally recognized by the Italian government as a recipient of public funding (Toronto 2008; Mezran 2013). In Italy there are no specific laws against religious garments, but the growing visibility of Islam has been addressed, for example, in debates about the construction of mosques. Because the Catholic

Church tends to hold the monopoly on cultural values in Italy, the presence of Islamic buildings is often framed as being against Italian identity (Saint-Blancat and Friedberg 2005).

Yalla was created by journalist Martino Pillitteri and professor Paolo Branca to talk about Italian Islam in relation to social and cultural change. They recruited six Muslim bloggers of Arab origins in the city of Milan. The blog's title, *Yalla*, is an Arab word that means "let's go" and was used to exhort second-generation Italians to establish their voices in public debates. Indeed, according to Branca (personal communication, 31 May 2015), media and social discourses in Italy tend to report only stereotypical depictions of Islam. Even if Italy did not suffer from terrorist attacks claimed by Muslim groups, Italian media often talk about episodes such as the 2015 attacks in Paris to frame Islam as violent and radical, or exclusively connected to migration waves. *Yalla* thus offers a space for Muslims to tell their everyday stories and opinions, implicitly contrasting dominant media representations.

Yalla is not connected to any established religious group. Different from the EMF, it is not a formal association and counts also various non-Muslim bloggers. However, similar to the EMF, the blog is often used as a platform to discuss different understandings of Islam in Italy, negotiate authorities, and describe religious practices in everyday life. In so doing, *Yalla* bloggers articulate "hybrid Muslim identities" that allow them to adapt to Western modernity without abandoning their culture of origin (Evolvi 2017a). Since it was founded, *Yalla* progressively included more contributors and increased its attention to topics that regard all second-generation Italians, such as the question of Italian citizenship. The following sections will describe *Yalla*'s negotiation of Islam in Italy and its effort to change the existing Italian citizenship law. *Yalla*'s interest in these topics creates networks of actors and actions that address various aspects of society, thus offering alternative narratives about Italian Islam.

Muslims and Italian Islam

Yalla is a public blog that discusses issues of multiculturalism and integration by offering comments on national and international news, and by telling personal stories through storytelling. According to blogger and founder Pillitteri (personal communication, 29 May 2015), storytelling is a style that reminds more of a personal journal rather than news reporting. This style helps the bloggers, who are not professional journalists, to connect their everyday experiences with society at large. By employing storytelling, *Yalla* aims at addressing social and cultural issues without complaining or making Muslims appear as victims. At the same time, the posts are often provocative in criticizing certain aspects of Italian society and eliciting social change through concrete propositions.

An example of storytelling is found in a post where a blogger of North African origins talks about her efforts to furnish a new apartment together with her Italian boyfriend. She writes that "a mixed couple (or better, a couple of mixed origins) needs a mixed house" and claims that her boyfriend wishes to buy traditional Italian furniture, while she desires a home with "wooden furniture, wind chimes, smell of mint or vanilla in every room" (*Yalla*, 22 July 2013). She ironically explains that the greater disagreement with her partner is about furniture, rather than culture or religion. While the post does not directly address social change, the blogger shows how people from different backgrounds can successfully live together, and how second-generations are not "other" to Italian culture. Written in a colloquial style, the post does not complain about social marginalization, but rather indirectly shows strategies of adaptations to the Italian culture for second-generations.

Storytelling allows for a colloquial language charged with emotions, and it is frequently employed to describe religious experiences. Religious change in Italy, indeed, is often addressed through stories about people's everyday approaches to practices and beliefs. A blogger, for example, describes her experience in a mosque in Italy, where she is forced to sit in the shadowy back of the room and prevented from fully listening to the Imam because of her gender. In describing the event in a blog post, she addresses gender equality within Muslim communities, explaining that many Imams refuse to acknowledge the role of women. She ironically describes the Imam as a "cave-dweller" with a long beard, who speaks only Arabic, and is dressed in a way that suggests "he came, yesterday, from Saudi Arabia." She concludes the post as follows:

> I can only say that this person [the Imam] doesn't represent me. I deserve more. Maybe I don't know the Muslim community in Italy, but I know my rights. I know that these old pompous guys need to beat feet. We need to substitute them, because we are the new generation, able to speak perfect Italian, we have a deep understanding of both cultures, both worlds, and both cultural codes.
>
> (*Yalla*, 31 August 2011)

In criticizing the lack of gender equality in certain Muslim communities, the post points to the heterogeneous character of Italian Islam. The blogger expresses anger because she was prevented from fully participating in a religious function, something that she deems incompatible with Italian values. In counterpoising the Imam to the "new generation" of Italian Muslims, she stresses both her belonging to the Italian culture and her understanding of religion. Indeed, the blogger does not refuse Islam, but she negotiates – and rejects – traditional religious authority in order to find her own personalized approach to Islam.

Yalla's religious-related posts often help bloggers and readers negotiate their views about Islam. The bloggers do not have a homogeneous understanding of Islam, as some are more engaged with religious practices – for example, observing Ramadan and, in case of women, wearing a hijab – and others only consider themselves as culturally Muslim, without practicing the religion. As a result, the bloggers might have disagreements with each other and use *Yalla* as a space to discuss the practice of Islam in relation to the Italian contest. A blogger, for example, explains that her friends often do not consider her an observant Muslim, but she nonetheless tries to fast for Ramadan. She frames her approach as follows:

> I don't change my dress habits (maybe I'm showing my décolleté a little too much?!?), I listen to music and I go dancing (obviously during the evening), I make exceptions one or two days to have lunch with my colleagues. . . . I admit I'm not the emblem of the perfect Muslim, I just commit sins like everybody, don't I?
>
> (*Yalla*, 17 August 2012)

In describing Ramadan, the blogger gives insights on her understanding of Islam. She tends to personalize the practice of Islam by "committing sin" and tries to observe the fasting while negotiating her everyday life and her Muslim faith. This attitude unveils a willingness to adapt Islam to the Italian and European context, thus finding strategies to be Muslim in a non-Muslim environment where, for instance, Ramadan is not celebrated. Pillitteri defines this religious behavior, common to many bloggers, with the expression "*Musulmano a modo tuo*" ("Muslims in your own way," personal communication, 29 May 2015). Being "Muslim in your own way" means selectively choosing certain aspects of Islam over others in a personalized way and negotiating the position of religious practices in the public sphere.

In this respect, some bloggers define themselves as "secular Muslims," because their religion does not necessarily guide their everyday behaviors and decisions. Blogger Oussama Mansour (personal communication, 9 June 2015), for example, explains that he was born in a Muslim family that places great importance in belonging to a Muslim community. However, he feels that certain Muslim groups in Italy tend to be excessively conservative, lacking the heterogeneity of viewpoints and approaches that characterizes Islam in general. In assuming a critical attitude towards religion, he explains that he considers himself "Muslim in the same way many Italians are Catholics" (*Yalla*, 29 October 2014). With this expression, the blogger describes his cultural belonging to Islam but, at the same time, he criticizes certain Muslim practices and beliefs. This attitude is similar to that of many Italian Catholics, who do not regularly attend religious services and do not necessarily follow all the precepts of the Vatican, but consider themselves as culturally Catholic.

The idea of being "Muslim in your own way" often leads to discussions about religious authority and gender. The majority of *Yalla* bloggers are indeed women, and they often talk about gender equality and misogyny both within Islam and in the Italian society. The predominance of female bloggers might be explained by the greater need for Muslim women to express themselves in non-traditional venues, especially if they struggle to find a voice within traditional religious communities. Therefore, *Yalla* becomes a venue to discuss religious practices and authorities from a non-institutional viewpoint and to collect reflections on different understandings of Islam.

By talking about similarities between Islam and Catholicism and negotiating religious authority, *Yalla* suggests that Islam can adapt to secularism and Western values exactly as other religions do. Instead of criticizing the cultural hegemony of Catholicism in Italian society, the bloggers find similarities between Islam and Catholicism. Therefore, *Yalla* functions as a space of normalization where, through a colloquial storytelling style that is emotionally charged, Islam is portrayed in an unthreatening way and as compatible with Italian society. The blog becomes an alternative space where non-conventional stories about Muslims are told, and where the position of Muslim Italians is negotiated in relation to mainstream culture. Being "Muslim in your own way" helps the bloggers also to articulate their identities as Italian citizens, and for this reason they often address the question of Italian citizenship.

Muslims and Italian citizenship

The majority of *Yalla* bloggers are born in Italy and consider themselves as fully belonging to Italian culture. However, not all of them hold Italian citizenship. Indeed, citizenship in Italy is granted on the principle of *Jus Sanguinis*, which sanctions that children automatically inherit the citizenship of their parents. Children born in Italy from immigrant parents who do not hold Italian citizenship, which is the case of many of *Yalla* bloggers, need to apply for citizenship when they reach the age of 18. The process of obtaining Italian citizenship is often expensive and bureaucratically complicated, resulting sometimes in years of waiting.

Second-generation Italians who do not hold citizenship have fewer opportunities than their peers in terms of employment and political engagement. In addition, they often feel symbolically excluded from Italian culture. It is for this reason that *Yalla* addresses the question of citizenship collecting the experiences of second-generation Italians. A blogger describes her feelings in the following way:

> I was born in Italy exactly like my friend Chiara. Both born in 1985, same musical tastes, same ideals. I still remember our first trip back-packing together when we were underage, ready for adventures with our ID cards in our pockets. But my ID card was different. I couldn't expatriate, because I was a foreigner in my own country.
>
> (*Yalla*, 3 July 2015)

In the post, the blogger explains that she perceived a difference with her peers for the first time when she realized that she was not a European Union citizen, and therefore she could not expatriate with her identity card only, as Italians can do. Apart from citizenship, she does not feel any different from her friend, with whom she shares "musical tastes and ideals." She takes the description of her trip abroad as an occasion to discuss the unfairness of not being considered a citizen of a country where she is born, raised, and educated.

Yalla discusses possible models to expedite the procedure for Italian citizenship. The bloggers often advocate for the principle of *Jus Soli*, which automatically grants citizenship to children according to their birthplace, and exists in many European countries. They published on the blog a proposal called *Jus Soli Temperato* (tempered *Jus Soli*), suggesting that children born in Italy could automatically gain Italian citizenship after completing compulsory education (*Yalla*, 8 April 2014). With this proposal, *Yalla* was able to intervene in the public debate about citizenship, also attracting the attention of then-Prime Minister Matteo Renzi.

The question of citizenship regards all second-generation Italians and does not have a direct connection with Islam. However, in the public debate about citizenship, Italian identity is often described in religious terms. Xenophobic political parties and opinion makers, indeed, tend to reiterate that Muslims are "other" to Italian culture in order to refuse the *Jus Soli* principle. Intrinsic in this approach is the idea that second-generations need to prove their acceptance of Western values, and that Muslims allegedly fail to do so. Therefore, the issue of citizenship is often discussed in posts that address the sense of marginalization that Muslim Italians feel, especially when they are considered as "non-Italian" by virtue of their religion.

In a post, a blogger describes a negative experience that she had when voting for national elections, after she gained Italian citizenship. In Italy, people vote in person and need to be identified by a poll clerk. The blogger explains that the clerk gazed at her hijab and asked her, "Why are you voting?" When the blogger explained that she is an Italian citizen, the clerk inquired, "How can you be Italian if you are Muslim?" (*Yalla*, 26 May 2017). This episode shows how national identity is often understood in religious terms. Being ethnically non-white and wearing visible religious symbols, such as the hijab, can be perceived as incompatible with Italian citizenship. While Islam in Italy is growing, there is a part of the public opinion that considers its visibility as unable to change the terms of national identity. These opinions are often expressed in comments to *Yalla* posts that address the question of citizenship:

> A wise and civil country, because of the EVIDENCE of Islam as persecutor, invader and violent, would NEVER give Muslims the citizenship. Not because of religion but because of politics and the impossibility they have of [reaching] INTEGRATION and becoming really Italian. A Muslim will NEVER be Italian even if he is born here because he

is Muslim and he will follow the Islamic law, which is not limited to religion only.

(*Yalla*, comment to a post, 30 December 2014, emphasis in original)

This Islamophobic comment shows how a part of the Italian population believes that Muslims cannot accept Western values and secular democratic principles. The commentator frames Islam as necessarily "persecutor, invader and violent" and considers Muslims as following the Islamic law rather than Italian laws. *Yalla* is often attacked by anonymous readers that oppose the *Jus Soli* principle solely on the basis of Islamophobic motivations, also mistakenly think of all second-generation Italians as Muslims. This approach unveils a lack of knowledge of the complex reality of Islam and the heterogeneity within Muslim communities, and it is likely influenced by superficial media and social representations.

Pillitteri, the blog moderator, usually publishes all the comments, even if they are disrespectful or offensive. In this way, the blog becomes a space of discussion where the bloggers can try to engage in conversation with Islamophobic readers. The bloggers employ various strategies to show these readers the compatibility of Islam with Italian and European citizenship. For example, a blogger replies to Islamophobic comments by saying, "We are even more Italian because we choose to be Italian, you are born Italian and never questioned it, but we questioned our identity and chose to be Italian. . . . WE ARE ITALIAN" (*Yalla*, 13 March 2013, emphasis in original). In asserting her feelings of belonging to the Italian culture, the blogger explains that she – as well as many other second-generation Italians – not only is born in the country, but also negotiates her identity in a way that can conciliate different cultures and religions. From this perspective, Italian citizenship ceases to be only a matter of documents, and becomes a symbolic choice that Muslim Italians do in an implicit endorsement of Italian values and culture.

In order to contrast Islamophobia and to show their Italianness, the bloggers tend to highlight the positive effects of religious change rather than complain about Italian society and politics. *Yalla*, indeed, often describes second-generation Italians as people that speak multiple languages and can bridge different cultures. This is the case of blogger Lubna Ammoune (personal communication, 4 June 2015), who explains that she always considered her foreign origins as a potential rather than a disadvantage. In discussing the expression "second-generation Italian," she asserts that she would prefer to be referred in other terms. While "second-generation" is a useful word to describe *Yalla* bloggers, it can also be perceived negatively. Ammoune explains that Italians with foreign parents are "second to none," and that they should not be considered different from other Italian citizens.

The blog *Yalla*, therefore, becomes a space where narratives about Italian Islam aim at normalizing the presence of Muslims within society and address their marginalization in relation to the dominant Catholic culture. It is a space for bloggers to confront pacifically Islamophobic and racist people. *Yalla* is alternative because the stories it tells – albeit mostly focused on the everyday lives of young people – show a facet of Islam that is often ignored in Italy. The bloggers, on the one hand, refuse to be considered terrorists or fundamentalists, as they show that their understanding of Islam is compatible with Italian culture; on the other hand, they do not want to be labeled as migrants, as they have been raised and educated in Italy and feel Italian. In addition, *Yalla* describes hybrid religious and cultural identities able to produce a positive impact on Italian society.

In *Yalla*'s efforts to negotiate a personalized type of Islam that can adapt to Italian culture, by being "Muslims in their own way," the bloggers describe their visibility in unthreatening terms and show how Islam may be compatible with secularism. I addressed the bloggers' propositions to modify the existing citizenship laws, which were able to make their voices emerge in political debates. The internet has a central role in helping young Muslim bloggers going beyond dominant media representations. It allows for an unconventional and colloquial storytelling style that emotionally appeals to the audience, likely inviting the readers to identify with the bloggers' experiences and opinions. In so doing, *Yalla* changes the terms of mainstream conversations: instead of Italian Muslims being a marginalized minority, they are able to improve the country's culture and society. Therefore, *Yalla* represents a facet of religious change in Italy and Europe because it seeks to establish alternative spaces for Muslim self-representations.

Conclusion: imagining a multifaith society

The *#NousSommesUnis* video is an example of how digital media can help to articulate and describe hybrid religious identities. European-born Muslims often use the internet to show that they wish to conciliate their religion and the European culture in which they live, rather than choosing between the two. Articulating a Muslim and European identity can thus become a strategy to counteract dominant stereotypes. The negotiation of authorities and practices within Islam, which often happens in hypermediated spaces of discussion, helps some young Europeans to be "Muslims in their own way" and adapt their religion to the European context. By so doing, they describe an unthreatening type of Islam and advocate for a society where multiple faiths can coexist.

This chapter has analyzed the website of the French association *Etudiants Musulman de France* and the Italian blog *Yalla*. They are written by young Muslims who are prevalently second-generation Europeans, meaning that they are born and raised in Europe. The two groups address different issues: EMF, for example, refers more explicitly to Islam and is mainly concerned with the visibility of Muslim identities in relation to the French *laïcité*, while *Yalla* focuses on citizenship and multiculturalism in Italy. However, they similarly aim at adding nuances to representations of Islam in Europe, refusing to be labeled exclusively as violent terrorists or powerless migrants. In the case of the Paris terrorist attacks, for example, national media tended to focus on negative and violent aspects of Islam, thus providing a monolithic portrayal of Muslims and ignoring groups such as EMF and *Yalla*. Through internet spaces, and the circulation of hashtags, videos, and narratives, European Muslims can partially challenge this representation and gain agency on their own religious biographies. In this way, they arguably normalize the presence of Muslims in European society, fighting Islamophobia and advocating for the creation of multifaith spaces.

EMF and *Yalla* do not speak for all European Muslims, but rather represent a specific aspect of European religiosity: a type of Islam that is embedded with European values and that coexists with secular norms. Studying these groups helps to understand the heterogeneity of Islam in Europe and to analyze the articulation of hybrid identities. Homi Bhabha (2004) finds hybridity in the negotiation of post-colonial identities in between the colonizer and the colonized. The intersection of two cultures constitutes what Bhabha defines as "third space," a terminology also employed by Stewart Hoover and Nabil Echchaibi (2014) to describe digital religion. European Muslims need to negotiate their faith and culture in order to create a hybrid religiosity that is compatible with the environment in which they live. EMF and *Yalla*'s discourses about the meaning of the veil and the personalization of religious practices, I would argue, help to create third spaces. In these third spaces, young Muslims discuss hybridity by seeking both to modify Islam from inside and to change the mentality of many Europeans about Islam.

The internet helps to create hypermediated spaces where hybrid identities are discussed and described. Social networks and blogs can function as safe spaces where European Muslims can freely express themselves without incurring in Islamophobic attacks. They can also offer venues to narratively elaborate on what it means to be Muslims in Europe, and discuss practices and beliefs beyond traditional authorities and outside predominantly Islamic countries. Because many Muslim discourses do not fit mainstream media representations, they often find alternative spaces of expression on the internet. In the case of the *#NousSommesUnis* video, Muslims succeeded in capturing the attention of the general public as they found a digital venue for their narratives. The creation of such discourses is important both because it addresses the need of Muslims to express their feelings, especially in situations of violence and distress, and because it establishes alternative representations of Islam that can help in modifying social perceptions.

The immediacy of internet communications facilitates this type of discursive creation. Young Muslims, indeed, can employ multiple platforms, spacing from videos, to short messages and hashtags, to novels and personal stories. In this way, they can benefit from the speed of the internet for fast reactions to social discourses. When they are able to navigate the language and logics of digital communication, for example creating videos that can potentially become viral, European Muslims can respond to social and cultural stimuli in real time even if they do not have direct access to mainstream media. Because they use different platforms, they can engage in conversations with a number of people, both Muslims and non-Muslims, expanding their communication possibilities and directly responding to Islamophobic and discriminatory claims.

The success of certain discourses is likely connected to their emotional character. Islamophobic and racist narratives often employ emotions as a strategy to turn the population against those that are framed as "others" (Ahmed 2014). Through digital platforms, young Muslims arguably seek to employ emotions against this type of discrimination. Videos that embed poems and music, as well as storytelling of personal experiences, invite the readers to connect with Muslims in an intimate way and to see them as persons beyond stereotypical and Islamophobic representations, thus creating affective publics (Papacharissi 2014). From this perspective, sharing personal feelings, as well as eliciting others' emotions, can help to connect with society at large and find alternative ways to establish a public voice.

Muslim hypermediated spaces are alternative because they are created by people who are often not perceived as part of mainstream culture. As per Chantal Mouffe's (2013) analysis of agonistic and antagonistic spaces, Muslims sometimes struggle to address power relationships as they are excluded by dominant forms of consensus. Creating spaces of multiculturalism and multireligiosity on the internet is arguably a way to enter in agonistic relations with other social groups: by so doing Muslims do not present themselves as "public enemies," but rather as a minority that seeks to establish conversations with, criticize, and ultimately change the dominant hegemonic culture. The majority of these hypermediated discourses, indeed, criticize society while accepting its values, and elicit cultural change in a provocative way without being aggressive, even when dealing with Islamophobic people. In this way, groups such as EMF and *Yalla* can seek to agonistically intervene in public debates without posing themselves as "other" to European society.

As alternative spaces, Muslim digital venues engage with mainstream religious institutions. These European Muslims do not usually criticize the privileged position of Christianity in the public sphere, but rather find similarities between Islam and Catholicism in an interfaith effort to promote a multifaith Europe. In so doing, they implicitly criticize Catholic secularism for not being sufficiently inclusive with other religions. At the same time, these spaces are alternative not only in respect to Catholic and secular culture, but also within Islam itself: they negotiate Muslim authorities and personalize religious practices in a non-institutional way. As a result, digital spaces such as EMF and *Yalla* constitute counterpublics created in response – and, sometimes, in opposition – to dominant discourses about religion.

In creating digital counterpublics, these European Muslims also address the question of public and private spaces. Because of the public visibility of Islam, and in particular of the hijab-wearing female body, Muslims are often accused of manifesting a form of religiosity that is incompatible with *laïcité*. Hypermediated spaces help to address this issue by offering a platform for alternative negotiations of the meaning of public and private. The hijab is framed as a private choice that is part of a woman's body and identity, and therefore unable to affect the secular character of public spaces. At the same time, videos, pictures, and personal stories of veiled women suggest that the public display of the hijab is not a social threat, but rather a normal facet of religious and cultural change. Digital spaces can become safe venues where the hijab is shown, discussed, and negotiated. Therefore, Muslim women may find on the internet a space of technology that can embed the material character of the hijab in order to gain agency on their own representations.

Discussions of Muslim bodies in between public and private spaces often lead to reflections on *laïcité*. Muslim groups such as EMF and *Yalla* indirectly advocate for a re-thinking of Catholic secularism by suggesting that Muslim symbols and values could publicly be displayed alongside Catholic ones. Because *laïcité* is generally understood as the neutrality of public and institutional spaces, these European Muslims propose that secularism should accept private – albeit visible – religious manifestations even when they do not belong to Christianity, as in the case of the hijab. In showing that they accept secularism, they likely imply that their visible public presence would not compromise the principle of *laïcité*, but rather elicit a re-thinking of public religion in Europe.

These reflections about private and public religion point to the articulation of a European public sphere in between reality and social imaginations. Hypermediated spaces, indeed, function as safe venues where Muslims can control their representations and enter into dialogue with other users, trying to establish relationships with both like-minded readers and Islamophobic people. These digital spaces likely aim at creating venues of coexistence between Islam and other faiths – including secularism – outside of the internet. From this perspective, Muslim hypermediated spaces pose the basis for imaginaries of a multifaith society. While episodes of Islamophobia may prevent many Muslims to be fully integrated within European society and culture, spaces as EMF and *Yalla* show that it is possible for different religions to have the same access to public debates. By articulating hybrid identities, they show that a multifaith society is possible if Islam is accepted as compatible with European values. To employ Michel Foucault's (2004) language, they enact a heterotopia where they experiment the coexistence of Islam with other values and religions.

The realization of this heterotopia, however, arguably encounters obstacles: European Muslims may find difficulties in pledging alliance to their national belonging while maintaining the public visibility of their faith. Groups like EMF and *Yalla* only describe a specific aspect of Islam, that of young and educated Muslims generally born in Europe. They often criticize Muslim authorities and they are seldom connected with Muslim institutions. While this shows the willingness of these groups to personalize their religious practice, it risks marginalizing EMF and *Yalla* not only from mainstream society, but also from Islam. In addition, these are youth groups whose activities and existence often depend on the engagement of unpaid members; the fact that *Yalla* was put down in 2017 shows how they do not necessarily have the means to establish a long-lasting presence. This may complicate the realization of the heterotopia of a multifaith society and prevent these Muslim groups from being considered as able to represent Islam in interfaith dialogues.

The analyzed blogs employ various strategies to try to overcome these obstacles. For example, they often openly endorse European values though nationalistic claims. "I have pain in my France" said in relation to terror attacks, the reiteration of the French motto *liberté, égalité, fraternité*, as well as the efforts to gain Italian and European citizenship are likely ways to show the willingness of European Muslims to be integrated into society. From this perspective, they indirectly suggest a re-thinking of the nation-state as "imagined community" (Anderson 2006) that could be also inclusive with Islam. They tend to put emphasis on non-religious activities rather than explicitly talking about Islam. For example, the EMF insists on its educational character, while *Yalla* talks about second-generations more than religion. This exemplifies how European Muslims arguably can be better accepted when they show their unthreatening character both by focusing on non-religious topics and by employing a language that is compatible with secularism. From this perspective, they symbolically disprove the concept – as expressed by Davie (2013) – that Islam constitutes a totalizing way of life and cannot be confined to the private sphere.

In addition, these hypermediated religious spaces present processes of religious and identity hybridization as a social potential, rather than a disadvantage. By showing that French Muslim students are successful in building careers and engaging in volunteer work, and by describing second-generation Italians as able to bridge different cultures and languages, these narratives seek to "evolve the mentality" of Europeans. By overturning dominant conversations about Islam in Europe, these Muslims refuse to be considered as a social burden, but rather show that they can improve society. In describing a model of "Muslim secularism" that is compatible with *laïcité*, groups like EMF and *Yalla* establish themselves as potential interlocutors for multifaith issues and suggest that they can represent a new face of Islam in Europe.

Therefore, the creation of Muslim hypermediated spaces may lead to a "Muslim and European" identity that helps to fight Islamophobia and change existing media representations. The formation of these digital spaces may be considered as a tactical media use – as in the work of Rita Raley (2009) – to change the long-term perception of European Islam. By insisting on the positive character of Islam, as well as the potential of Muslim youth and the benefits of a multicultural society, these digital discourses can find strategies to go beyond the internet and reach a greater audience. Even if it might not have direct and measurable impacts and the groups involved might not last in time, the internet heterotopia of a multifaith society may create long-term social change in showing alternative representations of European Islam.

References

Anderson, Benedict. 2006. *Imagined Communities: Reflections on the Origin and Spread of Nationalism*. Revised edition. London; New York, NY: Verso.

Ahmad, Waqar I. U., and Venetia Evergeti. 2010. "The Making and Representation of Muslim Identity in Britain: Conversations with British Muslim 'elites'." *Ethnic and Racial Studies* 33 (10): 1697–717. https://doi.org/10.1080/01419871003768055.

Ahmed, Sara. 2014. *The Cultural Politics of Emotion*. Revised edition. New York, NY: Routledge Chapman Hall.

Akou, Heather Marie. 2010. "Interpreting Islam Through the Internet: Making Sense of Hijab." *Contemporary Islam* 4 (3): 331–46. https://doi.org/10.1007/s11562-010-0135-6.

Allen, Chris. 2015. "'People Hate You Because of the Way You Dress': Understanding the Invisible Experiences of Veiled British Muslim Women Victims of Islamophobia." *International Review of Victimology* 21 (3): 287–301. https://doi.org/10.1177/0269758015591677.

Allievi, Stefano. 2003. *Islam italiano. Viaggio nella seconda religione del paese*. Torino: Einaudi.

Asad, Talal. 2003. *Formations of the Secular: Christianity, Islam, Modernity*. 1st edition. Stanford, CA: Stanford University Press.

Awad, Najib George. 2013. "Religio-Phobia: Western Islam, Social Integration and the Resurgence of Religiosity in Europe." *The Muslim World* 103 (4): 433–47. https://doi.org/10.1111/muwo.12032.

Bhabha, Homi K. 2004. *The Location of Culture*. 2nd edition. London; New York, NY: Routledge.

CESNUR. 2014. *Le Religioni in Italia*. Accessed July 25, 2016. www.cesnur.com/.

Davie, Grace. 2013. "Belief and Unbelief: Two Sides of a Coin." *Ecclesiastical Law Journal* 15 (3): 259–66. https://doi.org/10.1017/S0956618X13000410.

Davies, Peter. 2010. "The Front National and Catholicism: From Intégrisme to Joan of Arc and Clovis." *Religion Compass* 4 (9): 576–87. https://doi.org/10.1111/j.1749-8171.2010.00237.x.

Dostal, Jörg Michael. 2015. "The Pegida Movement and German Political Culture: Is Right-Wing Populism Here to Stay?" *The Political Quarterly* 86 (4): 523–31. https://doi.org/10.1111/1467-923X.12204.

Echchaibi, Nabil. 2011a. "From Audio Tapes to Video Blogs: The Delocalisation of Authority in Islam." *Nations and Nationalism* 17 (1): 25–44. https://doi.org/10.1111/j.1469-8129.2010.00468.x.

Echchaibi, Nabil. 2011b. *Voicing Diasporas: Ethnic Radio in Paris and Berlin Between Cultural Renewal and Retention*. Lanham, MD: Lexington Books.

Echchaibi, Nabil. March 2013. "Muslimah Media Watch: Media Activism and Muslim Choreographies of Social Change." *Journalism*. https://doi.org/10.1177/1464884913478360.

el-Aswad, el-Sayed. 2013. "Images of Muslims in Western Scholarship and Media After 9/11." *Digest of Middle East Studies* 22 (1): 39–56. https://doi.org/10.1111/dome.12010.

Evolvi, Giulia. April 2017a. "Hybrid Muslim Identities in Digital Space: The Italian Blog Yalla." *Social Compass* 0037768617697911. https://doi.org/10.1177/0037768617697911.

Evolvi, Giulia. 2017b. "#Islamexit: Inter-Group Antagonism on Twitter." *Information, Communication & Society*: 1–16. https://doi.org/10.1080/1369118X.2017.1388427.

Ferrara, Alessandro, Volker Kaul, David Rasmussen, and Seyla Benhabib. 2010. "The Return of Political Theology: The Scarf Affair in Comparative Constitutional Perspective in France, Germany and Turkey." *Philosophy & Social Criticism* 36 (3–4): 451–71. https://doi.org/10.1177/0191453709358546.

Foucault, Michel. 2004. "Des espaces autres." *Empan* 54 (2): 12–19.

Fraser, Nancy. 1990. "Rethinking the Public Sphere: A Contribution to the Critique of Actually Existing Democracy." *Social Text* 25/26: 56–80. https://doi.org/10.2307/466240.

Fredette, Jennifer. 2011. "Social Movements and the State's Construction of Identity: The Case of Muslims in France." In *Special Issue: Social Movements/Legal Possibilities*. Edited by Austin Sarat. Bingley: Emerald Group Publishing Limited.

Fredette, Jennifer. 2014. *Constructing Muslims in France: Discourse, Public Identity, and the Politics of Citizenship*. Philadelphia: Temple University Press.

Fredette, Jennifer. 2015. "Becoming a Threat: The Burqa and the Contestation Over Public Morality Law in France." *Law & Social Inquiry* 40 (3): 585–610. https://doi.org/10.1111/lsi.12101.

Gatti, Mauro. 2016. "The Log in Your Eye: Is Europe's External Promotion of Religious Freedom Consistent With Its Internal Practice?" *European Law Journal* 22 (2): 250–67. https://doi.org/10.1111/eulj.12162.

Hackett, Conrad. 2016. "5 Facts about the Muslim Population in Europe." *Pew Research Center* (blog). Accessed July 19, 2016. www.pewresearch.org/fact-tank/2016/07/19/5-facts-about-the-muslim-population-in-europe/.

Hoover, Stewart, and Nabil Echchaibi. 2014. "Media Theory and the Third Spaces of Digital Religion." Working Paper Center for Media, Religion, and Culture.

Kavakci, Elif, and Camille R. Kraeplin. November 2016. "Religious Beings in Fashionable Bodies: The Online Identity Construction of Hijabi Social Media Personalities." *Media, Culture & Society*. https://doi.org/10.1177/0163443716679031.

Linehan, Thomas. 2012. "Comparing Antisemitism, Islamophobia, and Asylophobia: The British Case." *Studies in Ethnicity and Nationalism* 12 (2): 366–86. https://doi.org/10.1111/j.1754-9469.2012.01161.x.

Maeder, Evelyn, Julie Dempsey, and Joanna Pozzulo. 2012. "Behind the Veil of Juror Decision Making: Testing the Effects of Muslim Veils and Defendant Race in the Courtroom." *Criminal Justice and Behavior* 39 (5): 666–78. https://doi.org/10.1177/0093854812436478.

Mezran, Karim. 2013. "Muslims in Italy: The Need for an 'Intesa' with the Italian State." *The International Spectator* 48 (1): 58–71. https://doi.org/10.1080/03932729.2013.758915.

Mouffe, Chantal. 2013. *Agonistics: Thinking the World Politically*. 1st edition. London; New York, NY: Verso.

Pace, Enzo. 2013. "Achilles and the Tortoise. A Society Monopolized by Catholicism Faced with an Unexpected Religious Pluralism." *Social Compass* 60 (3): 315–31. https://doi.org/10.1177/0037768613492280.

Papacharissi, Zizi. 2014. *Affective Publics: Sentiment, Technology, and Politics*. 1st edition. Oxford; New York, NY: Oxford University Press.

Peterson, Kristin M. 2016. "Beyond Fashion Tips and Hijab Tutorials: The Aesthetic Style of Islamic Lifestyle Videos." *Film Criticism* 40 (2). https://doi.org/http://dx.doi.org/10.3998/fc.13761232.0040.203.

Raley, Rita. 2009. *Tactical Media*. Minneapolis: University of Minnesota Press.

Roy, Olivier. 2013. "Secularism and Islam: The Theological Predicament." *The International Spectator* 48 (1): 5–19. https://doi.org/10.1080/03932729.2013.759365.

Runnymede Trust. 1997. *Islamophobia: A Challenge for Us All*. London: Runnymede Trust.

Saint-Blancat, Chantal, and Ottavia Schmidt di Friedberg. 2005. "Why Are Mosques a Problem? Local Politics and Fear of Islam in Northern Italy." *Journal of Ethnic and Migration Studies* 31 (6): 1083–104. https://doi.org/10.1080/13691830500282881.

Toronto, James A. 2008. "Islam Italiano: Prospects for Integration of Muslims in Italy's Religious Landscape." *Journal of Muslim Minority Affairs* 28 (1): 61–82. https://doi.org/10.1080/13602000802011069.

Vaccari, Christian. 2009. "Immigration and Diversity: Missed Opportunities: The Debate on Immigrants' Voting Rights in Italian Newspapers and Television." In *Beyond Monopoly: Globalization and Contemporary Italian Media*. Edited by Michela Ardizzoni, and Chiara Ferrari. Lanham, MD: Lexington Books.

Werbner, Pnina. 2009. "Revisiting the UK Muslim Diasporic Public Sphere at a Time of Terror: From Local (benign) Invisible Spaces to Seditious Conspiratorial Spaces and the 'failure of Multiculturalism' Discourse." *South Asian Diaspora* 1 (1): 19–45. https://doi.org/10.1080/19438190902719609.

Wood, C., and W. M. L. Finlay. 2008. "British National Party Representations of Muslims in the Month after the London Bombings: Homogeneity, Threat, and the Conspiracy Tradition." *British Journal of Social Psychology* 47 (4): 707–26. https://doi.org/10.1348/014466607X264103.

Zinn, Dorothy Louise. 2011. "'Loud and Clear': The G2 Second Generations Network in Italy." *Journal of Modern Italian Studies* 16 (3): 373–85. https://doi.org/10.1080/1354571X.2011.565640.

Zoonen, Liesbet van, Farida Vis, and Sabina Mihelj. 2011. "YouTube Interactions Between Agonism, Antagonism and Dialogue: Video Responses to the Anti-Islam Film Fitna." *New Media & Society* 13 (8): 1283–300. https://doi.org/10.1177/1461444811405020.

Web sources

CNEWS YouTube Channel: www.youtube.com/user/itele
EMF Asso YouTube Channel: www.youtube.com/user/EMFASSO
Etudiantes Musulmanes de France: www.emf-asso.com
Forum of European Muslim Youth and Student Organization: www.femyso.org
Nous Sommes Unis: www.noussommesunis.com
Yalla Italia: www.yallaitalia.it

4 Thank God I'm an atheist

Digital spaces for the promotion of laïcité

Soile Lautsi is an Italian citizen who does not believe in god. In 2009, she asked for the Catholic crucifix to be removed from the walls of the public school her children attended. While Italy formally recognizes the separation of church and state, Catholic crucifixes are displayed in public and institutional buildings, such as city halls, hospitals, and schools. The legal case *Lautsi vs Italy* quickly became controversial at the national and European level. The Second Chamber of the European Court of Human Rights agreed with Lautsi that the crucifix is not compatible with the state principle of religious neutrality. However, the Italian government framed the crucifix as a symbol of national identity, democracy, and Western civilization, rather than in religious terms. In 2011, the Grand Chamber stated that the crucifix, even if religious in nature, is a "passive symbol" that cannot lead to indoctrination and therefore can be displayed in secular spaces such as public schools (Leigh and Ahdar 2012).

Soile Lautsi acted with the support of the Italian atheist association *Unione degli Atei e degli Agnostici Razionalisti* (UAAR, Union of Atheists and Agnostic Rationalists), of which she is a member. The UAAR argues that public spaces, such as schools, should not display a symbol that openly refers to a religious ideology. The association published on its blog a press release wrote together with other national atheist organizations. In criticizing the European Court of Human Rights' decision about the crucifix, the post explains,

> We are concerned that the presence of a religious symbol in the school environment would justify the existence of a "prevalent" religion; this would result in a privileged role of the Roman Catholic Church and its hierarchies in the Italian social and political reality, as we have noticed and reported multiple times in the last years. We are also concerned that the government . . . intends to preserve a sort of hierarchy between religious faiths, placing Catholicism, which is the former state religion, at the top.
>
> (UAAR, 2 April 2011)

The quotation shows how Italian atheist associations, such as the UAAR, are concerned with the symbolic and hegemonic role the Catholic Church holds in Italian society. Catholicism, indeed, is often considered as *de facto* state religion in Italy, also because of the presence of the Vatican siege in the country. The *Lauti vs Italy* case was widely discussed throughout Europe from different viewpoints. The European Humanist Federation (EHF), an umbrella organization that counts the UAAR among its members, stated in a press release that the judgment was "highly regrettable." The press release explains that the crucifix is "a portrayal of the execution of Jesus Christ, the founder of the Christian religion" and "a very powerful image and potentially a highly disturbing one to put before children" (European Humanist Federation, 18 March 2011). According to the EHF, the decision of the European Court of Human Rights is not only factually and conceptually mistaken, but it breaches human rights imposing on Lautsi and her children a symbol they reject. By displaying the crucifix in public buildings, the Italian government goes against state secularism, which the EHF considers as the only principle that is able to guarantee freedom of religion.

The Belgian *Centre d'Action Laïque* (CAI, Center for Secular Action) reiterated the opinion of the EHF by producing a video and disseminating it on the association's YouTube Channel, as well as through the blog of the association *Action Laïque Belgo-Italienne* (ALBI, Belgian-Italian Secular Action), co-founded by the UAAR. According to CAI president Jean de Bruecker, the European Court of Human Rights' decision does not only regard Italy, but could jeopardize the church-state separation in Europe (CAI, 4 May 2011). The French atheist association *Union des Familles Laïques* (UFAL, Union of Secular Families) commented the case on its blog to talk about the French national context. While French public schools do not display religious symbols, the association explains that the crucifix should be removed also from private schools when they function as seats for public examinations. Therefore, the UFAL employed the Italian case to reiterate that the French government needs to define spaces where religion may – or may not – be present in order to enforce and protect *laïcité*.

The *Lautsi vs Italy* case is relevant to understand how secular and religious spaces may occupy controversial positions in the European public sphere, and how the concept of public and private is often ambiguous in relation to institutional decisions about religion. At the origin of this case there are disagreements on the meanings of a material religious object – the crucifix – and its impact on the surrounding space. Indeed, various media sources framed the controversy in different ways: the crucifix in public schools has been framed as a religious symbol incompatible with state secularism, a positive symbol of Italian (and European) culture, as well as a symbol against an alleged "Muslim invasion" (Ozzano and Giorgi 2013). The crucifix has been described as a powerful image that can charge space with religious meanings, or as a "passive" object that cannot indoctrinate children. In this debate, atheist associations not only discussed the negative meanings they attribute to the crucifix, but also denounced its public presence as a symbol of the religious hegemony they perceive in European public spaces.

These debates about the crucifix point to the ambiguities of Catholic secularism in Europe, mentioned in this book's introduction. If, on the one hand, state secularism protects citizens' rights to believe or not believe in a religion, on the other hand, Catholicism often occupies a prominent role in the European public sphere and informs secular values. The principle of Catholic secularism tends to inform mainstream culture, for example, influencing juridical decisions in *Lautsi vs Italy* case. The final verdict of the European Court of Human Rights, indeed, shows how Europe is still far from being completely secular, rather it is characterized by religious and post-secular spaces, where Catholic and secular values coexist.

The European Humanist Federation and its member associations exist to safeguard and enforce the principle of *laïcité* in Europe. This type of organized atheism is a facet of European religious change. While non-believers have arguably always existed, it is in the last decades that they started to become more vocal and visible, and more organized. This shows that religious change is represented not solely by new religions arriving and growing in Europe, but also by people abandoning religion and actively promoting a secularist ideology. In defining the space of the secular in Europe, atheist associations create community structures that coexist and interact with religious organizations, thus articulating networks of beliefs and actions. As a result, religious groups often find themselves competing with forms of atheism that are increasing more visible in the public sphere.

Atheist groups, creating internet discourses, often articulate hypermediated religious spaces. They elaborate communication strategies that combine online narratives with offline actions. They discuss material religious symbols – such as the Catholic crucifix and the Muslim veil – to address a perceived religious hegemony and to negotiate atheist identities. By defining the role religion should occupy in society, atheist associations discuss the boundaries between private and public spaces, and they imagine a European society where the principle of *laïcité* has a privileged role in respect to religious beliefs.

This chapter will describe these hypermediated discourses by analyzing the blogs of two atheist associations: the Italian UAAR and the French UFAL. After outlining a short story of the secular in Europe, it will discuss the association UAAR, explaining in particular its critique of the hegemonic character of the Catholic Church in Italy in relation to Italian media and politics. The chapter will then proceed to talk about the French UFAL, analyzing the associations' understanding of *laïcité*, especially in relation to the Muslim veil in public spaces. Lastly, it will explain why these blogs are examples of hypermediated religious spaces aimed at diffusing secularism in Europe, creating spaces for the formation of atheist communities, and articulating atheist identities based on non-religious values.

Atheism in Europe: a short summary

Atheism is becoming increasingly visible in Europe, entering the arena of civic engagement and actively shaping people's identities (Taira and Illman

2012). This does not mean that religion in Europe is disappearing, but rather that the progressive deprivatization – or re-publicization – of religion is followed by a similar growth of atheist organizations; as religion becomes more public, atheists also become more vocal in expressing their ideas. Indeed, according to the European Humanist Federation, between a quarter and half of the European population has no religious belief. In quoting the data of the research agency Eurobarometer, the EHF explains on its website that in the European Union only 52 percent of the population believes in god, 46 percent thinks that religion has a too-important place within society, and only 40 percent tends to trust religious institutions.

However, these data do not tell the whole story of atheism in Europe. In certain circumstances, for example, people refuse to self-identify as atheists even if they do not believe in god (Zuckerman 2007). Arguably, this happens because people may have different understandings of what "atheism" means. In general, "atheism" indicates an active engagement with non-religious, or even anti-religious, perspectives. "Secular" is usually understood as the absence of religion, in terms that tend to be less anti-religious than "atheism" (Knott and Poole 2013). At the same time, "secularism" can be considered as an independent political doctrine that seeks to influence state decisions (Asad 2003). While "*laïcité*" (*laicità* in Italian) can be used at times as a synonym of "atheism" and "secular," it usually describes the separation of church and state that is peculiar to the French context. However, as Grace Davie (2013) notes, *laïcité* can be understood in different ways, because "at one end of the spectrum it is a relatively neutral concept; at the other it denotes a militant, anti-clerical stance – at times tipping over into a mistrust of all religion" (4). This chapter will analyze the UAAR blog, which predominantly talks about "atheism," and the UFAL blog, which focuses more on "*laïcité*."

The different understandings of various terms show how atheism is not only growing, but it is also increasingly heterogeneous. In Western contexts, indeed, there are many ways of being an atheist. In certain cases, atheism coincides with an interest in science, as in case of the so-called "New Atheism" (Thomas 2010; Pigliucci 2013). Based on books of prominent atheist authors, mostly male and from the UK and the US, New Atheism gains visibility for the controversial positions of characters such as Richard Dawkins (Schulzke 2013). Media often focus on the more aggressive stances of New Atheism and on its charismatic leaders, who also tend to have a prominent internet presence (Taira 2015). New media, indeed, contribute to the visibility of New Atheism, helping to organize events and to articulate atheist "imagined communities" (Cimino and Smith 2011; Smith 2013)

Alongside New Atheism, other forms of atheism emerge in different contexts. The Sunday Assembly, for example, organizes atheist meetings that follow the structure of Protestant worship. These secular communities, popular mainly in Europe and the US, aim at eliciting emotional involvement through social gatherings, without necessarily engaging in social or political change (Smith 2017). Therefore, these meetings conceptualize atheism as a form of belief, rather than an anti-religious movement (Dick 2015).

This chapter focuses on atheist organizations that promote a secular worldview and try to have an impact on society, for example, challenging the presence of religious symbols in certain spaces. These associations usually do not only seek to create a secular society, but also promote human rights and a secular ethical worldview. This type of European organized atheism tends to challenge religious institutions rather than focusing on specific personalities. In this respect, they differ from more anti-religious and community-oriented phenomena such as New Atheism and Sunday Assembly. The European Humanist Federation (www.humanistfederation.eu) was founded in 1991 with the aim of establishing an institutional type of atheism. The association, which is based in Brussels and primarily works in English, has two main purposes: contrasting religious conservatism and preventing religious organizations from lobbying European institutions. The EHF thus aims at safeguarding the separation of church and state in Europe, protecting freedom of religion and beliefs, as well as going against discriminations of all kinds. The EHF gathers more than 60 associations from 20 countries. These various associations do not usually directly collaborate with each other, but adhere to the EHF' principles and translate them into national contexts, usually employing national languages. This chapter focuses on two associations that are members of EHF and share many of its aims: UAAR and UFAL.

The UAAR (*Unione degli Atei e degli Agnostici Razionalisti*) was founded in 1987 and, according to its website (www.uaar.it), is the only national atheist association in Italy. As its name suggests, it groups people that are atheist and agnostics and puts emphasis on rationality. The association is organized in local chapters that respond to a central administration in Rome, whose headquarters I had the occasion to visit in summer 2015. The UAAR counts about 4,000 members, who pay a yearly membership fee. Apart from being a member of the EHF, the UAAR has international collaborations, for example, through connections with the aforementioned Belgian-Italian association ALBI. The UAAR's blog, *A Ragion Veduta: Il Mondo Osservato dall'UAAR* (With Hindsight: the World Observed by the UAAR, www.blog.uaar.it), reaches an audience larger than the association's membership, and, according to former President Raffaele Carcano, it is among the 100 most influential blogs in Italian (personal communication, 10 June 2015). The blog, founded in 2005, is updated two to three times a week and offers opinions and press releases from an atheist viewpoint. The editorial staff is formed by Carcano, Treasurer Massimo Maiurana, and two paid employees that are in charge of communication and public relations; the editorial staff also moderates the posts' comments. The blog posts are peer-reviewed by other association's members and sometimes are written by guest writers. Posts are circulated through Facebook and Twitter accounts, and the association has a YouTube channel. On the UAAR's blog it is also possible to find digital versions of the association's bimonthly magazine, *L'Ateo* (the Atheist), and information about its printing company *Nessun Dogma* (No Dogma).

The UFAL (*Union des Familles Laïques*, www.ufal.org) is an association of families inspired by the principle of *laïcité*. Founded in 1988, the association aims at both safeguarding social security and promoting *laïcité*. The association was created with the purpose of representing non-religious families, given that the majority of family organizations in France are religious in scope. The UFAL is, alongside other organizations, a member of the French *Collectif des Associations Laïques* (Collective of Secular Associations). The association is organized both geographically and thematically: it has regional and local chapters, as well as commissions working on different themes (*laïcité*, families, school, healthcare, feminism, ecology, youth, and housing). The association's website, written in French, functions also as blog. It is structured alongside these themes and collectively written by around 30 members of the commissions and the association's administration, as explained by President Christian Gaudray (personal communication, 6 August 2017). The blog, whose first posts date 2007, offers opinions on a number of issues, comments to national and international news, as well as links to other media sources. The UFAL counts around 3,000 members – membership is assigned to families, not individuals – but its newsletter, called *Ufal Flash*, is sent to 30,000 people. It also produces a magazine, *UFAL Info*, which is published four times a year and counts 2,500 subscribers, and it is available on the website. The magazine is written by Gaudray and other members who are also bloggers for the association. The UFAL organizes various activities for its members, such as the *Semaine de la Laïcité* (*Laïcité* week), which includes conferences and educational meetings.

While they operate in national contexts that are characterized by different models of church-state relations, the UAAR and the UFAL have a similar structure and often discuss the same issues. Both blogs are predominantly written by men, and they mainly target an educated and left-wing audience. They are frequently updated and talk about a variety of different topics; for example, they discuss and support freedom of speech, gender equality, and LGBTQ rights. They do not include all European non-believers, but rather target those who openly identify as atheists and actively engage in the promotion of *laïcité* at the public and institutional level. In so doing, they often discuss values that serve as resources to articulate atheist identities. The following sections will illustrate how the Italian UAAR addresses in particular the hegemonic role of Catholicism, while the French UFAL tends to be concerned with the presence of Muslim symbols in public spaces. These discourses are hypermediated in articulating alternative atheist identities and communities and in negotiating the position of religion in public spaces.

UAAR: fighting the Italian *papolatria*

The *Lautsi vs. Italy* case shows what position religion occupies in the Italian public sphere. As the UAAR blog explains, *laicità* is one of the main principles of the Italian Constitution. However, the Italian state is not neutral when it comes to religious matters, as it also safeguards religious freedom and religious pluralism. Through a tax system called *otto per mille*, for example, citizens may devolve financial support to religious institutions that have an agreement (*concordato*) with the Italian state. Therefore, the Italian *laicità* does not entail a strict state-church separation, and it is slightly different from the French *laïcité*, which I will describe later in the chapter. The UAAR often criticizes the principle of religious pluralism in Italy as leading to favoritism for the Catholic Church. The Vatican, also because of its historical and geographical position, has a strong political influence in the country and occupies a privileged social role, even if Catholicism is no longer the state religion. In public schools, for example, the only religious symbol that is exposed is the Catholic crucifix, which the Italian government framed as "part of national identity" in the *Lautsi vs. Italy* case.

The UAAR defends the principle of *laicità* as providing equality to all citizens and as helping them to think critically and rationally. It criticizes the influence of all religions (including Islam, growing in the country) in the public sphere, framing religion as incompatible with cultural and social progress. In so doing, the association often focuses on the hegemonic power of the Catholic Church in Italy. In specific, it challenges both the actual political and social power of the Vatican, and the symbolic power of the Catholic Church in Italians' everyday lives. Indeed, even if they do not necessarily believe in god, the majority of Italians self-identify as Catholic, attend religious services and perform rituals – such as weddings and baptisms – in an approach defined as "belonging without believing" (Marchisio and Pisati 1999). As a result, only around 14–15 percent of Italians openly self-identifies as atheists (Zuckerman 2007).

In its blog, the UAAR criticizes the Italian social and cultural attitude towards the Vatican by ironically calling it *papolatria* (papolatry). This neologism, a portmanteau of "Pope" and "idolatry," indicates the tendency to portray the Pope in an overwhelmingly positive way, without leaving room for criticism. Intensified with the election of Pope Francis in 2013, the Italian *papolatria* is the result of the Vatican's hegemonic position in Italy, the UAAR claims. The neologism *papolatria* is paired with the concept of *ateofobia* (atheophobia), which indicates the public marginalization of atheists. While atheists are not officially discriminated in Italy, the UAAR often denounces social stigma against non-believers and their underrepresentation in mediated discourses. This chapter discusses the Italian *papolatria* in relation to Italian politics, which the UAAR considers as deeply entangled with the Vatican, and to media, which it blames for being biased against atheist positions, and also mention activities, such as the *sbattezzo* (de-baptism), which the UAAR organizes to get more visibility and to negotiate atheist identities.

Atheism and Italian politics

The UAAR often criticizes the entanglement of Catholicism and Italian politics. For example, the Christian Democratic Party contributed to the transition to the Republic during the post-war period and influenced for decades the Italian public radio and television broadcasting (Padovani and Richeri 2007). According to the UAAR, even if the Christian Democratic Party does not exist anymore, Catholicism continues to inform the agenda of many Italian politicians. The association does not criticize the private behaviors of politicians, who are considered free to believe or not believe in god, but blames them for their public display of religious faith. In a blog post, for example, the UAAR talks about Luigi Di Maio, a prominent member of the Five Star Movement party, who once attended the mass in honor of the patron saint of the city of Naples, Saint Gennaro. As it is custom in this occasion, Di Maio kissed the shrine containing what is believed to be Saint Gennaro's blood, which miraculously liquefies once a year.

According to the UAAR Treasurer Massimo Maiurana, author of the blog post, Di Maio needs to recognize that his gesture goes beyond his private faith: "The concept of 'private' assumes another meaning when it is applied to a public character, especially [if he is a] politician" (UAAR, 28 September 2017). The post, which reflects on how the personal can become political, frames Di Maio's action as a political endorsement of the Catholic Church. It criticizes Di Maio for stating that Saint Gennaro is part of the Neapolitan culture, thus implicitly reinforcing the idea that Italian history and culture are entangled with Catholicism. In addition, because Di Maio asserted that the miracle of Saint Gennaro is authentic and not part of popular superstitions, the UAAR blames him for his lack of rationality, framing religious rituals as false and incompatible with critical thinking.

This case is connected with another issue that the UAAR laments in respect to Italian politics: while attending Catholic masses and meeting with Catholic leaders do not generally pose problems for politicians, they are often prevented – or refrain from – publicly identifying as atheists. Raffaele Carcano, former UAAR President, talked about this issue by providing the example of Giorgio Napolitano (personal communication, 2 June 2014). Prominent left-wing politician and a former President of the Republic, Napolitano is considered among the most visible Italian atheists. Indeed, the UAAR mentions Napolitano in a video, created by the association and circulated on its YouTube channel, which aims at showing that Catholicism did not always have a prominent role in Italian history and culture. Napolitano figures among other prominent characters, such as philosopher Antonio Gramsci and scientist Rita Levi-Montalcini, who self-identify as atheists and substantially contributed to create, develop, and shape contemporary Italian culture and society (UAAR, YouTube, 13 December 2012). However, the UAAR also criticizes Napolitano for not being vocal about his atheism. In a post about politics and religion, the issue is articulated as follows:

The problem of atheist politicians is that they prefer to not come out. Often, the few politicians who dare to do it are quick to ensure that they respect Catholicism and pay homages to the Church: this is the case of President of the Republic Giorgio Napolitano, a former member of the

Communist Party and non-believer, but who often displays religious behaviors.

(UAAR, 19 December 2013)

In the post, people's public display of atheism is referred to as "coming out" (in English in the original post). Exactly as homosexuals are tolerated as long as they do not publicly come out, the post argues, atheists often fear that they would suffer social stigma if they make their beliefs – or lack thereof – public. The blog offers examples of the "religious behaviors" of Napolitano in its weekly post *Clericalata della Settimana* (Clerical Item of the Week). Another neologism, *clericalata* is an ironic and derogative word that indicates the entanglement between Italian politics and the Catholic clergy. Once a week, the UAAR publishes a post that comments on national and international *clericalate*, negatively talking about political and institutional decisions that favor the Catholic Church. In 2013, the UAAR blog readers voted as "worse *clericalata*" the story of Napolitano attending a concert organized in the Vatican, and telling to Pope Benedict XVI that every Italian should listen to the messages of the Catholic Church (UAAR, 30 December 2013).

The UAAR's criticism of Italian politics, therefore, is twofold: on the one hand, Catholic politicians who manifest their faiths are criticized for implicitly making connections between religion and Italian culture, thus indirectly reinforcing the idea of Catholic secularism; they are also blamed for supporting "false" superstitions and for not being rational, as in the case of Di Maio believing in miracles. On the other hand, atheist politicians are criticized for not being more vocal about secular values. The attitude of Napolitano towards the Pope and the Vatican, the UAAR argues, negatively perpetuates the marginalization of atheists, who might fear social stigma if they "come out" in public. In addition, it indirectly enhances the hegemonic position of the Catholic Church in Italy, because it frames Italian politics as subordinated to the Vatican.

The entanglement of Catholicism and Italian politics, defined by the UAAR as "state papolatria," may result in an influence of the Vatican that extends also beyond religion: for example, in Italy there is no same-sex marriage because of a "clerical game" played by the Episcopal Conference and Pope Francis (UAAR, 17 September 2013). As will be noted in the next chapter, there are in Italy and France Catholic-inspired groups that criticize same-sex marriage and protest against LGBTQ rights. Challenging the activities of these groups is a way for the UAAR to frame the Vatican as homophobic and to create alliances with LGBTQ groups. Therefore, religion is criticized as preventing social and cultural progress, while secularism is considered as a principle able to safeguard citizens' rights.

Discussions about Italian politics are informed by the distinction between public and private spaces. The UAAR describes politicians as public characters whose faith can no longer be seen in private terms. Therefore, religion occupies institutional spaces in virtue of the actions and beliefs of people who hold institutional roles. The Vatican reinforces its hegemony when it symbolically occupies public roles and situates itself near the political sphere. In this context, the UAAR frames atheists as marginalized because they struggle to be recognized in the political and institutional public spaces that religious occupies. The situation is further complicated by the alleged lack of visibility of atheist positions in media representations.

Atheism and Italian media

The UAAR considers that the hegemonic position of the Vatican in Italy is supported not only by politics, but also by national media. According to the association's blog, Italian media give greater attention to religious topics rather than secular themes and treat religion in an uncritical way. This criticism is not addressed to religious media, but towards the so-called secular media, which despite their formal neutrality often report Catholic viewpoints. In articulating this criticism, the UAAR also seeks media attention in alternative ways, for example, by organizing events that establish a public atheist presence.

In 2014, the UAAR organized a petition to AGCOM, the organ that regulates the Italian public broadcast system. Raffaele Carcano talked about this petition in an editorial of the left-wing magazine *Critica Liberale* (Liberal Critique), as well as in various blog posts. Employing data collected by the research institute Geca Italia, *Critica Liberale* (October-November 2014) shows that the near totality of religious news and TV shows are centered on Catholicism, with rare and sporadic exceptions for Judaism and Protestantism. According to Carcano, this data suggest not only a privileged position of the Catholic Church and a lack of religious pluralism in the Italian public sphere, but also a tendency to overlook secular topics and atheist positions. Indeed, in an open letter to Italian Members of Parliament, published on the UAAR blog, he writes, "We believe that a country cannot be defined democratic if it is not able to ensure pluralism of information. And we believe that a country cannot be defined secular [*laico*] if it cannot ensure this pluralism for religious matters" (UAAR, 18 December 2014).

However, the UAAR's petition has been rejected by AGCOM with the motivation that secular themes are absorbed within non-religious television programs. The case of this petition indirectly shows different understandings of atheism: while for AGCOM atheism is embedded in all those topics that are non-religious, the UAAR advocates for a media system that actively talks about secularism and amplifies the voice of atheist people. Therefore, the UAAR frames *laicità* as something that needs to be discussed alongside religious issues. Indeed, according to the UAAR, atheists are seldom invited to give their opinion or to intervene in debates together with religious leaders.

In addition, the association criticizes how the media portrayal of Catholicism tends to be overwhelmingly positive, contributing to the national *papolatria*. According to the UAAR, the Pope's actions and the Vatican decisions are reported only when they can gain the consent of the audience. As a result, certain news that would connote the Vatican negatively are overlooked, as happens with stories of members of the clergy accused of pedophilia. Also, the Pope's messages tend to be oversimplified to be more appealing to the national audience. A blog post articulates the issue as follows:

> When they [the media] talk about the Pope, every Pope, everybody seems to hold similar ideas. It is difficult to read opinions that do not appreciate the Pope, and the election of Bergoglio seems to enhance this *papolatria*, also because of his communication style that is much friendlier compared to that of his predecessor. Therefore, each word [of the Pope] is framed as leading to an alleged opening of the Church towards socially relevant matters and to a general modernization. Is this the truth? We don't think so. We actually think that there will be no concrete change within the Church in the near future.
>
> (UAAR, 23 September 2016)

The blog proceeds by offering examples of how media misleadingly report the Pope's words. For example, Pope Francis once stated that women who had an abortion should be able to confess and be forgiven by a priest. Such position was interpreted by many national newspapers as an openness of the Pope on the topic of abortion, something that would distinguish him from his predecessors. However, the UAAR argues, Pope Francis clearly opposed abortion in multiple cases, and its alleged openness is only limited to possibly forgiving women who underwent an abortion. This example is used, on the one hand, to underline the inability of the Catholic Church to accept modernity, since women are only seen as potential mothers and their reproductive rights are opposed or ignored; on the other hand, it shows the positive attitude of national media towards the Pope, who is always framed as progressive, even when he shows conservative attitudes. As the quote explains, this happens also because Pope Francis is able to navigate media logics through a communication style that captures the interest of the general public.

The UAAR reacts to the perceived flaws of the national media system through actions that are arguably aimed at attracting media attention. This is the case of *sbattezzo* (de-baptize), a symbolic renounce of faith done by former Catholics. Started in the 1990s, *sbattezzo* is a formal notification of atheism sent to parishes; the UAAR established and diffused this practice by providing information about the process and creating letter templates for the parishes. The aim of *sbattezzo* is to contrast the potential indoctrination of the Catholic baptism, which in Italy is usually celebrated when children are too young to give their consent.

Sbattezzo holds a symbolic role, rather than a practical function: in Italy there are no official national statistics about the number of baptized people – estimated to be as high as 97 percent of the population (CESNUR 2012) – and the Catholic Church likely ignores requests for "de-baptism." However, the UAAR blog employs the *sbattezzo* as a way to raise awareness about atheism in Italy and help people to actively engage with their non-religiosity, offering them a practical opportunity to withdraw from the Catholic Church. They aim at symbolically contrasting the hegemony of the Vatican by showing that there are ways of resisting its rituals. Therefore, while *sbattezzo* is, in theory, a private decision, the association tries to make it public by organizing dedicated events. It distributes letter templates and provides information during yearly *sbattezzo days*. In these occasions, local chapters of the UAAR may gather groups of atheists that publicly and collectively compile their *sbattezzo* letters, thus performing a symbolic "coming out" as atheists. Such events, usually amplified on the blog, arguably reinforce the sense of belonging to an atheist community, characterized by similar feelings and needs.

When collectively performed, *sbattezzo* charges the public space of gathering with atheist values, which are shown in a way that is not entirely dissimilar to a public display of religiosity. Together with *sbattezzo*, the UAAR organizes also other events: an example is the Darwin Day, inspired by atheist associations in the UK and in the US, which celebrates the birthday of Charles Darwin with talks and conferences. In addition, it organizes secular ceremonies for important life moments, such as births, weddings, and funerals. These ceremonies, similarly to the aforementioned Sunday Assembly meetings, tend to follow the structure of religious events, for example, including secular "godfathers" and "godmothers" within celebrations of birth. Therefore, people are symbolically invited to withdraw from baptism in a collective ceremony and to celebrate important moments of life with alternative rituals. By promoting these "anti-rituals," the UAAR indirectly criticizes religious rituals and offers spaces of gathering that help to establish atheist communities.

Sbattezzo and other ceremonies likely serve also the purpose to attract media and social attention and to challenge the perceived lack of secular discourses in mainstream media. Because of its unconventional and provocative character, *sbattezzo* was talked about by international media outlets, including the British BBC (BBC News, 20 November 2014). Even if Italian mainstream media tend to ignore it or describe it in an ironic way, the UAAR argues that *sbattezzo* may concern the Catholic hierarchies because it gives the association an international visibility that challenges the Vatican hegemony (UAAR, 23 December 2012).

In this sense, the internet holds an important role as the venue to promote alternative information and to amplify events such as the *sbattezzo*. Raffaele Carcano explains that the UAAR gained popularity starting from the 1990s precisely because the internet helped atheists to enter in contact with each other and organize communities of like-minded people (personal communication, 10 June 2015). In addition, the internet can enhance international connections. For example, the UAAR has representatives in Belgium and created the Belgian-Italian organization ALBI. Similarly to the UAAR, ALBI also has a blog that amplifies news about atheism and religion, for example, commenting the *Lautsi vs Italy* case, and it is written in Italian, French, and English. These connections may help to establish a voice beyond Italian mainstream media's lack of interest for atheism and to describe secularism in countries where the Vatican sustains less influence.

Therefore, the internet helps to challenge the perceived media *papolatria* and its connections with Italian politics. I have described how the UAAR blog criticizes the hegemonic position of the Catholic Church in Italy, focusing in particular on the connections between religion and politics and the tendency of media institutions to privilege religious viewpoints. According to the UAAR, the national media system is dependent on political influence and perpetuates the religious status quo rather than challenge it. As a result, media diffuse and support Catholic secularism and reinforce Catholic hegemonic power. This often prevents social changes and promotes a religious mentality that the association considers as incompatible with rationality. The UAAR blog is a space where an alternative atheist identity against the perceived mainstream Catholicism can be articulated. By embedding and amplifying events like *sbattezzo*, and through connections with other media platforms, the blog arguably tries to establish a voice that could interact with media and political institutions. By showing how events such as *sbattezzo* can help the formation of atheist communities and attract media attention, the UAAR implicitly states that media should talk about atheism as an independent topic of discussion, rather than only embedding it in other topics.

The UAAR blog often employs an ironic style – exemplified by neologisms such as *papolatria* and *clericalata* – but also quotes official statistics and data in order to support its claims. As a result, it arguably does not target the Italian population at large, but rather educated atheist people. In doing so, the UAAR articulates an atheist counterpublic that is based on the consumption of similar content and on discussions of similar ideas. While this counterpublic is not homogeneous, as it may group people that have a different understanding of what atheism is and how it should be represented in the public sphere, it includes people that similarly criticize mainstream Catholic values. Though the articulation of a digital atheist counterpublic, the UAAR tries to have an impact on Italian society and diffuse a type of *laicità* that exists in other countries, for example, drawing from the French model of *laïcité*.

UFAL: exercising a *gymnastique laïque*

Laïcité indicates the separation of church and state that is peculiar to the French context. French law 1905 establishes the concept of *laïcité* as non-interference of the state in religious matters and as protecting religious freedom. Many describe France as a non-religious country: between 44 percent and 48 percent of the French population, indeed, does not believe in god. However, only 19 percent self-identifies as atheist (Zuckerman 2007). This data can be explained by how the terms atheism and *laïcité* are perceived in France: while many people do not believe in god, they do not necessarily public identify as atheists. Indeed, atheist associations, such as the UFAL, tend to engage only those people that aim at actively promoting state-church separation. Differently from the UAAR, which is the only Italian national association, the UFAL does not represent all French secular positions, and it is not the only atheist organization in France. Rather, it is an active voice of a part of French non-believers engaged in the promotion of a particular understanding of *laïcité*.

Despite law 1905, France is a predominantly Catholic country and the Catholic Church holds an important social role. The French state sustains agreements – similar to the Italian *concordato* – with the Vatican in the Alsace-Moselle and in other regions. The UFAL, therefore, aims at challenging the public role of the Catholic Church in French society. For example, being an association of families, it promotes a re-thinking of the concept of family in non-religious terms. It supports LGBTQ associations in advocating for same-sex marriage and civil unions, something the UAAR also does. This support is also a way to define the UFAL's views about the concept of family and criticize the perceived religious hegemony. Indeed, the UFAL considers Catholicism as mutually exclusive with LGBTQ rights and aims at giving non-traditional families – including "single parents, blended families, divorced families, and homosexual parents" (UFAL, 4 November 2012) – the possibility of being represented by a non-religious association. In so doing, the UFAL advocates for freedom of conscience and implicitly rejects the idea that Catholicism defines European culture and lifestyle.

Together with activities and discourses against the perceived Catholic hegemony, the UFAL is concerned with increasing religious re-publicization, which in contemporary France often regards Muslims. As analyzed in the previous chapter, the French Muslim population represents one of the largest minorities in Western Europe, especially because of French colonial past. This is probably the reason why French atheists tend to discuss Islam more than Italian secular organizations do. Following this trend, atheist associations in France frequently focus on Islam when they discuss *laïcité* and negotiate the public role of religion. The following sections will discuss how the UFAL approaches the presence of Islam in France and how it addresses Muslim people in general, in particular supporting atheists in predominantly Muslim countries. By discussing Islam, the UFAL conceptualizes *laïcité* as tight to spatial understandings of religion and the secular. This type of *laïcité* is concerned with the distinction between private, public, and institutional spaces, and it is entangled with French values.

French laïcité and Islam

The UFAL often discusses *laïcité* in relation to Islam in France and abroad. The UFAL, alongside other atheist associations, supported law 2004 which prohibits public school students and civil servants from wearing "ostensible" religious symbols (Maeder, Dempsey, and Pozzulo 2012). While formally targeting all religions, this law mainly responds to the growing number of hijab-wearing students in public schools. As analyzed in the previous chapter, the visible presence of Islam, and in specific hijab-wearing Muslim women in public spaces, often elicits reflections on the implications of the principle of *laïcité*. The UFAL blog also discusses the issue in posts about atheism in relation to Islam.

A case that is debated on the UFAL's blog is that of the nursery *Baby-Loup*. The nursery is a private association for child's care that adheres to the principle of *laïcité*. When an employee came back from maternity leave wearing an Islamic veil, *Baby-Loup* director asked her to change clothing in respect to the nursery's non-confessional character. The employee refused to do so and, when she was eventually fired, denounced *Baby-Loup* for discrimination. The case was widely discussed by atheist associations because it shows the ambiguities of the position of religious symbols in the French public sphere. Indeed, *laïcité* may assume different nuances in private and public establishments, as well as in different social and institutional spaces. In addition, the case kindled debates about public funding to confessional and non-confessional private schools. In offering support to *Baby-Loup*, the UFAL's blog frames the matter in these terms:

> Religious neutrality is the only way to develop a sense of "common living" (*vivre ensamble*) for little children, [especially] in a district where different nationalities and religions coexist. The UFAL reminds that *laïcité* is primarily freedom of conscience. It includes the rights of non-believers, and every type of beliefs, as long as they don't display their beliefs: only the "neutralization" of working spaces can guarantee rights for all. Therefore, a company or an association should be able to legally impose on its employees the respect of religious neutrality.
>
> (UFAL, 20 Mars 2013)

In discussing the implications of religious symbols, the post frames *laïcité* as the principle that protects freedom of conscience and leads to tolerance of other beliefs. However, this tolerance is symbolically limited by the presence of visible religious objects, such as the hijab. This is particularly relevant because the nursery is in a multiethnic district: the UFAL considers that *laïcité* would help children's integration in a multiethnic environment, while the display of religious symbols may prevent it. This approach does not seem to consider the question of ethnicity as entangled with religion, perhaps echoing the "racialization" of Islam – a focus on religion rather than color or race (Ahmad and Evergeti 2010) – mentioned in the previous chapter. The cultural background of children and teachers comes after their religiosity and the importance of state secularism. Because the nursery *Baby-Loup* includes children from different cultural backgrounds but adheres to secular principles, the UFAL argues that it needs to impose *laïcité* on its employees.

In addition, *Baby-Loup*'s veiled employee is not seen as manifesting her religiosity privately, but as doing so while invested in a public educational role. The case *Baby-Loup* is in this respect compared to that of Muslim mothers who participate in school activities. Because of law 2004, instructors and pupils cannot wear religious symbols such as the hijab in public schools, but this rule does not concern parents. The law reveals itself controversial when hijab-wearing mothers volunteer to take part in school trips to help teachers looking after the pupils. While the mothers are not part of the school establishment, and therefore can wear religious symbols as private individuals, they are sometimes prevented to do so when participating in school activities.

The UFAL comments on such cases by drawing parallelisms with the *Baby-Loup* controversy. As in the case of the nursery, the UAAR claims that Muslim women should not wear veils when they assume an educational role. Even if veiled mothers are usually not subject to law 2004, they need to follow the principle of *laïcité* when they are in the symbolic space of the school. In its blog, the UFAL explains that wearing a hijab when engaging in school activities would threaten the "neutrality of the public sphere," which is the "real core of the *laïque* Republic" (UFAL, 17 June 2015). In doing so, it narratively differentiates between institutional spaces – in this case, the school and the venues where school activities take place – and public spaces that are not charged with any institutional meaning.

The UFAL's attention to veiled women often leads to debates about gender equality, which is described as one of the values embedded in the principle of *laïcité*. Indeed, the visibility of Muslim hijabs is framed as mutually exclusive with sexual and gender equality. In commenting the cases of veiled mothers in school trips, the UFAL's blog writes, "If dignity means to defend the headscarf and to impose it in school trips, what men and women who fought for contraception should think, what Simone Veil who fought for the right to abortion should think?" (UFAL, 16 May 2011). By connecting the Muslim veil to contraception and abortion, the post frames the hijab as a symbol of the patriarchy that is incompatible with feminism. It is not seen as a material object that regards the individual's body and the private sphere of religious practice, but rather as a symbol that can charge the space into which it is situated, in a way equally powerful – or even more powerful – than the Catholic crucifix. Therefore, the veil allegedly contributes to creating a repressive culture that prevents the emancipation of women.

The promotion of *laïcité* regards also Islam in places other than France, in particular in relation to persecuted atheists in predominantly Muslim countries. The UFAL, indeed, places great emphasis on people's freedom of conscience and their emancipation from religion, especially in non-democratic places. For example, it adheres to international campaigns for Raif Badawi, a Saudi Arabian blogger that has been found guilty of apostasy because of his criticism of religious beliefs and institutions. Condemned to 1,000 lashes and ten years of prison, Badawi gained the support of the international community as a symbol of Saudi Arabia's lack of respect for human rights, and his story was reported by many atheist associations in Europe, including the UAAR. In addition, the UFAL created a fundraising campaign to support Sobak, nickname of a Bangladeshi blogger who, after repeatedly receiving death threats, escaped to Nepal with his family. According to president Gaudray, the campaign does not directly appeal to the association's members, and it has no influence on the French situation, but it is part of the very *raison d'être* of the UFAL (personal communication, 6 August 2017). Blog readers, indeed, are invited to show solidarity and identify with Badawi and Sobak, persecuted for holding ideas similar to those of UFAL. These cases elicit also indirect reflections on the medium of blogging, so powerful in circulating ideas that it can even result in death and violence.

The UFAL arguably talks about the cases of bloggers in Muslim countries also to stress the importance of human rights and democracy. Badawi and Sobak are praised for their bravery in challenging non-democratic systems, indirectly showing how *laïcité* could also be promoted in Muslim contexts. These narratives about Islam also help to reflect upon the values that inform *laïcité*. In specific, the cases of Badawi and Sobak emphasize the importance of freedom of speech, which the UFAL defends both in France and abroad as part of a larger effort to support human rights. In order to promote freedom of speech, the UFAL engages in petitions and campaigns to abrogate anti-blasphemy laws. Blasphemy, which is the act of hurting, offending, or ridiculing religious feelings, is debated in France in relation to the killing of several journalists of the *Charlie Hebdo* magazine in Paris in January 2015. Notorious for publishing anti-religious satirical images, *Charlie Hebdo* was attacked by terrorists who declared themselves outraged by caricatures of the Prophet Mohammed. In mourning the victims of the attack, many debates focused on the need of allowing, or restraining, anti-religious satire. For the UFAL, both the persecutions of bloggers in other countries and the debates about *Charlie Hebdo* in France are occasions to reiterate that freedom of speech needs to be protected over religious feelings.

Therefore, talking about Islam becomes an occasion for the UFAL to promote *laïcité* and values that are connected with secularism. As separation of church and state, *laïcité* involves that religious symbols, such as the Muslim hijab, are not displayed in certain public and institutional spaces. The association's understanding of *laïcité*, indeed, is tight to specific spaces and roles, and it does not admit religious manifestations that blur the line between public and private, as well as personal and professional spaces. At the same time, supporting *laïcité* means also helping people who want to abandon religion, especially when they are persecuted, as in the case of Badawi and Sobak. These discourses connote *laïcité* not as a neutral term, but as entailing certain values, such as gender equality and freedom of speech. These values are indirectly framed as mutually exclusive with religion. Therefore, reflecting on Islam in France and abroad elicits reflections that help the UFAL to define what *laïcité* means in relation to human and civil rights, as well as French national values.

Laïcité and the French republic

The UFAL often talks about *laïcité* as an intrinsic French value. However, since not all French citizens may agree on what *laïcité* means, many blog posts reflect on the implications of this value in contemporary France, indicating also its possible pitfalls. In commenting on the presence of women wearing a veil in public spaces, Charles Arambourou, director of the UFAL commission *laïcité* and blogger for the association, coins the expressions *gymnastique republicaine* (republican gymnastics). According to Arambourou, this *gymnastique* involves accepting *laïcité* as the principle regulating the public sphere and relegating religious manifestations in the private sphere (personal communication, 15 June 2017). Therefore, following this principle, a Muslim mother or teacher should take off her veil when in the institutional space of the school, and put it back on at home or in the street, where she is not holding a public role. This *gymnastique* applies also to political ideologies: a teacher, or a public servant, needs to adhere first to the principles of the French Republic, among which figures prominently *laïcité*; they may express ideas that go against these principles only in the private sphere, when they no longer hold a public role.

This approach reveals an understanding of *laïcité* as grounded in physical and symbolic spaces. This view is not necessarily universally accepted in France: other secular groups sometimes disagree with the UFAL's views, and they use its blog as a space of confrontation where *laïcité* is explained and negotiated. The UFAL defines *laïcité* as a doctrine that incorporates other ideologies, following the definition of French philosopher Catherine Kintzler, who collaborates with the UFAL blog:

> I say that *laïcité* is not a doctrine that people adhere to or not. You can be Muslim, Catholic, atheist, etc., and *laïque* at the same time. It is a philosophical concept that, differently from tolerance, is not concerned with the coexistence of different types of freedom in a society with different communities, but creates a space that allows *a priori* freedom of expression of everyone.
>
> (UFAL, 3 January 2011)

The UFAL considers *laïcité* as creating a space for the expression of different identities and ideologies and distinguishes it from the concept of atheism. While these two terms are often used interchangeably, as happens in the blog of the Italian UAAR, in this case *laïcité* is considered as a more nuanced principle that goes beyond religious beliefs and belongings, and that can be embraced by believers and non-believers alike.

Figure 4.1 Banner for the *Semaine de la Laïcité*. Retrieved from www.ufal.org/laicite/ programme-de-la-semaine-de-la-laicite-2017/ on the 27 February 2018

This definition of *laïcité*, and the idea of *gymnastique republicaine* that derives from it, is entangled with a specific form of French nationalism. It is important here to underscore that the concept of "republican" (*republicaine*), often mentioned in the UFAL blog, does not refer to a political ideology, but to the principles of the French Republic. According to the UFAL, the three principles of *liberté, égalité, fraternité* (freedom, equality, and fraternity), the motto of the French revolution, should embed also the concept of *laïcité*. Indeed, as Figure 4.1 shows, the association employs *Marianne*, the woman symbolizing the French Republic, to promote *laïcité*. In the picture, which is a banner for the event *Semaine de la Laïcité* (*Laïcité* week), *Marianne* holds a French flag with "*liberté de conscience*" (freedom of conscience) written on it. In addition, various religious symbols are stopped by a road sign that denies entry. This image symbolizes how the UFAL considers *laïcité* as entangled with French values and posits it as occupying a position in the French public sphere that religion should not aspire at. While apolitical, the UFAL is close to left-wing nationalist positions that aim at giving greater emphasis to *laïcité* in the French Republic.

Laïcité, however, can be applied in society in different ways. Quoting French philosopher Catherine Kintzler, the UFAL explains that there are two potential pitfalls in the understanding of *laïcité* (UFAL, 6 October 2011). The first one is defined as *laïcité adjectivée* (adjectived *laïcité*), meaning a positive approach to multiculturalism that encourages the public presence of religion. According to the UFAL, this approach can dangerously lead to privileges of religious communities, as in the case of Muslim women who want to wear veils in public schools. This type of *laïcité* may give results similar to those of Catholic secularism, because it allows certain religions to occupy prominent roles in the public sphere and to influence social and political decisions. Arguably, that is the kind of *laïcité* for which the Muslim groups analyzed in the previous chapter advocate. The second pitfall is defined *extrémisme laïque* (secular extremism), and it entails the absolute rejection of religious symbols in any space. This approach, sometimes employed by right-wing and xenophobic political parties such as the

Front National, is criticized by the UFAL because it may lead to racism and Islamophobia.

The criticism of these two types of *laïcité* shows how the UFAL conceptualizes the public presence of religion in French society. Religion and religious symbols, according to the association, can be present in public spaces, but not in institutional venues. The UFAL distinguishes between the home and the public streets as spaces of civil society, where religious symbols can be displayed, and public schools and other similar institutions as republican spaces, where religion should not be manifested. Therefore, the UFAL blog does not only differentiate between public and private spaces, but also elaborates on this distinction in symbolic terms. Even if *laïcité* is presented as a mainstream French value, the UFAL frames it as potentially threatened by the public presence of religion, which needs therefore to be limited through laws and regulations. It is probably because the UFAL considers public religion as problematic that it seems to focus on Islam more than Catholicism: Islam tends to hold a visibility that openly manifests itself in those considered as republican spaces, while Catholicism may be less recognizable in certain public spaces.

This approach to *laïcité* is not free from criticism, especially on the UFAL blog. Olivier Nobile, responsible of the UFAL commission healthcare and social welfare, says that many non-believers – more than religious people – comment on the blog by criticizing the UFAL positions (personal communication, 3 August 2017). Members of other secular associations sometimes accuse the UFAL bloggers of being *laïcards*, a derogatory term used against people that have an uncritical approach to *laïcité* and hold anti-religious positions. While the UFAL rejects this term, it is symptomatic of the heterogeneity of French *laïcité* and of how even among secular associations there could be different understandings of the principle of church–state separation. The internet becomes an important space for discussion because the UFAL blog is used as the venue where various people articulate their ideas, discuss news from a secular perspective, and negotiate the meanings of *laïcité*.

This chapter has described the UFAL's efforts to define its understanding of *laïcité*, in particular in relation to the visibility of Islam. In discussing the public presence of the Muslim veil and in supporting atheist bloggers in Muslim countries, the UFAL frames *laïcité* as embedding values such as gender equality and freedom of speech. Employing a style that tends to be formal, *laïcité* is described through legal as well as philosophical sources. The UFAL does not consider atheists as marginalized in France, but it frames the visible presence of religion in the public sphere as potentially threatening *laïcité*. In addition, because it considers the French model as being the only one able to promote human rights and support multiculturalism, the association is concerned with the promotion of *laïcité* outside France. Olivier Nobile (personal communication, 3 August 2017) explains that France's understanding of *laïcité* is so unique in Europe that the UFAL sometimes struggles to establish a dialogue with atheists in other countries, but the association tries nonetheless to contribute creating a European secular public sphere.

Conclusion: imagining a secular society

The sentence "thank god I'm an atheist" (*grâce à Dieu, je suis toujours athée*), first pronounced by filmmaker Luis Buñuel, is often used in an ironic way by non-believers. For example, together with other jokes about atheism, the UAAR quotes it on its website archive under the section "humor." While it is ironic, the sentence tells something true about atheism in contemporary Europe. Atheists do not believe in god, and they do not belong to a church; however, they do hold certain beliefs, and they do create organizational structures that have something in common with religious institutions. Their beliefs and structures are often articulated in opposition to religion, and their discourses tend to mainly address religious institutions. Religion and god, therefore, arguably play an important role in atheist narratives.

This chapter has outlined some of the characteristics of organized atheism in Europe, focusing in particular on digital discourses based in Italy and France. The two associations UAAR and UFAL, without being representative of all European atheist positions, summarize some of the main trends of non-religiosity in Catholic Europe. The chapter has focused on two specific aspects of the associations, which respond to the characteristics of their national contexts: the criticism of the UAAR against the perceived hegemony of the Vatican in predominantly Catholic Italy, and the UFAL's negotiation of visible Muslim symbols in France, where the principle of *laïcité* was first established. These topics are emphasized because they exemplify some of the issues that non-believers have with Catholic secularism in Europe. The two associations, indeed, challenge the privileged position that they see religion occupying in relation to European politics and society. They also criticize the intertwinement of secular and religious values in the European public sphere, exemplified by the presence of religious symbols in public spaces, as in the *Lautsi vs Italy* case. Through their discourses and activities, the UAAR and the UFAL try to establish a type of secularism that does not only safeguard the separation between church and state – formally in place in most European countries – but also leads to an active engagement with atheist values.

The two associations often aim at creating spaces for the articulation of atheist identities. They offer physical venues – as in case of public squares for *sbattezzo* – and virtual spaces – for example, blogs – where atheists can gather and emotionally connect with like-minded people. While they put emphasis on rationality and science, atheist selves are arguably mostly framed around values such as gender equality and freedom of speech, frequently reiterated in campaigns for civil and human rights. In creating spaces for atheist communities and identities, atheist associations provide their members with a set of shared ethical and moral resources that mirror some messages and structures of religious organizations. While based on the very rejection of religion and transcendental beliefs, these resources help to articulate a shared cultural system that forms a complex worldview. From this perspective, blogs are employed as hypermediated spaces where this atheist "religion" is elaborated and experienced, and therefore partially substitutes religious resources, authorities, and texts.

Atheism, indeed, is often framed as an ideology that needs to find a space of existence and expression alongside religious organizations. In criticizing Italian media for not granting enough attention to atheist voices, the UAAR indirectly claims that atheism is an ideology that needs to be taken into account independently, and not only the negation of religion. At the same time, *laïcité* is described as a supra-principle that can prove inclusive with other viewpoints, including religious positions. The UFAL, in discussing Muslim veils in public schools, states that *laïcité* is the only value that should enter educational institutions and that people should be able to embrace *laïcité* and religion at the same time. This approach implies that *laïcité* needs to be actively diffused and taught in those contexts where it is not already in place.

In this sense, the often-interchangeable terms "atheism" and "*laïcité*" are used to indicate slightly different concepts: while the first points to an active engagement of values and ideas that is comparable to religious worldviews, the second is a principle that should include all citizens, religious and non-religious alike. While they refuse to be defined as anti-religious, associations such as the UAAR and the UFAL indirectly frame *laïcité* as being more inclusive than religions, and atheist identities as better adapted to modernity and rationality than religious identities. Therefore, atheist associations represent an important facet of religious change in Europe because of their active engagement in diffusing *laïcité* and because of their effort to establish public atheist identities that exist alongside religious organizations. In trying to counteract the re-publicization of religion, they inevitably impact the European religious landscape and contribute to diffusing a certain type of secularization.

These atheist discourses are hypermediated as their main space of narrative production is the internet, and the activities of the analyzed associations exist between various physical and virtual spaces. While the UAAR and the UFAL were funded in the pre-internet era, digital spaces enormously increased their communication potential. In particular, because atheists do not traditionally have places of gathering, the internet offers a venue to debate with like-minded people and help find physical spaces to meet, for example, facilitating the organization of events. In addition, in a context of media ubiquity, blogs serve the purpose of offering updated and immediate responses to what happens in society, and constitute venues for timely discussions on religion and *laïcité*. From this perspective, the internet can become a collective place to discuss and negotiate secular ideologies.

While the two associations also publish printed magazines and books, it is only through the internet that they can receive readers' comments in real time, and start discussions about what *laïcité* means and how it could be diffused in the society. As the audience of the blogs is far bigger than the associations' memberships, they arguably function as platforms of exchange between people who, while self-identifying as non-believers, can hold different viewpoints on social and political issues. While seeking reflections on *laïcité*, these blogs rarely invite the viewpoints of religious people, thus becoming venues that primarily involve atheists. In so doing, they help readers form an active atheist counterpublic around the same texts and ideas. This counterpublic is created through unique spaces for the negotiation of atheist identities, and through a corpus of digital texts that inform atheist people's ideas and behaviors.

The hypermediated character of these atheist blogs is found in their approach to materiality, institutions, and technology in relation to national and European politics and society. In discussing religious symbols, they debate the place of material religion in Europe and reflect on how religious objects can charge a given space with religious meanings and create post-secular venues. Through events and gatherings, such as the Italian *sbattezzo*, they symbolically substitute religious venues with spaces charged with secular values. In so doing, they directly or indirectly criticize media institutions, which are often bypassed through the use of technology. By talking about the presence of the crucifix and the veil in certain spaces, they criticize religious institutions as well as individual and embodied forms of religiosity.

Atheist blogs are hypermediated when they discuss the alternative position of atheist identities in relation to mainstream religiosity. While atheists in Europe are seldom openly discriminated against and persecuted, as happens in places such as Saudi Arabia and Bangladesh, the analyzed blogs tend to describe secular selves as marginalized. When religious symbols enter institutional spaces, as in the case of the Muslim veil or the crucifix in public schools, they are framed as challenging atheists' freedom of choice by imposing values they do not accept. The symbolic re-publicization of religion is discussed as potentially preventing the visible articulation of atheist identities, as exemplified by politicians who do not dare "come out" as atheists. While in Italy the perceived hegemony of religion in the public sphere is stronger than in France, both the UAAR and the UFAL tend to frame their viewpoints as alternative in respect to either mainstream religious culture or other understandings of secularism. The growth of non-believers in Europe arguably eases the perceived stigma of atheists, but these associations still feel the need to create safe spaces of expression where they can discuss and criticize religion.

The blogs are also concerned with the distinction between public and private spaces. In discussing the place of religion in society, they operate a re-thinking of the concept of public sphere. They often imply that, while *laïcité* can rightfully occupy both private and public spaces, religion should belong primarily to the private sphere of practice and beliefs. According to the analyzed discourses, religion may be present in public spaces, but such spaces cannot become institutionally religious; therefore, atheist associations usually differentiate between public spaces where religion can have a role and those where religion should not be manifested. In specific, religion must be kept outside institutional spaces, such as public schools, which are considered domains of *laïcité*. Such view of public and private is often incompatible with certain forms of religiosity, such as the Muslim veil. By inscribing religious garments within the category of public religiosity, rather than considering them as concerning the private body, atheist associations implicitly advocate against the public visibility of religion. Because they tend to frame the question of secularism as leading to religious privatization, the Muslim hijab is often seen as a religious manifestation whose proselytizing role is "active" and problematically public.

Atheist hypermediated spaces offer venues for non-believers to gather and address their perceived marginalization, thus articulating "imagined communities" – to employ Benedict Anderson's (2006) terminology. These virtual and physical communities serve the purpose of reinforcing atheist identities and framing them as more resourceful than religious selves in the negotiation of national and European identities. *Laïcité*, indeed, is positively associated with modernity and described as creating better living conditions, for example, advancing human rights. On the contrary, by connoting religion as belonging to the private sphere of experience and not able to adapt to rationality and modernity, atheist associations suggest that society would inevitably benefit from a more extensive application of *laïcité*. In so doing, they enforce a heterotopia (Foucault 2004) of a secular Europe by imagining a society that is entirely secular, and where religion exists only in private spaces and does not hold a hegemonic role in media and society.

This viewpoint is tied to a negative vision of religion as monolithic and unable to be inclusive. While framing *laïcité* as the only principle able to safeguard tolerance, the UAAR and the UFAL seldom seek a dialogue with religious institutions. They negotiate various meanings of *laïcité*, but sometimes fail to see the changes within religious communities and the possibilities of engaging with them for common aims. Similarly, they are involved in a number of social issues, and look for external allies, but tend to overlook certain interconnections. For example, by framing feminism and religion as mutually exclusive, they usually do not engage in dialogue with self-identified religious feminists, and the terms of gender equalities are often discussed by males only. Also, while rejecting Islamophobia, they usually do not take ethnicity into account, thus tending to overlook various facets of European Islam. The risk is that, avoiding engaging with certain groups, atheist associations fail to create what Chantal Mouffe (2013) defines as agonistic confrontations, establishing instead antagonistic relations that tend to marginalize and exclude certain minorities, such as Muslims.

The hypermediated religious spaces created through atheist blogs, therefore, tend to enforce a separation between religion and non-religiosity. The sentence "thank god I'm an atheist" can also be read as follows: not only are atheists grateful because they already reached the rational thinking that is allegedly needed in modern Europe, but they also articulate their identities by separation from religious institutions. Even if they frame *laïcité* as an independent principle, spaces and identities continue to mirror and address religious organizations. To quote Stewart Hoover and Nabil Echchaibi's (2014) theory of third space, they act "as if" their digital spaces are religious-like communities for the exchange of ideas and the definition of values. Without religion, and without god, atheists would probably not be able to actively articulate their selves in terms of specific secular values and emerge within the public sphere in opposition to mainstream culture. This strategy might reveal successful in giving greater emphasis to *laïcité* in public spaces and in advocating for civil and human rights. Because atheist identities are often framed as more rational and resourceful than religious ones, the UAAR and the UFAL blogs suggest that Europe is inevitably going towards a growth of secularism. It is for this reason that organized atheism, and the digital spaces that it employs as venues for communication, may represent one of the more relevant and visible facets of religious change in Europe in the near future.

References

Ahmad, Waqar I. U., and Venetia Evergeti. 2010. "The Making and Representation of Muslim Identity in Britain: Conversations with British Muslim 'Elites'." *Ethnic and Racial Studies* 33 (10): 1697–717. https://doi.org/10.1080/01419871003768055.

Anderson, Benedict. 2006. *Imagined Communities: Reflections on the Origin and Spread of Nationalism*. Revised edition. London; New York, NY: Verso.

Asad, Talal. 2003. *Formations of the Secular: Christianity, Islam, Modernity*. 1st edition. Stanford, CA: Stanford University Press.

Cimino, Richard, and Christopher Smith. 2011. "The New Atheism and the Formation of the Imagined Secularist Community." *Journal of Media and Religion* 10 (1): 24–38. https://doi.org/10.1080/15348423.2011.549391.

CESNUR. 2012. *Le Religioni In Italia*. Accessed July 25, 2016. www.cesnur.com/.

Davie, Grace. 2013. "Belief and Unbelief: Two Sides of a Coin." *Ecclesiastical Law Journal* 15 (3): 259–66. https://doi.org/10.1017/S0956618X13000410.

Dick, Hannah. 2015. "Atheism in Religious Clothing? Accounting for Atheist Interventions in the Public Sphere." *Culture and Religion* 16 (4): 372–91. https://doi.org/10.1080/14755610.2015.1090466.

Foucault, Michel. 2004. "Des espaces autres." *Empan* 54 (2): 12–19.

Hoover, Stewart, and Nabil Echchaibi. 2014. "Media Theory and the Third Spaces of Digital Religion." Working Paper Center for Media, Religion, and Culture.

Kavakci, Elif, and Camille R. Kraeplin. November 2016. "Religious Beings in Fashionable Bodies: The Online Identity Construction of Hijabi Social Media Personalities." *Media, Culture & Society*. https://doi.org/10.1177/ 0163443716679031.

Knott, Kim, and Elizabeth Poole. 2013. *Media Portrayals of Religion and the Secular Sacred*. New edition. Burlington, VT: Routledge.

Leigh, Ian, and Rex Ahdar. 2012. "Post-Secularism and the European Court of Human Rights: Or How God Never Really Went Away." *The Modern Law Review* 75 (6): 1064–98. https://doi.org/10.1111/j.1468-2230.2012.00933.x.

Maeder, Evelyn, Julie Dempsey, and Joanna Pozzulo. 2012. "Behind the Veil of Juror Decision Making: Testing the Effects of Muslim Veils and Defendant Race in the Courtroom." *Criminal Justice and Behavior* 39 (5): 666–78. https://doi.org/10.1177/0093854812436478.

Marchisio, Roberto, and Maurizio Pisati. 1999. "Belonging Without Believing: Catholics in Contemporary Italy." *Journal of Modern Italian Studies* 4 (2): 236–55. https://doi.org/10.1080/13545719908455008.

Mouffe, Chantal. 2013. *Agonistics: Thinking the World Politically*. 1st edition. London; New York, NY: Verso.

Ozzano, Luca, and Alberta Giorgi. 2013. "The Debate on the Crucifix in Public Spaces in Twenty-First Century Italy." *Mediterranean Politics* 18 (2): 259–75. https://doi.org/10.1080/13629395.2013.799344.

Padovani, Cinzia, and Giuseppe Richeri. 2007. *A Fatal Attraction: Public Television and Politics in Italy*. Lanham, MD; Oxford: Rowman & Littlefield Publishers.

Pigliucci, Massimo. 2013. "New Atheism and the Scientistic Turn in the Atheism Movement." *Midwest Studies in Philosophy* 37 (1): 142–53. https://doi.org/10.1111/misp.12006.

Schulzke, Marcus. 2013. "New Atheism and Moral Theory." *Journal of Global Ethics* 9 (1): 65–75. https://doi.org/10.1080/17449626.2012.756420.

Smith, Jesse M. 2013. "Creating a Godless Community: The Collective Identity Work of Contemporary American Atheists." *Journal for the Scientific Study of Religion* 52 (1): 80–99. https://doi.org/10.1111/jssr.12009.

Smith, Jesse M. 2017. "Can the Secular Be the Object of Belief and Belonging? The Sunday Assembly." *Qualitative Sociology* 40 (1): 83–109. https://doi.org/10.1007/s11133-016-9350-7.

Taira, Teemu Patrik. 2015. "Media and the Nonreligious." In *Religion, Media, and Social Change*. Edited by Kennet Granholm, Marcus Moberg, and Sofia Sjö. London: Routledge.

Taira, Teemu Patrik, and Ruth Illman. 2012. "The New Visibility of Atheism in Europe." https://helda.helsinki.fi/handle/10138/162153.

Thomas, Owen C. 2010. "The Atheist Surge: Faith in Science, Secularism, and Atheism." *Theology and Science* 8 (2): 195–210. https://doi.org/10.1080/14746701003675561.

Zuckerman, Phil. 2007. "Atheism: Contemporary Rates and Patterns." In *The Cambridge Companion to Atheism*. Edited by Michael Martin. 1st edition. New York, NY: Cambridge University Press.

Web sources

Action Laïque Belgo-Italienne: www.albi.be
Centre d'Action Laïque: www.laicite.be
European Humanist Federation: www.humanistfederation.eu
Uaarit Youtube Channel: www.youtube.com/user/uaar
Union des Familles Laïques: www.ufal.org
Unione degli Atei e degli Agnostici Razionalisti: www.blog.uaar.it

5 Who is afraid of gender?
Catholic anti-gender spaces of public protest

Around 500 people stand in a square in the center of Milan, the second biggest city in Italy. They remain still for an hour, approximately one meter (three feet) from one another, as it can be seen in Figure 5.1. They do not speak or move, and they read a book. Each person holds a different book: I notice that many read volumes about Christianity, such as Papal Encyclicals and the books of Catholic journalist Costanza Miriano, but I also spot the Quran, the "Prison Notebooks" (*Quaderni dal Carcere*) from communist thinker Antonio Gramsci, and a novel from Pier Paolo Pasolini, a homosexual and atheist author. The people occupying the square are both men and women, from different age groups, and they appear to be all white. There is a quasi-religious atmosphere in the square, but the way people stand may also remind of a military parade. With their presence, the people confer a solemn atmosphere to the space of the square and attract the

Figure 5.1 A gathering of *Sentinelle in Piedi*. Retrieved from www.facebook.com/pg/sentinelleinpiedi/photos/?ref=page_internal on the 26 February 2018

attention of passersby. When counter-protestors start screaming slogans and play music to disturb the event, the protesters would not talk or move. Similarly, they do not appear to be bothered or look for shelter as it starts raining. Around the square, a few men with matching orange vests take photos and videos, place banners, and distribute flyers about the demonstration. As a flyer explains, the people are part of the group *Sentinelle in Piedi*, inspired by the French organization *Veilleurs Debout*; the name of these two associations, the first in Italian and the second in French, can be translated in English as "Standing Watchmen." *Sentinelle in Piedi* are performing what they call as *veglia* (watch). They are silently protesting against the law on same-sex unions that was under debate in Italy at the time, in May 2015.

A small group of women stand on one side of the square and seem to be in charge of the *veglia*'s organization. I have contacted some of them via email and social networks for interviews, but they refused to meet with me. Instead, they invited me to observe a *veglia*, because they prefer to answer questions and engage with people collectively and publicly. Among the women, one gives directions with a megaphone to the people standing in the square. At the beginning of the *veglia*, she delivers a speech:

> *Sentinelle in Piedi* are here in Milan and in other 99 squares [across the country]. We're here to say no to a law that would equate gay unions with marriage, which would let two same-sex persons raise a child, depriving this child of his mother and father. This bill on civil unions is not civil at all. It destroys civilization by annihilating its most important element, which is family. It would lead to the abominable practice of surrogacy for pregnancy. All this happens in a context of general indifference, and with the complicity of mainstream media, which are aligned with the "single thought."
>
> (*Sentinelle in Piedi*, Milan 23 May 2015)

The speech mentions some of the core ideas and values of the group *Sentinelle in Piedi*. The group opposes the so-called "gender theory" that is considered as a pro-LGBTQ conspiracy that seeks to undermine traditional family values. It is defined as "single thought" (*pensée unique*) because it does not accept different viewpoints. Pope Francis also condemned gender theory by saying that it could "destroy civilization" by undermining the institution of marriage (*Il Messaggero*, 1 October 2016). *Sentinelle in Piedi* are part of a larger network of similar associations against gender theory, among which the French *La Manif Pour Tous* (LMPT, Demo for Everybody) is particularly prominent. Started as a series of public protests against same-sex unions, LMPT became soon known throughout Europe; similar organizations were established in other national contexts where the Catholic Church sustains a strong presence, such as Germany, Italy, and Croatia. Some members of LMPT created the group *Sentinelle in Piedi/ Veilleurs Debout*, which soon grew in popularity, especially in Italy.

These organizations are not formally religious in scope. The criticism of gender ideology, indeed, is framed as a collective effort to protect a certain set of values and to support traditional families and their children. They refuse a connection with the Vatican, which also does not formally recognize them; they claim to be non-traditional citizen movements and networks of people with similar aims rather than associations. In this chapter I refer to protesters as "members" because they share the same values, but these organizations do not have a formal membership system. They are also inclusive of people from different religions, ethnicities, and political orientations, as exemplified by the various books read during the *veglia* described above.

However, the ideology behind the European anti-gender effort is inspired by Christian values and by the opinions of Catholic leaders – including Pope Francis – about gender. Not only these groups' messages often quote Catholic sources, but their more prominent members are Catholic, as will be analyzed in this chapter. In addition, they implicitly or explicitly criticize secularism and atheist groups. As analyzed in the previous chapters, many atheist associations are in favor of same-sex unions and other rights for homosexuals; they challenge and are challenged by Catholic-inspired groups in a clash that is arguably not only about gender and sexual norms, but also about the influence of religion in society. Groups such as LMPT and *Sentinelle in Piedi*, therefore, employ Catholic values to react to social and cultural changes in late modernity.

These groups constitute a form of religious change because they establish a new type of lay engagement with Catholic values and find new strategies to make religion visible in non-traditional ways and spaces. Religious change, indeed, is constituted not only by the growth of non-Christian religions or atheism, but also by new ways of publicly engage with Catholicism. In addition, these groups show the heterogeneity of Catholicism because they are inspired by Catholic values but act independently from the Vatican; they do not include all European Catholics and, albeit increasingly visible, they do not aim at representing mainstream Catholicism. In so doing, anti-gender groups complicate the concept of Catholic secularism: they often do not accept the idea that European secularism and Christianity can coexist, advocating instead for a greater role and visibility of religion in the public sphere and rejecting certain forms of secularism. While Pope Francis in Lampedusa and in Strasbourg showed a friendly attitude to politicians, as mentioned in this book's introduction, these groups tend to criticize and keep a distance from secular institutions. Even if they operate in predominantly Catholic countries such as Italy and France, they consider Catholicism as threatened by the increasing privatization of religion and the secular character of national and European institutions.

Because these groups criticize secular media as supporting gender theory, they often seek non-traditional modes of expression, for example, privileging the internet rather than national media. In this way, they create hypermediated religious spaces in between public demonstrations and internet-based communications. They produce discourses that are hyper-mediated because they challenge what they perceive as hegemonic mentality. They seek a social impact through various activities, such as the *veglie*, where they embed materiality and technologies in their public use of space. They try to resist certain manifestations of secularism and imagine a society where Catholicism has a greater public role.

This chapter explores the digital discourses of LMPT and *Sentinelle in Piedi* in Italy and France, first providing a summary of literature about groups against gender theory in Europe (which, for the sake of brevity and mirroring discourses on their blogs, will be referred to as "anti-gender groups"). It will then describe the activities of LMPT, focusing in particular on its conceptualization of Christian values and the articulation of Catholic identities, and proceeds by talking about the group *Sentinelle in Piedi*, analyzing its innovative use of space and communication technologies, as well as its negotiation of authority. In conclusion, the chapter will describe how these groups create hypermediated spaces to discuss sexual and gender norms in contemporary Europe, resist certain aspects of secularism and modernity, and find strategies to make religious identities more visible in the public space.

Anti-gender groups in Europe: a short summary

The Catholic Church is a global institution that adapts to local contexts and to historical changes. With modernity, Catholicism has progressively found new ways to engage with the public sphere and interact with media and politics (Casanova 1996). The public visits of Pope Francis and his meetings with political characters, as described in this book, suggest the willingness of the Vatican to establish a dialogue with secular institutions and to contribute shaping contemporary European culture. This public form of Catholicism may help to define hegemonic social and political values in many European countries. The Pope, as unique leader of the Catholic Church, represents and speaks for all Catholics, who are supposed to follow his precepts.

However, despite having a unique leader, the Catholic Church is heterogeneous and its members may hold very different viewpoints. The Catholic Church, indeed, has often tolerated and incorporated popular and folk beliefs (Pace 2007) and recognizes a number of groups that organize various social and cultural activities in a more or less independent way (Ballardini 2011). As mentioned in Chapter 2, the heterogeneity of contemporary Catholicism can be understood through Raymond Williams' (1973) conceptualization of residual and emergent elements, which may or may not be incorporated in a hegemonic structure. The Catholic Church, from this perspective, functions as a hegemonic structure that embeds different practices and attitudes on social and cultural issues, in a way that can also define political participation.

The anti-gender movement takes inspiration from debates about gender and sexuality among European Catholics. The Vatican started to talk about gender ideology already in the 1990s (Paternotte 2016), but it is in 2003, with the publication of the "Lexicon," a dictionary of terms that are problematic and ambiguous for the Church, that the Vatican officially condemned LGBTQ activism and gender theory (Pittà and De Santis 2005). In 2013, a few months after his election, Francis was the first Pope to openly use the word "gay," declaring, "If someone is gay, and searches for the Lord and has good will, who am I to judge?" This sentence has been interpreted in different ways: while some speculated that Pope Francis was accepting homosexuality, others argued that the Church would include gay people only at the condition of them repressing their sexuality (Evolvi 2016). Pope Francis, indeed, also condemned gender ideology, confirming the views of his predecessors (*Il Messaggero*, 1 October 2016).

Catholics can have different attitudes when it comes to LGBTQ issues (Kirby and Michaelson 2008). On the one hand, many Catholics conciliate their beliefs with other social and political viewpoints; this is the case of Catholics that identify as part of the LGBTQ community and ignore some of the Vatican's positions on homosexuality, or find strategies to conciliate different sexual orientations with Catholicism (Bertone and Franchi 2014; Clague 2014; Clements 2014). On the other hand, some Catholics strictly follow the precepts of the Vatican and employ them as resources for social activism, for example, in case of pro-family movements (Reidel 2009; Hooghe et al. 2010). These different attitudes can be defined as "orientations," a term that indicates the degree people employ religious values to make sense of social norms (Hichy, Coen, and Marco 2015).

Groups such as *La Manif Pour Tous* and *Sentinelle in Piedi*, therefore, do not represent all Catholics, but rather what David Paternotte (2016) defines as a "radicalized" minority – whose number is not easily quantifiable – that engages in an anti-gender effort. In this book, I define this approach to religion as "conservative" because it sticks to certain aspects of religious doctrine in a non-negotiable way and often appeals to conservative political ideologies. These Catholics employ gender theory – sometimes referred to as "ideology" – as a rhetorical stratagem to criticize pro-LGBTQ positions (Garbagnoli 2014). They depict gender theory as a secular conspiracy, enforced by left-wing academia and feminist scholarship, against Catholic values and traditional families. Gender theory allegedly leads to a "single thought" (*pensée unique*), a set of hegemonic – and pro-LGBTQ – values that everybody is supposed to share and that are diffused through national media. While gender theory is not an actual anti-Catholic conspiracy, the European anti-gender movement considers it as threatening because it could potentially erase differences between men and women and undermine traditional values. In particular, the movement employs the Vatican's opposition to gender ideology as a resource to organize protests and actions against same-sex unions, adoption for gay couples, sexual education in schools, assisted reproduction, and pregnancy surrogacy (Paternotte 2015). The anti-gender movement can arguably be seen also as a response to the successes of LGBTQ activism – often supported by atheist groups – in obtaining the recognition of rights in a number of predominantly Catholic countries, such as Spain, Belgium, and France (Paternotte 2008).

This chapter focuses on the two movements *La Manif Pour Tous* and *Sentinelle in Piedi*. As mentioned above, these movements are connected and have the same aims, but different ways of expressing their ideas and protesting. The former is more prominent in France, while the second interests Italy in particular; national groups tend to work independently and respond to the needs of national contexts. However, it is important to keep in mind that these two groups exist in various European countries and often consider themselves as part of an international anti-gender movement.

LMPT (*La Manif Pour Tous*, www.lamanifpourtous.fr) began in Paris in 2012 as a series of public demonstrations, which involved predominantly Catholic youth and parishes. The movement opposed the law on same-sex marriages, deemed *marriage pour tous* (marriage for all), or *loi 1*, from the name of the politician who proposed it. Even if in 2013 *marriage pour tous* was approved in France, the movement did not disappear; on the contrary, it became more organized and rapidly shifted its focus from same-sex unions to assisted reproduction and surrogacy, claiming the importance of traditional family values and of children's needs. The movement's leadership also changed when humorist and comedian Frigide Barjot – born Virginie Merle – left her role as the main spokesperson of LMPT because her ideas did not align anymore with those of the other group members. After Frigide Barjot, the leadership of LMPT passed to Ludovine de La Rochère, former press officer for the Episcopal Conference of France. In this phase, LMPT became more institutionalized and created an increasingly influential online presence (Balas 2017). Since 2013, the LMPT website functions as a blog that collects news and opinions, is updated several times a week, and sometimes translates posts from French to other European languages. Posts often contain links to other platforms, such as the Catholic news outlet *La Croix*; they are generally written by the LMPT president or spokespersons, or are anonymous. While the LMPT website does not include comments, it is connected with various social network platforms, in particular Twitter and Facebook.

According to Ludovine de La Rochère, as reported by national French newspaper *Le Figaro* (27 May 2016), LMPT is the biggest social movement in France from 1968, able to gather one million protesters in a single demonstration in 2013. While these data are not official, LMPT has been undoubtedly able to create a massive social movement in a relatively short time. It established more than 90 local chapters and launched the association *Europe for Family* in order to lobby institution at European level and gather other organizations with similar objectives. In 2013, an Italian chapter of the group has been created in Rome, with Filippo Savarese as spokesperson and Jacopo Coghe as president. According to the organizers, pro-family protests in Italy are able to involve around one million people and influence the ideas of roughly five or six million citizens. While connected with the French movement and employing the same symbols, the Italian chapter eventually changed the name in *Generazione Famiglia* (Generation Family, www.generazionefamiglia.it) and organizes independent activities and demonstrations.

Within LMPT, other forms of protest started to take place. This is the case of the *Veilleurs Debout* (Standing Watchmen), created in 2013. Differently from LMPT, the *Veilleurs Debout* are an informal group with no clear leadership which gathers in public places to protest. Instead of traditional demonstrations, the *Veilleurs Debout* choose alternative modes of expressing their messages: they sit scattered on the ground reading books, listening to music, and singing, in a way that resembles boy scouts' gatherings (Balas 2017). The *Veilleurs Debout* inspired the creation of the *Mères Veilleuses* (Vigil Mothers), a group made up exclusively of women, with a greater emphasis on maternity and gender issues. The *Mères Veilleuses* usually gather in small groups in public spaces, where they pacifically protest for days and nights, engaging with passersby and talking about their ideas.

The mode of protest of *Veilleurs Debout* and *Mères Veilleuses* arguably aims at sidestepping accusations of homophobic speech, a crime under French law: standing scattered from one another, the protesters can claim that they are formally not demonstrating and are less likely of being arrested by the French police on the basis of anti-homophobia laws. However, as I was told during my interactions with members of *Sentinelle in Piedi* in Milan (23 May 2015), this unconventional mode of protest was successful in attracting media and social attention also beyond national borders. Therefore, in 2013, a group of Italians from the city of Brescia decided to create a local chapter of the *Veilleurs Debout*, even if in Italy there are no specific laws against homophobia that prevent anti-LGBTQ demonstrations. The group translated the French name into the Italian *Sentinelle in Piedi* and started to organize protests where participants read a book while standing in silence, without listening to songs or singing. According to some Catholic media outlets (*Tempi*, 4 October 2014), the group was also inspired by the words of Pope John Paul II during a mass at Washington Hall, where he exhorted people to "stand up" every time human life is threatened. *Sentinelle in Piedi* rapidly grew and became more influential than their French counterpart, arguably also because in Italy marriage for same-sex couples does not exist and civil unions for LGBTQs were only approved in 2016. There are no official numbers of *Sentinelle in Piedi*'s membership, but they organize multiple protests, sometimes in 100 cities simultaneously, attracting up to 600 participants for each *veglia*.

Similarly to their French counterpart, *Sentinelle in Piedi* are formally apolitical and areligious and use their website (www.sentinelleinpiedi.it) and social networks as main communication tools to organize demonstrations.

They lack a formal leadership, but there are a number of Catholic thinkers who are part of the group, such as journalist Costanza Miriano. A self-identified Catholic, Miriano often covers news about the Vatican and has an influential blog in Italian (*Il Blog di Costanza Miriano*, Costanza Miriano's blog, www.costanzamiriano.com), online since 2011. The blog is updated several times a week with posts written by Miriano herself or guest authors, and sometimes attracts more than 100 comments. It focuses on Catholicism and offers descriptions of the anti-gender movement in Italy and France and of the activities of *Sentinelle in Piedi*, often described from a personal perspective. While she refuses to be considered a formal leader of *Sentinelle in Piedi*, various media outlets identify Costanza Miriano as one of the most prominent members and organizers of the group.

La Manif Pour Tous and *Sentinelle in Piedi* express their messages in different ways, with the former being a more traditional association and the latter an informal protest group that employs alternative modes of demonstration. They also have a different approach to media, as LMPT tends to seek interactions with journalists, while *Sentinelle in Piedi* openly criticize mainstream media and avoid interviews. Indeed, I was not able to obtain formal interviews with members of *Sentinelle in Piedi*, but LMPT Italian spokesperson Filippo Savarese quickly agreed to be interviewed. However, both these groups represent a new mode of Catholic engagement in the public space, often entangled with conservative political views and criticism of modernity. Both movements have an official website which functions as a blog, and national and local social network pages that serve the purpose of organizing demonstrations and articulating anti-gender discourses. The initial success of these movements partially decreased, probably because laws about same-sex unions were approved in Italy, France, and other European countries. The website of *Sentinelle in Piedi*, for example, closed in 2017. However, the groups continue to hold a social media presence and organize protests, and the visibility they were able to reach in a short time suggests that they might have a longer social impact. This chapter will first analyze the LMPT blog and then will proceed by talking about *Sentinelle in Piedi*, analyzing also the blog of journalist Costanza Miriano. The first part focuses more on France and the second on Italy, even if the two groups coexist in both countries. The examples show how hypermediated religious spaces can try to resist the speed of modernity and indirectly advocate for a slowing down of the peace of life, thus re-appropriating certain spaces in religious terms.

LMPT: protesting against *familiphobie*

La Manif Pour Tous organizes demonstrations in various French and European cities. While during the *veglia* of the *Sentinelle in Piedi* described above people remain still and in silence, in LMPT's gatherings people march in the streets and shout slogans. This is the case of a protest organized in

Figure 5.2 LMPT gathering in Paris. Retrieved from www.facebook.com/pg/
sentinelleinpiedi/photos/?ref=page_internal on the 26 February 2018

January 2013 in Paris against the law for same-sex unions. A video created by the French newspaper *Le Monde* (13 January 2013) shows some moments of the demonstration, where people carry pink or blue LMPT flags, as can be seen in Figure 5.2. The flags are printed with the LMPT logo, which, as Figure 5.3 shows, represents a traditional family with a silhouette of two parents and two children, a boy and a girl. In some cases, protesters also wave the French flag. The video created by *Le Monde* includes interviews of several young men and women, many with the LMPT symbol painted on their faces, who talk about the need of protecting traditional families, Christian values, and children.

The Italian chapter of LMPT also produced a video with various images from a 2016 demonstration in Rome, called *Family Day* (Generazione Famiglia La Manif Pour Tous, YouTube, 14 June 2016). As in the case of the demonstration in Paris, protesters sing and wave flags; many of them, generally young men and women or families with small children, smile while wearing t-shirts with LMPT logo. The video, accompanied by a song about the event, shows protesters assembling around a stage whose entire side is occupied by the slogan *vietato rottamare la famiglia* (it is forbidden to demolish family), as shown in Figure 5.4. Various people, including journalist Costanza Miriano, appear on the stage to give speeches about the importance of family. LMPT was among the event's organizers together with other groups, mostly Catholic associations. While it was not directly connected with the Vatican, religious media gave great resonance to the 2016 *Family Day*, and the Catholic channel TV2000 broadcasted it (TV2000it, YouTube, 30 January 2016).

Figure 5.3 LMPT logo in a square. Retrieved from www.generazionefamiglia.it/ foto-gallery/ on the 26 February 2018

Figure 5.4 Family Day in Rome. Retrieved from YouTube www.youtube.com/ watch?v=uyDPMCB7ZcM&t=748s on the 26 February 2018

LMPT websites and social networks offer detailed accounts of the demonstrations in Paris and Rome, with pictures and videos that show the visual impact of the protesters in public spaces. Images of demonstrations are often employed to recruit new potential protesters. A blog post of LMPT (27 September 2014), for example, exhorts people to join demonstrations in Paris and Bordeaux, and includes a video that shows images from past protests and ends with the words "come and change history." The post explains that it is necessary to "stop the demolition of family" and employs the neologism *familiphobie*. A portmanteau of the words "family" and "phobia," *familiphobie* indicates the alleged tendency of secular media and society to privilege non-traditional families – such as those created by same-sex unions – rather than families based on traditional Catholic values. Fighting *familiphobie* is likely a reaction to social changes in late modernity, where the proliferation of different life choices compels certain Catholics to re-think their position in the public sphere. The following sections will analyze how LMPT's anti-gender (and anti-*familiphobie*) effort directly or indirectly embeds religion, and how group members articulate Catholic identities.

LMPT *and the anti-gender effort*

LMPT blog discusses gender theory and the perceived hostility against traditional families. In so doing, it frames certain types of Catholic identities as socially marginalized in an increasingly secular environment. These discourses focus on families and children rather than sexuality. Therefore, they do not criticize members of the LGBTQ community for their individual sexual orientation, but because of their willingness to create families – through marriage and parenting – as heterosexual couples do. The Italian *Generazione Famiglia*, for example, writes in its online manifesto (La Manif Pour Tous Italia, homepage) that the association refuses any "humiliation, derision, and violence against all human beings," including homosexuals. However, it defends the "fundamental right" of children to have a father and a mother and of all citizens to "protect families, for the sake of society." This approach poses the rights of traditional families above those of same-sex couples and frames LGBTQ rights as mutually exclusive with the well-being of children. Indeed, LMPT considers that only traditional – and Catholic-inspired – families can provide children with a positive living environment.

It is for this reason that LMPT, alongside same-sex unions, criticizes also adoption for homosexual couples, assisted reproductive technology (where fertilization occurs in a laboratory), and surrogacy (when a woman carries a pregnancy for others). While laws on same-sex unions do not necessarily include these options, and while assisted reproduction and surrogacy also interest heterosexual couples, LMPT tends to associate them solely with LGBTQ activism. It frames the issue in the following terms:

> Because of indecent and outrageous practices such as assisted reproduction, which deliberately deprives a child of a father, or surrogacy,

which is nothing more than slavery and renting of the uterus, politicians urgently need to find ways of dissuading this commodification of babies.

(LMPT, 13 June 2014)

The quotation shows how LMPT's main aim is to protect children, framed as weak victims of a process that treats them as merchandise. The post, as many others published on LMPT blog, employs a highly emotional language that suggests strong images: children are "commodities," surrogate mothers are "slaves" and their uteri are "rented." Because LMPT considers that children need both a father and a mother, it often frames those adopted from same-sex couples as "orphans" who lack either a masculine or feminine figure.

This emotional language, together with the neologism *familiphobie*, narratively frames LGBTQs as threatening the existence of traditional families. Digital narratives of LMPT connote same-sex unions, together with assisted reproduction and surrogacy, as a consequence of gender theory. In order to challenge gender theory, LMPT often calls for stricter gender roles and for emphasis of femininity and masculinity. The association, therefore, also criticizes sexual education in school, as well as educational programs that inform children of different sexual orientations. In a post, for example, it is written, "The human being is either man or woman: why would it be problematic to say it?" It continues as follows: "The state, in addition, should not interfere in intimate subjects as sexual identity and impose to children concerns that regards only adults" (LMPT, 13 January 2014). The post criticizes the way homosexuality is talked about in public schools. By saying that the state "should not interfere" with topics such as sexual identity, it indirectly connotes the family as the space of children's education, also regarding sexuality. Therefore, this approach considers that public institutional spaces – in this case, the school – should not be concerned with matters that regard the individual private life, such as sexuality. At the same time, gender ideology is considered to be so pervasive that it is even diffused by the state and able to enter public and institutional spaces.

The idea that the secular state increasingly promotes gender ideology is often connected with the concept of a "gay lobby." In various posts, LMPT talks about a powerful lobby that includes governments and corporations and has interests in promoting LGBTQ rights. While there is no proof of the concrete existence of the "gay lobby," the term is likely connected with anxieties about the changing notion of family and the privatization of religious values. LMPT members, indeed, often frame themselves as being a minority within European society. While it is not clear why the promotion of LGBTQ rights would affect members of LMPT, they often perceive themselves as socially marginalized. They claim that a certain type of Catholicism is progressively disappearing and that the "gay lobby" tries to silence them in expressing their religious ideologies in the secular public space.

The articulation of alternative – and marginalized – identities is often discussed on LMPT blog through personal stories. For example, it talks about Nicolas Bernard-Buss, a French student who is a prominent member of LMPT, as well as one of the founders of the *Veilleurs Debout*. Bernard-Buss was arrested with others in 2013 while he was demonstrating and wearing a t-shirt with the LMPT logo. Arrested by the police for homo-phobic demonstration, he resisted by refusing to provide his identity and fingerprints and was sentenced to four months in prison. LMPT reports this episode as an example of how anti-homophobia laws can prevent people's free speech and of how governments and hegemonic culture publicly oppose certain ideologies. Ludovine de La Rochère, commenting on the perceived victimization of LMPT members, directs a plea to the then-President of the French Republic, François Hollande:

> About the arrests of last months and last days, Mr. President, how many have been imprisoned only for wearing a t-shirt with a logo that repre-sents a family? For walking and singing some slogans (if not the *Marseil-laise*, the French anthem), that you surely don't like? For biking through our cities with a flag? For putting little flags along the streets? For recit-ing poems on a lawn or in a square? . . . Mister President, it is because of your obstinate refusal to listen to us that we actually started a resistance.
>
> (LMPT, 1 June 2013)

With these words, de La Rochère contributes to framing members of LMPT as victims of a system that does not tolerate certain ideas, suppos-edly because of its *familiphobia*. Describing protests as "resistance" against mainstream authority, LMPT employs once again a strong and emotional language, which probably helps members of the association to feel as part of a social movement against an unjust hegemony. By creating alternative identities and promoting positions that often criticize mainstream culture, LMPT overturns the terms of dominant conversations. Its members refuse to think of LGBTQs as a marginalized community, but rather accuse them of depriving children of their rights. Similarly, they do not frame Catholi-cism as belonging to the mainstream culture, denouncing instead the per-vasive role of the *laïque* state in matters of private identities. This identity articulation often takes place through online discussions about Catholicism in relation to changing cultural and social values.

LMPT and Catholic values

The fight against *familiphobie* draws on Catholic values to support a tra-ditional (and Catholic-inspired) model of family. However, LMPT does not openly situate itself within mainstream Catholicism and claims to be for-mally areligious. Rather than openly talking about Catholicism, many of the LMPT discourses mention spirituality and moral values that belong to the whole humanity. In so doing, they talk about the religious identities of LMPT members, including President Ludovine de La Rochère, and negoti-ate the Pope's influence on the movement.

The LMPT blog often counterposes spiritual meanings to secularization. For example, a post claims that there is a need to resist the government's "unfair laws" with "spiritual force." This force is described as inhabiting "every human being, not only believers" (LMPT, 18 April 2013). The post talks about spirituality as being a form of resistance that even the government cannot oppose. Mentions of spirituality often serve the purpose to celebrate diversity within the association and include non-Catholic members. In addition, it likely suggests that certain spiritual values, albeit fundamental to society, are missing in the (secular) institutional spaces. Therefore, direct and indirect references to religion point to the need to engage with a spirituality that goes beyond institutional decisions. While the group rarely criticizes *laïcité* directly, their focus on religion and spirituality is arguably an indirect critique of the secularist character of the European public sphere. This spirituality is framed as a natural part of humanity and described as a positive identity trait of LMPT members.

While this type of spiritual engagement is formally areligious, members of LMPT are often described as Catholics. They are usually lay people who consider traditional Catholic values as relevant to inform their life choices and behaviors, and therefore engage in anti-gender protests. Among blog posts that describe personal stories and testimonies of LMPT members, one focuses on the experience of a young member called Camille:

> Behind her ideas there is, as happens for many of LMPT members, an education where Catholicism plays an important role. "My parents are practicing Catholics" confirms Camille, but she also promptly adds that "we do not care." She tries to convince that "It is not because we're Catholic that we're protesting."
>
> (LMPT, 5 October 2014)

The quote shows how Camille is motivated by religious convictions. At the same time, it refuses to connote the associations' activities and recruitments exclusively in relation to Catholicism, preferring to frame them in terms of universal human values and spirituality. The post proceeds by explaining that many of the movement's leaders are motivated by religion, but their main focus is the protection of children. By so doing, it shifts the conversation from religion to human beings and children, indirectly claiming the universal character of traditional Catholic values, which should inform ethics and morality of all citizens, beyond the activities of religious institutions.

This type of religiously inspired activism is arguably incarnated by LMPT President Ludovine de La Rochère. The first president of the association, Figide Barjot, is described as an extravagant and flamboyant comedian. She is not Catholic and has ideas that go against the official doctrine of the Vatican, for example, supporting the right to abortion (LMPT, 1 May 2013). Frigide Barjot resigned from her role because her ideas did not match with those of the majority of LMPT members. Differently, Ludovine de La

Rochère seems to perfectly respond to the expectations of the association, not only in terms of ideology – being more conservative than Barjot – but also on a personal level. A blog post talks about her in the following terms:

> Her profile is reassuring. Mother of four children, former press officer for the Episcopal Conference of France, practicing Catholic, her style contrast with the extravagance of a Frigide Barjot. Disappointed for being dismissed, Barjot accuses her of representing the most right-wing part of the anti-*marriage pour tous* fight. Ludovine de La Rochère shrugs her shoulders and talks about her deep attachment to the Church, without identifying as a "traditionalist Catholic," as many describe her.
>
> (LMPT, 13 September 2013)

The post describes a type of religious identity that is probably common to many LMPT members. De La Rochère is "reassuring" because of her large family and her Catholic faith. At the same time, her "deep attachment to the Church" is not considered as a form of extremism, but as a normal religious involvement. While framing LMPT as a non-mainstream voice in respect to the predominant *laïcité*, these discourses refuse to consider the association as representing a conservative ("traditionalist") type of Catholicism. On the contrary, the Catholic faith of LMPT members is often framed as responding to the mainstream messages of the Vatican and Pope Francis. Its blog, indeed, often quotes the words of Pope Francis, for example, in occasion of his meeting with Ludovine de La Rochère during a visit to Paris in 2014:

> Ludovine de La Rochère assured to the Pope that family is "attacked from everywhere" in France, referring in particular to the 2013 Taubira Law that allowed adoption for same-sex couples. The Pope told her . . . that he would think about the best way of addressing a message to French people. She thanked him for his "support" and gave him a t-shirt with LMPT logo.
>
> (LMPT, 12 June 2014)

The quote suggests that LMPT is influenced by Catholicism, but at the same time it situates the organization outside of the hierarchies of the Catholic Church. Giving the Pope a t-shirt with the LMPT logo, de La Rochère arguably shows her close relationship with the Vatican, also in virtue of her former role within the Episcopal Conference. However, the association is lay and independent, and Pope Francis' "support" (between quote marks in the original post) seems to be symbolic rather than concrete. This description suggests a willingness of LMPT to employ Catholic values to create a lay-based activism that can mobilize people outside the clergy.

Filippo Savarese, the spokesperson of LMPT (*Generazione Famiglia*) in Italy, explains the reasons of this approach to Catholic authority (personal communication, 17 August 2017). While the founders of *Generazione*

Famiglia are Catholic, they chose to create a lay association following Pope Francis' directives. Differently from his predecessors, Pope Francis tends to refrain from directly leading Catholic associations to social action; however, he also said that Catholics should have a role in public life and that the bishop should be a "pastor" rather than a "pilot" (*La Stampa*, 19 May 2015). Savarese and the other founders of LMPT in Italy interpreted these words as an exhortation to draw from Catholic principles for a new and more independent form of public engagement that involves lay protesters rather than traditional Catholic associations. The Catholic clergy has the role of being "pastor" for the spirituality of believers, and not directly leading them into action as "pilot." LMPT thus seeks to constitute a "third pole" in between Catholic Church and the state. LMPT sustains relationships with Catholic associations, as national demonstrations take place after a number of encounters in local parishes and contacts with priests, but it is not directly dependent on the Catholic Church. In so doing, it creates a militant type of Catholicism, often conservatively and right-wing oriented, aimed at social change and at establishing a new voice that did not exist before.

The LMPT considers the so-called gender ideology as threatening for Catholicism, and it embeds Catholic values. LMPT arguably exists in between mainstream and alternative forms of religiosity, because it claims that traditional family values are marginalized with respect to hegemonic culture. According to LMPT, indeed, mainstream culture supports LGBTQs – through the so-called "gay lobby" and "gender theory" – against certain types of religious ideas. It tends to talk about religion in general terms, associating Catholicism with spirituality. By so doing, it indirectly claims that Catholic-inspired family values – differently from secularism – are universal, appeal to other religious faiths, and should hold a more hegemonic role in the public sphere. LMPT's relationship with religious authority is ambiguous: it acts outside the hierarchies of the Vatican, but its beliefs are often framed as responding to the mainstream messages of Pope Francis. It is also unclear how the Vatican approaches LMPT: the meeting between Pope Francis and Ludovine de La Rochère suggests that he shares the association's effort, but at the same time prefers to keep it outside its direct influence.

This negotiation of mainstream and alternative types of religiosity is intertwined with private and public understandings of faith. Catholicism is considered to be "under threat" because it risks losing privileges in the public sphere. LMPT is not directly against secularism, but it challenges the ways in which a secular mentality – incarnated by political characters and secular governments, as well as the so-called "gay lobby" – changes the traditional perception of family and forces Catholicism in the private sphere. Protesting against same-sex unions and gender theory is likely a way to establish a public Catholic voice that could influence politics and society. LMPT publicly scrutinizes the private sphere of sexuality while claiming that the secular state should not interfere with such private matters. The appropriation of public spaces of protest urges national media and politics to notice new forms of religious engagements that simultaneously belong to mainstream religiosity and find alternative ways to connect with the public sphere. LMPT's novelty, indeed, does not lie in the values in which its members believe – which draw from traditional Catholicism – but in the public ways they carry on their actions.

LMPT's anti-gender engagement is often expressed through the internet, which helps to inform people about demonstrations, enter in conversation with other media platforms, and establish a voice in the public debate. Internet discourses often employ an emotional language. Digital spaces embed images of young people protesting in a loud, determined, and cheerful way, as well as personal experiences told through a storytelling style. At the same time, many blog posts talk about same-sex unions and children of LGBTQ parents in an extremely emotional and negative way, urging readers to challenge the perceived *familiphobie* with an unconventional type of lay and public Catholic activism. Other groups, such as the *Veilleurs Debout / Sentinelle in Piedi*, employ emotions and spaces in a similar way. However, they often organize public protests and elaborate online and offline discourses in a different way.

Sentinelle in Piedi: screaming in silence

When I observed a *veglia* of the group *Sentinelle in Piedi* in Milan, I was surprised by their unconventional way of protesting and communicating. While LMPT is innovative in proposing a new type of Catholic engagement – based on lay activism and visibility in the public space – *Sentinelle in Piedi* add to these features a style of protest that entails silence, stillness, and book-reading. Their public and temporary appropriation of city spaces and the bodily presence of protesters in the square attract people's attention in a way that other forms of protest would probably not be able to achieve. It is for this reason that, I would argue, *Sentinelle in Piedi* are not to be considered as a branch of LMPT, but rather a group that communicates the same messages in a different way. LMPT blog talks about the *Veilleurs Debout/ Sentinelle in Piedi* in the following way:

> Who are they [the *Veilleurs Debout*]? They are young and not-so-young people, mostly Catholic, conservative, and coming from an intellectual environment. Many have been scouts. . . . "We are neither a prayer group, nor a partisan gathering, we don't have a moral or a program to carry on" says Gaultier, spokesman of the *Veilleurs* in Lyon. "We are not museum keepers, watchers of an ancient world, and we are not only outraged. We are lovers of life."
>
> (LMPT, 8 April 2014)

The description shows that, similarly to LMPT, the group's members come from a Catholic background and focus on social engagement. The expression "lovers of life" ("*amoureux de la vie*") suggests a willingness to positively connoting the group beyond the fight against same-sex unions. However, the post also mentions the *Veilleurs Debout*'s lack of organized structure and defined program. These characteristics are even more prominent in the Italian case of *Sentinelle in Piedi*. When I contacted the group via email and social networks, I could not find an official spokesperson, as the members act collectively and without following any traditional hierarchy. Even if I was able to talk with some *Sentinelle in Piedi* members both in person – after the *veglia* I observed – and on the phone, none of them wanted to speak for the entire group. They also firmly refused to be connected to political parties or religious groups, with some of them refusing interviews after hearing about my interest in religion. The hostility I encountered when I tried to obtain interviews suggests a strong criticism to both national media and academia, and a willingness to convey messages in non-conventional spaces. *Sentinelle in Piedi*'s protests entail an ambivalent media use, negotiation of authority, and resistance to the speed of modernity, as well as willingness to find alternative ways to make religious identities visible. I will here describe the ambiguous media use of *Sentinelle in Piedi*, and how they negotiate Catholic and lay authority. I will analyze *Sentinelle in Piedi*'s discourses drawing also from the blog of journalist Costanza Miriano, a prominent member of the group.

Sentinelle in Piedi and media

Sentinelle in Piedi refuse to give interviews to journalists and academics, criticizing certain aspects of society. In addition, they also remain silent during *veglie*: protesters do not move or interact with passersby, even if they are provoked and insulted for their homophobic ideas. Only certain people, who are not leaders but are designated specifically for each protest, publicly answer questions. The choice of silence is described in the group's blog as a way to "contrast the noises of today's society" (*Sentinelle in Piedi*, 18 June 2015), in what is likely a form of resistance against modernity and technology. A blog post, published on *Sentinelle in Piedi* website and Costanza Miriano's blog (21 May 2015), explains, "Many journalists ask to interview us, invite us to take part in television shows or radio debates. We are gathering here all the information that helps to understand why we say no to your invitations." The post continues by clarifying that *Sentinelle in Piedi* are not an association, but rather a lay people movement. It explains that the group avoids interactions with media outlets because

> We do not seek visibility, we are not interested in television talk shows. We only want to express one action, the action of [gathering in] the square. This action educates us in our everyday lives and shakes our consciousness, because it is a public gesture. The space we want to re-appropriate during our *veglie* is public, as well.
>
> (*Sentinelle in Piedi*)

As the website explains, the gesture of gathering in a square constitutes a public testimony that aims at avoiding national media and going beyond traditional forms of communication. According to the website, reading a book completes the silent performance because it reminds of the "permanent education" that everybody needs, thus adding an intellectual element to the group's protests. The symbolic gesture of reading in silence, which is collectively performed in a quasi-meditative fashion, is perhaps an indirect critique of digital technologies in favor of paper books. My interactions with members of *Sentinelle in Piedi* confirmed that the association considers mainstream media as being LGBTQ-friendly and overlooking the activities of the anti-gender movement. Therefore, the refusal to engage with media is an implicit critique of the secular character of media institutions, and a resistance against a public sphere which is perceived as hostile to certain voices.

However, *Sentinelle in Piedi*'s silence paradoxically attracts media attention. While standing in silence may be a form of resistance against media, it creates a visual performance that responds well to media logics. Indeed, a number of national television channels and newspapers talk about *Sentinelle in Piedi*, sometimes claiming that their unconventional mode of protest might be more effective than a traditional demonstration. The national Italian newspaper *La Repubblica* (30 March 2014), for example, dedicates an article to a *veglia* in the city of Turin. In explaining that *Sentinelle in Piedi* represent a novelty within Italian conservatism and act with the approval of Catholic authorities, the article defines them as "hypermediated." In this case, the newspaper employs the term "hypermediation" to describe how silent performances can attract attention more than actual words. Similarly, the Catholic magazine *Tempi* talks about *Sentinelle in Piedi*'s communication style as follows:

> The *Sentinelle* took Mcluhan's "medium is the message" concept in a literal way: standing in squares, and surrounded by crazy contesters, they prefer to use a powerful and archaic symbolic language rather than slogans. Silence, order, and harmony, are responses to chaos. They represent the Apollonian spirit against the Dionysian one, they chose balance and purity as [preferred] categories of the spirit. In [Catholic] liturgy things are covered not to be hidden, but rather to be shown in their true nature. Similarly, the silence of *Sentinelle* is able to speak and cry. It does it against crazy secularism, against totalitarianism that does not tolerate other ideas, against the exploitation of human life.
>
> (*Tempi*, 4 October 2014)

According to the article, silence is a powerful form of communication as it reminds of Catholic "balance and purity" and can "speak and cry" louder than secularism. While *Sentinelle in Piedi* refuse to directly interact with both Catholic and secular media, these articles show how the group is able to make a media impact that is considered by many as successful. Therefore, if silence becomes a medium of communication that confers values to the physical space of the square, it is also indirectly amplified by different media.

Sentinelle in Piedi's relationship with media is ambiguous as they refuse to engage with them but, at the same time, benefit from media popularity. This ambiguity is further complicated by the group's extensive use of digital media. Together with public performances, website and social networks often represent the only spaces where *Sentinelle in Piedi* express their ideas. Digital spaces have a double role for *Sentinelle in Piedi;* first, they provide information about the group's aims and goals, articulating their anti-gender ideology. The official blog, for example, lists the reasons why people gather, providing pictures, videos, and descriptions of protests. Second, blog and websites diffuse information about *veglie*, letting members know where and when protests are organized and helping new potential members to get in contact with each other. When I asked a *Sentinelle in Piedi* spokesperson in Milan how they are able to coordinate their demonstrations, she explained that they mainly employ Facebook. Started by a group of friends who were inspired by the French *Veilleurs Debout, Sentinelle in Piedi* reached nationwide diffusion mostly because of the circulation of images and texts through social media.

Therefore, the internet both provides information about the group to media practitioners and the general public and facilitates internal communications among members. *Sentinelle in Piedi* criticize national media such as television and newspapers, but do not necessarily avoid digital media. They arguably do so because of the greater agency in digital media practices: while media institutions – both secular and religious – usually reproduce certain viewpoints, *Sentinelle in Piedi* blog and social networks can directly feature the opinions of the group. The greater audience involvement in digital spaces might make them feel able to control their own narratives and representations. If certain media – such as newspapers – are criticized for their secular ideologies, the internet might allow for the creation of spaces that are charged with religious values.

Sentinelle in Piedi's protests in public spaces are organized alongside – and against – various media spaces. Silent performances in squares are situated in between public and private spaces, embedding the private act of reading with public visibility. They likely appropriate the square in religious terms, through a quasi-meditative silence. These performances also implicitly criticize the speed of modernity and symbolically slow down the pace of life through one hour of stillness. These public spaces are closely connected with selected digital spaces where the group's representations are negotiated and displayed. Public spaces and internet spaces are therefore interconnected in an alternative media use aimed at conveying a message that, allegedly, cannot find a place in the public sphere. Paradoxically, this message is also amplified by the same national media *Sentinelle in Piedi* criticize. Through various media sources, *Sentinelle in Piedi* also negotiate religious and lay authority.

Sentinelle in Piedi and religious authority

Sentinelle in Piedi are a collective protest movement that does not have an organized structure or a clear leadership. When I talked with some members, they defined *Sentinelle in Piedi* as a grassroots protest, which could be compared – for its lack of formal organization, not for its ideologies – to the *Occupy* movement. However, it is likely that the group does involve some kind of authority figures. Indeed, the militarist-inspired rigor, the well-structured media strategy, and the ability to coordinate local groups at the national level suggest that there probably is some sort of leadership. The *Veilleurs Debout* group in France, for example, started within LMPT, with whom the group continues to share aims, strategies, and media platforms. *Sentinelle in Piedi* is a more independent movement, but it probably relies on lay and religious authorities both to organize its protests and as intellectual resources.

Costanza Miriano, a prominent Catholic journalist who covers Vatican-related news, is likely one of the informal leaders of *Sentinelle in Piedi*. While she does not have an official role in the group, *Sentinelle in Piedi* Facebook and Twitter pages often mention her as an inspiration for the movement. When invited for a debate on the national Italian channel LA7, a journalist presented her as "one of the voices that the Catholic movement of *Sentinelle in Piedi* follows the most" (Catechista Duepuntozero, Youtube, 5 July 2015). Even if she specifies that she is not an official leader for the group but a simple protester, Miriano contributes to increasing the visibility of *Sentinelle in Piedi* and to attracting new members.

In particular, Miriano has a strong media influence. She is a public character who often engages with media, being a journalist and author of various books, such as *Sposati e Sii Sottomessa* (Marry Him and Be Submissive). Notwithstanding *Sentinelle in Piedi*'s refusal to sustain relationship with media institutions, she often offers her opinions to various media platforms as a private citizen who regularly attends pro-family *veglie*. While *Sentinelle in Piedi* are formally areligious, Miriano is vocal about her Catholic faith and about her conservative ideas. Because she is not an official leader of the group, her media personality does not seem to be at odds with *Sentinelle in Piedi*'s communication strategies. In her blog, Miriano often talks about *Sentinelle in Piedi* and *Veilleurs Debout* and describes her pro-family engagement, in particular through personal narratives about her family life as a Catholic mother of four. She addresses also her leadership role:

> After the book was published [*Sposati e sii sottomessa*] I became a sort of symbol of the battle to defend family. . . [I am no longer] a sister for my friends in trouble, but someone who knows all the answers; not someone who is struggling with her everyday life, but someone who went beyond struggle . . . . Can you believe it? But when you're walking and you realize that people are following you, what do you do? . . . So

I became a defender with a flaming sword, even if I am not physically strong enough for that.

> (*Il blog di Costanza Miriano,* 12 November 2014)

In the post, Miriano refers to her book *Sposati e sii Sottomessa,* which some members of *Sentinelle in Piedi* read during public protests. The book reiterates the differences between men and women and analyzes marriage from a traditionalist Catholic perspective, advocating for wives to be "submissive" to their husbands. Miriano explains how the book made her a sort of informal leader for *Sentinelle in Piedi* and ironically writes that she is not "physically strong enough" to lead a movement.

While Miriano's leadership role is ambiguous and she is reluctant to be identified publicly as a lay authority for *Sentinelle in Piedi,* she is nonetheless an intellectual resource for the group. Not only her personal stories and reflections arguably inspire *Sentinelle in Piedi,* but she often employs her blog to talk about Catholic authority in relation to the anti-gender movement. In a post, guest blogger Paolo Pugni criticizes many believers' superficiality in approaching religious matters, especially on social media. The criticism is articulated as follows:

> Christ said the Pope is His successor and Christ chooses the Pope. Isn't this right? If you don't believe in this, why do you believe in the Resurrection? And if you do believe in this, you shouldn't say that you "like" or "don't like" [the Pope]. You only have to love him and serve him.
>
> (*Il Blog di Costanza Miriano,* 10 April 2013)

The post talks about religious authority as being non-negotiable, because every Catholic should follow the Pope without questioning his words. In addition, it criticizes Catholics who treat religion superficially and implies that faith should be pervasive in believers' lives. Costanza Miriano, indeed, often refers to religious doctrines and their effects on Catholics' public engagement both in her books and on her blog. She puts emphasis on certain aspects of Catholicism, specifically the anti-gender effort of the Vatican. In so doing, Miriano identifies her beliefs – and, indirectly, those of *Sentinelle in Piedi* – among traditionalist and conservative forms of Catholicism.

In talking about Catholic authority, Costanza Miriano often quotes sources other than the Pope. For example, she mentions cardinals and priests who are active in the anti-gender movement and who constitute spiritual resources for *Sentinelle in Piedi.* She also recognizes other lay characters as offering spiritual guidance to herself and to the group. This is the case of Spanish painter Kiko Argüello, founder of the Neocathecumenal Way. A lay Catholic group, the Neocathecumenal Way gathers people that seek a communal spiritual experience and focuses in particular on family values. While *Sentinelle in Piedi* and Neocathecumenal Way are two distinct movements, their aims often overlap, and many Neocathecumenals take part in *veglie.*

Costanza Miriano specifies on her blog that she is not part of the Neocathe-cumenal Way, but she deeply respects the movement and his founder. She defines Argüello as a "man in love with Christ" and even "a saint" (*Il Blog di Costanza Miriano*, 24 June 2015). While Argüello is not a priest or a member of the Catholic clergy, Miriano and many members of *Sentinelle in Piedi* follow and respect him for his ideas and public engagement.

Miriano's frequent mentions of various sources of religious inspiration are symptomatic of the heterogeneity of modern Catholicism. *Sentinelle in Piedi* not only choose non-conventional forms of protest, appropriating public spaces through silent performances, but also draw from family-engaged and conservative forms of Catholicism. Other than the Pope, whose authority it never questions, the group follows alternative Catholic authorities. These authorities, as is the case of Kiko Argüello, benefit from a certain degree of autonomy from the Vatican when it comes to social engagement. In following these authorities, *Sentinelle in Piedi* indirectly claim that believers should engage with religion in a totalizing way and employ their religious convictions as resources for social action. From this perspective, they articulate alternative Catholic identities that slightly differ from mainstream Catholicism in being more conservatively oriented and in connecting social actions and behaviors with religion.

Sentinelle in Piedi often frame themselves in opposition to mainstream society and media. I have analyzed how *Sentinelle in Piedi* center their actions on the visibility of public protests, something that attracts attention but makes it more difficult to communicate messages clearly. They arguably also need media spaces and informal leaders to connect with society at large. Miriano's blog, for example, constitutes a digital space the group seems to consider trustworthy and legitimate, arguably because of her deep religiosity. Together with the *Sentinelle in Piedi* blog and social networks, Costanza Miriano's blog represents one of the rare media spaces where the group articulates its ideas and establishes a public presence. In symbolically offering a voice to the silent protesters, Miriano creates a public message for the group, thus helping to connect its alternative communication style with mainstream society.

Sentinelle in Piedi digital spaces employ different narrative styles. While Costanza Miriano often talks about her personal experiences and her family life, *Sentinelle in Piedi* official blog is more formal and impersonal, with posts that tend to be anonymous. Both digital venues, similarly to *LMPT* blog, feature pictures and videos of protests, thus emphasizing the symbolic connection between physical and virtual spaces. Even through different styles, these media spaces' narratives tend to be emotional in character. By employing militaristic metaphors, *Sentinelle in Piedi* – as well as *Veilleurs Debout* – urge people to engage in the anti-gender movement, implying that certain types of religious beliefs are under threat. The symbolic act of reading in silence creates a powerful visual impact, which emotionally invites people to think about certain values and behaviors. In so doing, they try to make certain religious beliefs more prominent in the public sphere.

Conclusion: imagining a Catholic society

"Who is Afraid of Gender?" is the title of a 2016 song by Italian singers Immanuel Casto and Romina Falconi, used as the official theme of the LGBTQ club "Gay Village" in Rome. The song, which is in English, makes fun of the anti-gender movement through a parody of *Sentinelle in Piedi* in its music video (ImmanuelCastoVEVO, YouTube, 6 June 2016). The video narrates the vain efforts of a fictitious doctor to make a lesbian woman straight and depicts *Sentinelle in Piedi* as shallow and motionless characters that are eventually replaced by a joyful dance of LGBTQ people. While the song and the video are ironic, the attention they accord to the anti-gender movement shows how a certain type of Catholic engagement is gaining visibility and entering into mainstream culture. The title of the song says something true about movements like *La Manif Pour Tous* and *Sentinelle in Piedi:* the urge of these groups to establish a public presence and a public voice likely responds to anxieties concerning modernity. Gender theory is a scapegoat to criticize social changes that certain groups perceive as diffusing secularism and threatening religious identities. Therefore, fighting the so-called *familiphobie* is arguably a way not only to protect traditional family values, but also to address a type of religious change that increasingly relegates religious beliefs in private spaces.

This chapter has described anti-gender groups in France and Italy. In France the anti-gender movement is mainly represented by *La Manif Pour Tous*, which organizes massive protests where people march, wave flags, shout slogans, and sing songs. LMPT has a clear leadership structure, with Ludovine de La Rochère, former press officer for the Episcopal Conference of France, as president. Founded within LMPT, the groups *Veilleurs Debout/ Sentinelle in Piedi* pursue the same aims through different performances. Standing in silence and reading a book in public squares, participants seek to attract attention going beyond traditional media platforms. They act collectively, and they do not recognize official authorities, even if they are inspired by certain public characters such as journalist Costanza Miriano. *Sentinelle in Piedi* are more successful in Italy, where same-sex unions have been approved later than France and where the anti-gender movement was inspired by the French example. These groups show how religious change in Europe regards also internal changes of the Catholic Church and new ways of engaging with Catholicism.

While the two groups have different characteristics, LMPT and *Sentinelle in Piedi* also share multiple traits in common. They do not only hold the same anti-gender ideologies, but they also create hypermediated spaces through public protests and an extensive use of digital technologies. In particular, they create spaces that resist – or try to resist – the speed of modern communications by embedding materiality and technology. Anti-gender public protests establish a temporary presence in public spaces, charging them with religious-inspired values. These spaces could be regarded as becoming post-secular because, for the time of a protest, they make religious ideas and identities visible in what is normally a secular space. Arguably, this type of performance is resistive against certain aspects of modernity, in particular the increasing speed of social life. By taking the time of gathering and protesting, LMPT and *Sentinelle in Piedi* members symbolically seek to stop social and cultural changes, and to criticize medical and scientific progress that would allow same-sex couples having children. In particular, *Sentinelle in Piedi* express this criticism through silence, which often functions as a medium for communication. Silence may help to create spaces by charging it with implicit meanings, thus becoming an "absence made present" (Meyer 2015, 13). The use of silence entails a critique of traditional mediated discourses – as shown also by members' refusal to accord me an interview – and to certain forms of communication. Reading a paper book is a material performance that likely challenges the pervasive use of digital technology and re-appropriates a space that is lost in secular modernity. This engagement might be a symbolic response to the risks of increasing social acceleration in contemporary society, a concern expressed by Hartmut Rosa (Costa 2017).

LMPT and *Sentinelle in Piedi*'s performances are also emotional. Their gatherings – both in case of young people cheerfully shouting or singing, and silent readers remaining still – attract people's attention in non-conventional ways. As for Sara Ahmed's (2014) work, the use of emotions can result in processes of "othering" of given social groups. In this case, the circulation of mediated images of these protests via social networks and blogs contribute to discriminate LGBTQs. Digital narratives often elicit emotions by associating homosexual families with the exploitation of children and women, framing same-sex unions as potentially threatening for society. At the same time, digital spaces also offer venues to talk about personal experiences of protesters, often describing their religious beliefs and indirectly inviting readers to sympathize with and join them.

This intertwinement of protests in physical spaces and digital discourses is often ambiguous. The material presence of protesters' bodies – and, in case of *Sentinelle in Piedi*, their books – symbolically contrast the pervasiveness of media technologies and institutions. This type of resistance against certain aspects of modernity, however, cannot truly avoid the media ubiquity that characterizes contemporary hypermediated societies. Indeed, LMPT and *Sentinelle in Piedi* need to extensively use digital media to communicate their messages and organize physical protests. In addition, in order to establish a public voice, they also engage with national media. Therefore, while the use of materiality might at first seem a critique of media, the groups actually employ physical performances together with media platforms. It is for this reason that these groups create hypermediated narratives that negotiate the meanings of mainstream and alternative, public and private, real and imaginary spaces.

LMPT and *Sentinelle in Piedi* members situate themselves in between mainstream and alternative spaces, in relation to both religion and society at large. They protest because they feel increasingly socially marginalized, and frame LGBTQ rights as supported by a secular mentality that threatens religious identities. They arguably consider secularism – represented by gender ideology – as a mainstream force that involves institutions and governments and promulgates a "single thought" that does not admit criticism; they symbolically protest against groups, such as those analyzed in Chapter 4, that connect LGBTQ rights with secularization. Therefore, anti-gender groups arguably do not consider Catholicism as holding hegemonic power, but rather as losing its hegemony. They address this situation through alternative strategies: they often refuse traditional forms of leadership, situate themselves in between Church and state, and seek public attention in unconventional ways, especially in the case of *Sentinelle in Piedi*. For example, the paradoxical fact of publicly reading both Catholic books and books by Antonio Gramsci might suggest a symbolic connection between religiosity and counter-hegemonic movements. Indeed, members of anti-gender groups often frame their conservative political ideologies as subversive and innovative. This type of engagement results in the articulation of non-traditional Catholic identities that do not criticize mainstream religiosity, but rather protest against what they perceive as hegemonic secularism.

Anti-gender groups often talk about prominent members, such as Ludovine de La Rochère and Costanza Miriano, to indirectly define their positions in relation to mainstream Catholicism. De La Rochère and Miriano are women with a strong Catholic faith, large families, and great charisma, and their discourses often assume a gendered perspective on motherhood, which may explain why many members of these groups are women. Blogs describe them as belonging to mainstream Catholicism, albeit with some conservative ideas. At the same time, they indirectly frame Catholicism as a spiritual force that appeals to everyone; it is probably for this reason that they claim to be formally areligious and occasionally include people from other religions. Narratives about de La Rochère and Miriano often operate also a negotiation of Catholic authority: LMPT and *Sentinelle in Piedi*, while following the authority of the Pope, are also inspired by lay leaders and by pro-family movements such as the Neocathecumenal Way. In so doing, they situate themselves within mainstream Catholicism, showing at the same time that Catholicism is not a homogeneous cultural framework, but promotes various kinds of social engagements and beliefs.

This religious engagement has a public character. The appropriation of spaces of protest, both in case of LMPT's marches and *Sentinelle in Piedi's* performances, might be a way to make Catholicism publicly visible. Indeed, these groups also respond to Pope Francis' exhortations to create a type of publicly engaged religious faith against religious privatization. This type of publicness regards the private sphere of the body, because it is the physical presence of protesters that attracts attention on their messages. At the same time, they also publicly scrutinize citizens' private lives: they protest against a certain understanding of sexuality, and they discuss decisions about people's bodies, including same-sex relations, assisted reproduction, and surrogacy. While LMPT and *Sentinelle in Piedi* claim that the secular state should not interfere with the private sphere of the family, they implicitly advocate for a public control of people's bodies, advocating for the discrimination of citizens on the basis of their sexual orientation. In so doing, they implicitly assert that religious faith should have a more prominent social role in citizens' private decisions, thus controlling their bodies and sexuality. They force a re-thinking of the concept of public and private in relation to gender and sexuality, creating – to employ Michael Warner's (2005) definition – a resistive counterpublic through the display of their own private self in public squares.

In publicly negotiating their religious-inspired ideas, LMPT and *Sentinelle in Piedi* exist in between physical spaces and digital spaces. The internet amplifies the offline protest and the ideologies behind them, and circulates narratives and images. At the same time, it also helps to create social imaginaries about a different society. These groups' digital narratives, indeed, indirectly comment on Catholic secularism: while European *laïcité* might be inspired by Christianity, it can marginalize these Catholic believers who follow their faith in a strict and non-negotiable way. Therefore, from this perspective, secularism and Catholicism are not necessarily compatible. Through protests and online discourses, LMPT and *Sentinelle in Piedi* advocate for a society where religion has a greater role, also in influencing political and social decisions. Their defense of traditional family might unveil a nostalgia for the past, when the Vatican was more powerful in the public sphere and there was less tolerance for certain types of gender and sexual identities. This nostalgia is a utopia rather than a reality, because it often refuses to acknowledge social changes. Anti-gender groups, however, do not consider themselves as backward or against modernity, but rather as preserving values that are allegedly important for the future development of European society. Through digital and physical spaces, they create a heterotopia (Foucault 2004) to influence modernity in their own terms, trying to make it less secular and to give religion a more prominent role.

This heterotopia, however, can exist only at the expenses of other groups. LMPT and *Sentinelle in Piedi* consider LGBTQs – indirectly associated with a secular mentality – as social enemies and try to marginalize them as a scapegoat for social problems. They promote what Chantal Mouffe (2013) defines as "antagonistic relationships," as they would like to enter the public sphere by silencing other groups. This type of mentality can certainly influence social and political decisions, but would inevitably create a society with more tensions and less equality, in terms of both religious and sexual identities. This might be the reason why these groups' protests are becoming more sporadic and *Sentinelle in Piedi* blog closed down in 2017.

However, these movements have arguably contributed to making a certain type of Catholicism visible and will probably leave a social impact. LMPT and *Sentinelle in Piedi* might be mocked because they are "afraid of gender," but they started a conversation about gender and sexual orientations that probably had an impact on decisions about LGBTQ rights. LMPT spokesperson Filippo Savarese (personal communication, 17 August 2017) commented on the decrease of public protests by saying that the association now aims at creating a permanent social presence and a new type of public engagement. Whether anti-gender groups will be successful in the long run is difficult to determine; by far, they were able to employ physical and online spaces to create hypermediated religious spaces which became visible in a very short period and, arguably, contributed to making some European citizens more afraid of gender and secularism.

References

Ahmed, Sara. 2014. *The Cultural Politics of Emotion*. Revised edition. New York, NY: Routledge Chapman Hall.

Balas, Maria. 2017. "From Anti-Gender to Political Causes: Nationalism Among Young Catholics from La Manif Pour Tous." Paper presented at the *Gender – Religion – Nation Internationaler Workshop des Exzellenzclusters 'Religion und Politik'*. Münster, Germany, 28–29 June 2017.

Ballardini, Bruno. 2011. *Gesù e i saldi di fine stagione. Perché la Chiesa non "vende" più*. Milano: Piemme.

Bertone, Chiara, and Marina Franchi. 2014. "Suffering as the Path to Acceptance: Parents of Gay and Lesbian Young People Negotiating Catholicism in Italy." *Journal of GLBT Family Studies* 10 (1–2): 58–78. https://doi.org/10.1080/15504 28X.2014.857496.

Casanova, José. 1996. "Global Catholicism and the Politics of Civil Society." *Sociological Inquiry* 66 (3): 356–73. https://doi.org/10.1111/j.1475-682X.1996. tb00225.x.

Clague, Julie. 2014. "Catholics, Families and the Synod of Bishops: Views from the Pews." *The Heythrop Journal* 55 (6): 985–1008. https://doi.org/10.1111/heyj.12224.

Clements, Ben. 2014. "Research Note: Assessing the Determinants of the Contemporary Social Attitudes of Roman Catholics in Britain: Abortion and Homosexuality." *Journal of Contemporary Religion* 29 (3): 491–501. https://doi.org/10.1080 /13537903.2014.945733.

Costa, P. 2017. "Se il nostro problema è l'accelerazione, la "risonanza" può essere la soluzione? La crisi della stabilizzazione dinamica e le prospettive di una critica del presente." *ANNALI DI STUDI RELIGIOSI* 18: 7–36.

Evolvi, Giulia. 2016. "Is the Pope Judging You? Digital Narratives on Religion and Homosexuality in Italy." In *Lgbtqs, Media and Culture in Europe*. Edited by Alexander Dhoest, Lukasz Szulc, and Bart Eeckhout. London: Routledge.

Foucault, Michel. 2004. "Des espaces autres." *Empan* 54 (2): 12–19.

Garbagnoli, Sara. 2014. "'L'ideologia del genere': l'irresistibile ascesa di un'invenzione retorica vaticana contro la denaturalizzazione dell'ordine sessuale." *AG About Gender – Rivista internazionale di studi di genere* 3 (6). www.aboutgender. unige.it/index.php/generis/article/view/224.

Hichy, Zira, Sharon Coen, and Graziella Di Marco. 2015. "The Interplay Between Religious Orientations, State Secularism, and Gay Rights Issues." *Journal of GLBT Family Studies* 11 (1): 82–101. https://doi.org/10.1080/1550428X.2014.914005.

Hooghe, Marc, Ellen Claes, Allison Harell, Ellen Quintelier, and Yves Dejaeghere. 2010. "Anti-Gay Sentiment Among Adolescents in Belgium and Canada: A Comparative Investigation into the Role of Gender and Religion." *Journal of Homosexuality* 57 (3): 384–400. doi:10.1080/00918360903543071.

Kirby, Brenda J., and Christina Michaelson. 2008. "Educating About Homosexuality: What Do American Catholics Think?" *Sex Education* 8 (2): 225–35. https://doi.org/10.1080/14681810801981282.

Meyer, Morgan. June 2015. "A Space for Silence: Exhibiting and Materialising Silence Through Technology." *Cultural Geographies.* https://doi.org/10.1177/1474474015588708.

Mouffe, Chantal. 2013. *Agonistics: Thinking the World Politically.* 1st edition. London; New York, NY: Verso.

Pace, Enzo. 2007. "A Peculiar Pluralism." *Journal of Modern Italian Studies* 12 (1): 86–100. https://doi.org/10.1080/13545710601132979.

Paternotte, David. 2008. "Les Lieux d'activisme : Le 'mariage Gai' En Belgique, En France et En Espagne." *Canadian Journal of Political Science/Revue Canadienne de Science Politique* 41 (4): 935–52. https://doi.org/10.1017/S0008423908081092.

Paternotte, David. 2015. "Catholic Mobilisation Against Gender in Europe." In *Anti-Genderismus: Sexualität und Geschlecht als Schauplätze aktueller politischer Auseinandersetzungen.* Edited by Sabine Hark, and Paula-Irene Villa. 1st edition. Bielefeld: Transcript.

Paternotte, David. 4 April 2016. "From the Vatican to Madrid, Paris and Warsaw: 'Gender Ideology' in Motion." Ensemble video, 01:11:27. https://ensemble.dickinson.edu/Watch/kExYXqpHtkCchmMFPCJ9RA

Pittà, Maurizio De, and Rita De Santis MD. 2005. "Rome, Italy: The Lexicon – An Italian Dictionary of Homophobia Spurs Gay Activism." *Journal of Gay & Lesbian Issues in Education* 2 (3): 99–105. https://doi.org/10.1300/J367v02n03_10.

Reidel, Laura. 2009. "Religious Opposition to Same-Sex Marriage in Canada: Limits to Multiculturalism." *Human Rights Review* 10 (2): 261–81.

Warner, Michael. 2005. *Publics and Counterpublics.* New York, NY; Cambridge, MA: Zone Books.

Williams, Raymond. 1973. "Base and Superstructure in Marxist Cultural Theory." *New Left Review: London* 1 (82): 3–16.

Web sources

Catechista Duepuntozero Youtube Channel: www.youtube.com/user/CATHECHISTADUEPUNTO0

Generazione Famiglia: www.generazionefamiglia.it

Generazione Famiglia La Manif Pour Tous YouTube Channel: www.youtube.com/channel/UCIn50l9teTREkePtno5H_tQ

Il Blog di Costanza Miriano: www.costanzamiriano.com

Immanuel Casto YouTube Channel: www.youtube.com/ImmanelCastoVEVO

Le Monde Blogs: www.lemondefr/blogs

Manif Pour Tous: www.lamanifpourtous.fr

Sentinelle in Piedi: www.sentinelleinpiedi.it/category/blog

TV2000IT YouTube Channel: www.youtube.com/user/TV200it

6 Conclusion

Creating hypermediated spaces of religious change in Catholic Europe

In the last episode of *The Young Pope*, the drama television series discussed at the beginning of this book, fictional Pope Pius XIII gives a public speech to a crowded St Mark's Square in Venice. He decides to show his face and, finally, become the media event he spent ten episodes building. He meets the same publicity that Pope Francis, in real life, constantly sustains. This book mentioned events that involve Pope Francis, such as his first papal visit to the island of Lampedusa, as examples of how media describe, amplify, and comment on a certain type of mainstream Catholicism. Media events are not only performances that national television channels broadcast, but they can also be those actions – some of which described throughout this book – that seek media attention in alternative ways and in non-conventional spaces.

The same space where Pope Pius XIII gives his speech in *The Young Pope* hosted another media event, this time not fictional. Valeria Solesin was a 28-year-old doctoral student who lived in Paris. Her funeral was celebrated in St Mark's Square after she was killed in the Paris terrorist attacks of 13 November 2015, which young Muslims condemned in the *#NousSommesUnis* video described in Chapter 3. As the only Italian victim of the attacks, Valeria Solesin's funeral attracted national and international media attention and assumed a symbolic value that elicited some reflections about religion. The way the funeral was structured and commented upon in physical and media spaces can arguably summarize some of the trends of religious change in contemporary Europe.

Valeria's parents, Alberto and Luciana Solesin, decided to hold a civil, non-religious funeral. Alberto Solesin explained this choice to the national newspaper *Corriere della Sera* (23 November 2015) by saying that Valeria did not receive a religious education. During the funeral, a band played both the Italian and the French national anthem, in honor of the country where Valeria Solesin was born and the one where she had chosen to live. In addition, the band played Beethoven Symphony n. 9, which is also used as the official anthem of the European Union. A number of local and national political authorities attended the funeral, including the President of the Italian Republic Sergio Mattarella. Roberta Pinotti, Italian Minister of Defense, read a message written by then-French President François Hollande.

Together with these secular authorities, various religious leaders were invited to give speeches at the funeral. Alberto Solesin, indeed, said that he and his family are non-believers, but they welcomed the presence of the representatives of the three main monotheistic faiths: the Catholic Patriarch Francesco Moraglia, the Jewish Rabbi Scialom Bahbout, and the Muslim Imam Hamad Al Mohamad. Each of the three condemned terrorism and participated in the mourning of Valeria Solesin. Alberto Solesin explained to *Corriere della Sera* that he precisely wanted a funeral that could create social union (between different faiths) rather than divisions (*idem*).

The president of UCOII, the Italian Union of Muslim Communities, formally thanked Alberto Solesin for inviting him and other Muslim leaders to the funeral; in this way, he said, Valeria's family proved that terrorist attacks failed in provoking hatred and divisions. Various media outlets, including the aforementioned *Corriere della Sera*, praised the Solesin family for their inclusivity and openness. The funeral arguably succeeded in creating a symbolic secular space where three religions could peacefully interact with each other and with people. Various media platforms made this physical space available for a public much larger than the people present in St Mark's Square. Valeria Solesin's funeral suggests a model in which physical and media spaces can facilitate the coexistence of secular and religious identities in contemporary Catholic Europe.

However, the heterotopia – to employ Foucault's (2004) concept – created during Valeria Solesin's funeral did not reach universal consensus. An article published in the conservative national newspaper *Il Giornale* (25 November 2015) and written by Renato Farina – a Catholic journalist who, in other occasions, positively covered the group *Sentinelle in Piedi* described in Chapter 5 (*Tempi*, 8 November 2014) – criticizes the funeral for two main reasons. First, the article claims that the secular character of the funeral goes against the Judeo-Christian roots of Europe. Second, it argues that the ceremony was characterized by a secular religion of the state that constitutes a "spiritual void"; this void may be filled by Islam, a violent religion allegedly incompatible with European values. According to the article, the funeral was "disrespectful" to Christianity and to the Catholic cross on top of the Cathedral of Saint Mark, in front of which the ceremony was held. In addition, it negatively reports how Imam Al Mohamad was the only religious leader publicly praying for Valeria Solesin, wishing Islam could be more discreet and leave space for Catholic prayers. A post on the blog of the atheist association UAAR, described in Chapter 4, criticizes the article and defends state secularism. The post compares the hegemonic Catholic culture in Italy with Islamic fundamentalism by explaining that both propagates symbolic and physical violence. It continues by denouncing how atheists are often challenged if they publicly choose secular ceremonies instead of religious ones (UAAR, 1 December 2015).

These reactions show how the place of religion in Catholic Europe is often controversial. While Valeria Solesin's funeral and its commentaries do not directly relate to the examples talked about in this book, they contribute to creating hypermediated religious spaces of dialogue about the position of religion in society. The event can be put in connection with the concept of Catholic secularism, the idea that Catholic values inform secular identities and discourses: Muslims are often denied public expressions of faith, because their religion is deemed incompatible with both secularism and Christianity; atheists tend to be criticized when they choose secular ceremonies for allegedly disrespecting the Christian character of European culture; and Catholics may feel marginalized by secularization when they are directly or indirectly excluded from events in the public sphere. These discourses do not capture all the facets of religious change in Europe, and do not regard all Muslims, atheists, and Catholics, but highlight some characteristics of contemporary religion that elicit academic inquiries. In particular, the concept of hypermediated religious spaces helps to explore the position of various religious groups in contemporary Europe, as well as to reflect upon the role of scholars in shaping some patterns of religious change.

The present of hypermediated religious spaces

This book described groups that seek to narrate alternative stories and to create media events that make them more visible. It looked for unconventional narratives that do not point to linear religious identities, but rather try to capture the ambiguities of religious and secular feelings in contemporary society. In so doing, this book did not describe traditional *religious spaces* – the conventional sacred spaces, the venues officially charged with religious meanings such as the Vatican – but *spaces of religion*. In offering a place to discuss identities and practices, these spaces of religion, in this case represented by blogs, allow various groups to articulate what religion means for them and what role it should sustain in society.

These spaces of religion can help to understand some facets of religious change in contemporary Catholic Europe. In this area, the hegemonic presence of the Vatican is often contrasted by non-traditional religious expressions in alternative spaces. In describing these spaces, this book focused in particular on Italy and France, exploring linguistic and cultural contexts that the existing literature in English on religion and media tends to overlook. It talked about six groups from these two countries, in order to describe specific ways of being Muslim, atheist, and Catholic in Europe. Because I focused on relatively small groups and organizations, I was able to combine textual analysis with interviews, thus coming to know in person some of the people I wanted to talk about and directly hearing their viewpoints. What emerged from my inquiries are stories that regard a small part of the population but, at the same time, tell something about the ways religion is perceived and experienced in contemporary Europe.

Italy and France seem to be at the opposite ends of a binary spectrum, with Italy heavily influenced by the presence of the Vatican, and France being the homeland of *laïcité*. Their different approaches to religion exemplify the inner heterogeneity of Europe in terms of religious regulations. However, in both countries there are groups that, without mentioning it directly, have similar problems with the concept of Catholic secularism, which this book employed as the cultural framework that helps the articulation of identities within European mainstream culture. The blogs analyzed in this book often address the same topics: the public presence of the Muslim hijab, the pro and anti-LGBTQ rights activities, the presence of religion in public educational establishments, just to mention a few. They comment on national issues, but often aim at addressing discourses at the European level. This arguably shows how, in the context of Catholic Europe, the strong symbolic role of the Vatican may result in different groups articulating similar actions and discourses and looking for international connections.

While these groups often tell the same stories, they do so from radically different perspectives. They all criticize Catholic secularism for different reasons: it is not sufficiently inclusive with other faiths, it is not secular enough, or it is not Catholic enough. This probably happens because Catholic secularism is not a fixed and defined concept; various groups may consider it in different terms, depending on their understanding of religion and the secular and on the national context in which they operate. For example, while certain atheist groups consider that mainstream media overlook secular topics, some Catholic groups criticize the same media for being excessively secular. This multiplicity of viewpoints exists in relation to religion, as well as to other concepts and ideologies. For example, all three groups discuss the importance of human rights in contemporary Europe, but they show very different understandings of what human rights are. For Muslims, gender equality is represented by women's right of freely wearing religious garments; for atheists, it is ensured only by the absence of religion in public and institutional spaces; for Catholics, it is the protection of traditional gender roles and family values. These discourses show that many topics – such as human rights – can be discussed both from secular and religious points of view.

Contemporary society, indeed, is often characterized by the entanglement of religion and the secular. This entanglement can interest spatial transformations, with given spaces being charged with or voided from religious meanings. The processes of transforming a secular space into a religious one, and vice versa, create post-secular venues. This trialectic have been described mostly in symbolic terms: physical and virtual spaces are made religious, secular, and post-secular by people's activities and the meanings they embed in their actions. Therefore, Catholic Europe does not undergo processes of secularization that result in an uncritical disappearance of religion; rather, it experiences religious changes that involve religious spaces fluidly coexisting with secular spaces. The case studies analyzed in this book rarely talk about god or religious practices directly, but they frequently mention religion (and the secular) when they describe the society they intend to create. As a result, their discourses and actions often embed religion in

politics, culture, activism. This does not mean that religion loses its specificity, but that it needs to be understood as entangled with the secular and
within the social and historical context of its existence.

This type of religion creates networks of actors and actions that target
various types of audiences and embeds different media forms. Therefore,
media are defined in terms of materiality, institutions, and technologies. This
book described digital media platforms – in specific, blogs – that discuss
material objects allowing for embodied religious experiences; they operate in a context that is saturated with media institutions and often target
these institutions with their discourses; and their claims are made possible
and amplified by technologies that become complementary to the religious
experience. Focusing on all these actions helps to contextualize the ways in
which the internet contributes to religious change, and to complete existing
theories of secularization in Europe with a media perspective. It is for this
reason that, in a media-saturated environment, it is arguably more useful to
look at connections between different media rather than concentrating on a
single media platform.

The theory of hypermediation has been explored to capture the encounters between the religious trialectic – religion, secular, and post-secular –
with the tree media forms – materiality, institutions, technologies. This book
explored hypermediation from a spatial perspective. By focusing on the concept of space, it is possible to understand hypermediation as both creating
venues of religious dialogue and enabling discussions about the space religion should occupy in Catholic Europe. Space is not necessarily a physical
location and does not have clear boundaries, but it is the venue where people practically or conceptually express a certain ideology and try to make
it tangible. The Pope's messages, for example, are amplified and negotiated
between physical spaces and various media platforms. This book considered
groups that employ hypermediated actions and discourses to create new
spaces of expressions, appropriate existing places with new meanings, and
seek venues to establish a public voice. In so doing, they subtly contribute to
placing religion into new spaces and to modifying its social role.

Digital spaces are hypermediated when they are unique in articulating
new values and identities, and when the adoption of digital technologies
induces changes in how religion is understood, perceived, and manifested
within certain groups. This uniqueness is often connected with the new
range of possibilities enacted by the internet. Physical actions are able to
attract attention when they clearly communicate a compelling message, but
today it is often the internet that amplifies them, circulates them, and makes
them relevant for society at large. The three groups explored in this book,
for example, elaborate internet-based strategies to express their ideas about
religion and reflect on their own religious identities. Therefore, the internet is not necessarily hypermediated, but groups that create and negotiate
hypermediated religious spaces would probably not be able to express themselves in the same way without the internet.

The uniqueness of hypermediated religious spaces is enhanced by some characteristics of the internet: differently from many other media forms, digital venues are connoted by increased speed and the display of emotions. The internet allows for fast communications that can amplify actions and discourses. Various groups can gather and comment news in real time, offer opinions that are overlooked by mainstream media, and enter in conversation simultaneously with users that hold similar or contrasting ideas. Sometimes, as the example of *Sentinelle in Piedi* analyzed in Chapter 5 illustrates, they may want to disconnect and criticize the speed of the internet. However, speed seems to be the necessary condition for certain types of discourses to exist in a media-saturated public sphere. At the same time, the internet creates emotional discourses because it allows embedding personal stories, pictures, and videos. Emotional narratives can invite other users to empathize with members of a group, support them, and, eventually, join their cause; or they may also instill fear and hate for a specific social group, thus contributing to its marginalization. Either way, emotions are often embedded in hypermediated discourses and help the articulation of religious identities.

These identities are hybrid when they exist in a third space – to employ Stewart Hoover and Nabil Echchaibi's (2014) theory – situated in between physical and virtual communities, in between religious and non-religious feelings, as well as in between local and global negotiations of religion. This "in-between-ness" exists also in the three dialectical pairings described in this book: hypermediated religious spaces emerge at the interstice of alternative and mainstream, private and public, imaginary and real spaces. The three pairings do not represent categories with clear boundaries or elements that are in antithesis with each other. Rather, they are lenses employed to analyze various blogs, explore the different facets of religious change in Europe, and understand the uniqueness of hypermediated religious spaces.

Hypermediated religious spaces often embed both alternative and mainstream values. Many groups employ the internet as the preferred venue of expression when they are overlooked by mainstream media and established religious institutions. This does not mean that these groups are necessarily a marginalized minority in society – atheists and Catholics in Europe, for example, are usually not – but rather that they feel excluded from mainstream debates. The creation of counter-hegemonic spaces often goes together with the definition of what is hegemonic in society. Among the case studies, atheists describe the predominant cultural role and privileged position of Catholicism in the public sphere; in so doing, they articulate alternative atheist identities in opposition to their definition of mainstream Catholicism.

The internet can also provide tools to address perceived marginalization. Groups may use digital spaces either to criticize mainstream culture – for example, challenging established religious authority – or to engage with it – as in the case of blogs that seek the attention of national media platforms. In so doing, various groups constitute counterpublics that arguably aim at changing the terms of mainstream conversations: as my case studies illustrate, Muslims describe themselves as able to improve society rather than representing a threat to European culture, atheists criticize secular states for not enforcing *laïcité*, Catholics consider LGBTQs as a threat to religious identities rather than a minority. These strategies arguably see digital spaces as potentially transcending the hegemony of the Catholic Church or, more precisely, of the Catholic secularism usually identified with mainstream culture. Hypermediated religious spaces, therefore, constitute venues to define hegemonic social values and aspire to occupy mainstream positions.

The definition of public and private religion is also a characteristic of hypermediated religious spaces. They are concerned with the position religion occupies in society, and often discuss whether religion should be publicly manifested or not. There are different opinions about the public character of religion: its visibility may be considered as able to publicly charge a space with religious values; at the same time, visibility embedded in embodied religious practices may be conceptualized as a private form of religiosity that regards the individual. This is the case of the Muslim hijab, which certain secular groups oppose as compromising the *laïcité* of public spaces, and some Muslim women consider as a private choice that only affects the individuals' body.

The case studies analyzed in this book also employ publicity to establish a voice in the public sphere. They do so by enacting actions and circulating discourses that arguably aim at making their claims more visible. Private experiences often help to create emotional narratives and to connect with the public sphere through performances of the self (Warner 2005). While certain groups, such as the Muslims analyzed in Chapter 3, establish a public presence by insisting on the private character of their religious practices, others, such as the anti-gender Catholics from Chapter 5, articulate a type of activism that closely connects private religious feelings with public actions. These different negotiations of public and private contribute to explaining why religion in Europe can be considered as simultaneously more public and more private than it was before: it is more visible, and this visibility is often mediated through multiple media platforms; but it is also more private, as religious identities are increasingly negotiated in relation to private experiences. This suggests that internet-based negotiations of religion in the public sphere may add nuances to the processes of religious privatization and deprivatization described by José Casanova (1994).

Hypermediated religious spaces often discuss reality by producing social imaginaries and creating "myths" about religion. The case studies, for example, employ digital venues to try creating a society where multiple religions coexist, or where religion is not visibly present in the public sphere, or where one religion has a predominant social role. The fact that these imaginaries are very different from each other shows how the internet can help to enact various ideas in a way that makes all of them seem possible. These imaginaries can be considered as responses to anxieties about modernity and fears for social change, which people try to address through collective reflections and discussions. These social imaginaries are defined as heterotopias because they usually exist only in certain specific spaces, such as blogs.

Even if their existence is spatially and conceptually limited, these heterotopias are real because they produce tangible outcomes. In particular, their activities arguably create what Birgit Meyer (2010) calls "aesthetic formations": hypermediated religious spaces form communities through aesthetic practices and the creation of shared identities. These communities are bound by digital communications rather than being based in a physical place. Hypermediated religious spaces also help to create "imagined communities" (Anderson 2006) in relation to national and European identities. They embed religious and secular ideas with national feelings, for example, showing the compatibility of Islam with European values or the importance of *laïcité* for nationalism. Because they form these communities, hypermediated religious spaces are considered as authentic venues that produce collective negotiations of social reality.

The three dialectical pairings of alternative and mainstream, private and public, imaginary and real are entangled with each other and help to understand processes of space formation. They define the ways in which different groups understand religion in society and the actions they undertake to promote certain social imaginaries. Considering these three pairings as the basis for the creation of hypermediated religious spaces, they are illustrated as indicated in Figure 6.1, already presented in Chapter 2 (Figure 2.2):

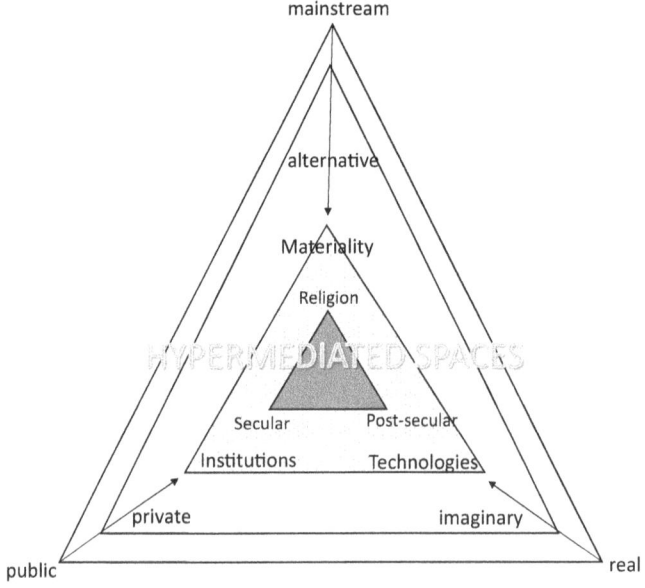

Figure 6.1 Hypermediated religious spaces

The illustration seeks to conceptualize hypermediated religious spaces by representing how contemporary religion exists and is experienced. I elaborated the concept of hypermediated religious spaces wishing that it could help scholars to explore both the actions of established religious institutions, such as the Vatican, and non-conventional forms of religion. I hope that the three dialectical pairings help to better understand secularization in Europe and digital media practices, as well as to explore new methodologies for digital religion. The concept of hypermediated religious spaces may allow analyzing geo-cultural contexts that tend to be marginal in the academic literature, as well as capturing the fluidity of social elements that are often entangled with religion. Hypermediated religious spaces may thus become venues to better conceptualize the new spaces, new modes of experience, and new stories that characterize today's religion.

The future of hypermediated religious spaces

Media and religion are both central to people's lives. They often contribute to shaping identities and social perceptions, even when people do not believe in religion and try to avoid using certain media platforms. Valeria Solesin's funeral, for example, was probably not meant to be a religious media event, but it elicited reflections about religion, and it was amplified by various media. The concept of hypermediated religious spaces can help to understand religious media events that are not officially staged, but that result from actions – such as the creation of a video, the contestation of a law, the organization of a protest – embedded in people's everyday existence. By looking at unconventional spaces of religion, the theory of hypermediation aims at contributing to the existing literature on religion and media both by suggesting new angles to look at spaces of religion, and by compelling reflections on the researchers' role as public scholars.

The concept of hypermediated religious spaces opens up possible topics of research besides those explored in this book. For example, it focused on single groups more than looking at contacts between different communities. This can open a fertile ground to explore how the creation of hybrid identities within a religious group may lead to the incorporation of elements from other traditions and religious encounters in hypermediated spaces. Furthermore, hypermediation was theorized in relation to the specific case of Europe, which is characterized by strong media institutions and a diffused presence of media technologies. Because of the global role of digital media in challenging hegemonies, hypermediated religious spaces can arguably be found also outside Europe. Venues for future research can include studies that look at transnational examples of digital religion, and that explore how the theory of hypermediation can be modified to be applied to other contexts. Lastly, this book focused on religion, but hypermediation regards various spheres of human existence. The analysis of the case studies saw gender, race, and ethnicity emerging as hypermediated discourses connected to issues such as the Muslim veil or anti-gender activism. Because religion cannot be separated from other social elements, gender and race are areas of exciting potential to better contextualize the theory of hypermediation in contemporary society.

Addressing these possibilities and looking into more empirical case studies would help to define how the concept of hypermediated religious spaces can be practically applied. In particular, there are two compelling questions about the theory of hypermediation. The first regards the impact of digital practices: What kind of social changes can hypermediated religious spaces create? This book argued that hypermediated religious spaces can be considered as examples of tactical media. To say it with Rita Raley's (2009) words, they cause

> The intervention and disruption of a dominant semiotic regime, the temporary creation of a situation in which signs, messages, and narratives are set into play and critical thinking becomes possible. Tactical media operates in the field of the symbolic, the site of power in postindustrial society.
>
> (6)

This definition applied to hypermediated religious spaces suggests that they are alternative venues of contestation that re-think certain aspects of society. They do so by creating internet-based actions and events that seek to have a social impact. The groups analyzed in this book make efforts that can arguably help to change people's mentality in relation to certain issues. Even if some groups might not be able to establish a lasting internet and social presence, they produce "tactical" actions and discourses that, by reaching a certain visibility, may change the way certain religious identities are perceived.

However, these groups also have antithetical opinions about the role of religion in society and are not always able to establish constructive dialogues with other actors. To employ Chantal Mouffe's (2013) definition, they often try to enter in agonistic conversation with mainstream culture, but they may create antagonistic relationships instead. Small groups that articulate actions and discourses prevalently on the internet may remain excluded from dialogic interactions when they are not considered as equal interlocutors and framed as "other" to mainstream culture. As a reaction, they sometimes try establishing a voice at the expense of other groups. The atheist, Muslim, and Catholic blogs analyzed in this book, for example, often do not seek a productive conversation with each other, even when they address the exact same issues. In some cases, they try attracting the attention of mainstream media and society through criticism and marginalization of other groups, framed as scapegoats for social problems. This is the case of anti-gender groups that protest against LGBTQs and feminist groups, as well as certain atheist organizations that criticize the public visibility of Muslims. In this way, they not only prevent the creation of consensus, but they may also fail to establish a productive (and "tactical") dialogue with mainstream culture because they remain isolated and without social alliances.

These hypermediated religious spaces can arguably be more successful if they establish relationships that go beyond their immediate interests. For example, they may create networks by putting together different goals in a model of "connective action" (Bennett and Segerberg 2012). This type of action, exemplified by the "we are the 99 percent" slogan of the *Occupy* movement, is able to maintain the individual claims of different groups and amplify them while appealing to a heterogeneous audience and find non-conventional digital strategies to establish voices. Hypermediated religious spaces may enhance cooperation with other religious minorities or with other social groups, improving mutual dialogic participation and creating a more powerful internet and social presence. In some cases, the groups described already do that, for example, when atheists collaborate with LGBTQ groups. In this way, they are more likely to be effective in engaging with society at large and in becoming trusted interlocutors for religious-related issues.

By so doing, hypermediated religious spaces may lead to new modes of political participation. The term "political" is here considered as in the work of Jaques Rancière (2009), who writes, "*Politics* is not primarily a matter of laws and constitutions. Rather, it is a matter of configuring the sensible texture of the community for which those laws and constitutions make sense" (8). This means that politics goes beyond the laws of a state, and it is embedded in actions and negotiations of members of a community. Religion, therefore, may be a tool for citizens of a democracy to represent themselves as alternative political subjects. In the case studies analyzed in this book, religion is discussed in relation to issues that are often political, as for example, citizenship or LGBTQ rights. Various groups approach these issues from new perspectives and indirectly propose a type of political participation that is disjointed from traditional political parties and based on religious identities.

The potential for hypermediated religious spaces to create connective actions and alternative modes of political engagement leads to a second question. How can researchers employ hypermediated religious spaces for public scholarship? Scholars at the Center for Media, Religion and Culture at the University of Colorado Boulder, for example, employ the theory of hypermediation to engage with public scholarship. Hypermediation not only describes the interconnectedness that enhances various groups' narrative potential, but also opens up new opportunities for scholars to engage with society and make their research more public. In so doing, academics may also blend research with activism and amplify certain causes. Nabil Echchaibi (2017) describes this opportunity as follows:

> Finally, hypermediation is not simply a technological or media challenge for our time. It is above all, an ethical provocation to mobilize its energies and affordances to build a better world. In academia, this

means turning this critical lens against our own practices to imagine new cultures of interaction with the public and an economy of contribution of and to knowledge. It is a call to reflect on the kind of theoretical practices and academic habits we need to capture the mobility and acceleration of communication in this deeply mediated context and respond to the urgency of our political, social and cultural time.

(3)

The quote suggests that researchers are responsible for establishing intellectual voices that have an impact also outside academic environments. The urge of becoming public intellectuals, therefore, compels further reflections about the role of theory in contemporary society.

This book has analyzed digital media practices and social phenomena rather than engaging in public scholarship. I explored different and, sometimes, antithetical events trying to be as objective as possible. Something that I – or other scholars – may do in the future is use research to describe, understand, and explain certain phenomena to the general public. Scholars may use the internet not only as a subject of study, for example, analyzing blogs, but also as a tool to create venues to share their research. In addition, it is possible to create digital spaces to amplify certain groups' claims and help them improve their political participation. A methodology that includes interviews and observations can strengthen this approach as it would let the researcher work *with* the subjects, and not only *on* them. In the case of my research, this involves both valorizing groups whose aims I share because they try to promote greater tolerance, and criticizing groups I disagree with because they tend to marginalize minorities and promote social inequalities. In this way, scholars may describe certain digital venues and also create themselves hypermediated spaces – such as academic blogs, websites, documentaries, social network accounts – to make their research available, to intervene in public debates, and to valorize their intellectual voice.

I started some of this book's chapters with descriptions of events that illustrate the activities of certain groups. The beginning of this chapter described the funeral of Valeria Solesin in Venice. I chose this event not only because it summarizes certain religious discourses in contemporary Europe, but also because it shows a model of coexistence of religion and the secular that I believe should be extended to other social spheres. The funeral exemplifies how it is possible to fully embrace *laïcité* while, at the same time, refraining from marginalizing Muslims as social "others." The space it created can be symbolically more inclusive than that established by Pope Francis in Lampedusa, because it is not based on the premises that one religion (Catholicism) holds a hegemonic social position on others. This is particularly compelling in contemporary Europe, where populist political formations employ religious identities as a way to establish a racist agenda, and where alternative modes of political engagements may be particularly needed. Valeria Solesin's funeral was an isolated event that represents a heterotopia more than a social reality, and it is unlikely that this model of religious interaction could be easily applied to society at large, given also the criticism it attracted. However, the role of the scholar could also be that of giving more relevance to a media event such as this one, and helping to promote other similar positive models of religious change in society.

I would like to conclude this book with a call for scholars to think about hypermediated religious spaces as a theoretical framework to understand contemporary religion, and as a possible tool to shape religious change. The contemporary pace of life transforms the spaces where religion exists, allowing alternative groups to emerge against mainstream culture and define new parameters for public and private religion. Scholars can intervene in this hypermediated reality and take part in collective social imaginaries, establishing their voices through the fast and emotional communications of contemporary life. They can wish for a society where both religious and secular identities are more inclusive and inclined to talk with each other, creating – to employ Alberto Solesin's words – "union rather than divisions." They can imagine models of religious change where the secular character of the state is valorized without excluding any religious, gender, ethnic, or sexual minority. They can help to create media events that show what needs to be changed in contemporary society. As I mentioned in this book's introduction, I cannot predict the future of Catholic Europe. But scholars in the field of religion and media can employ hypermediated religious spaces to try to find a role in shaping this future.

References

Anderson, Benedict. 2006. *Imagined Communities: Reflections on the Origin and Spread of Nationalism*. Revised edition. London; New York, NY: Verso.

Bennett, W. Lance, and Alexandra Segerberg. 2012. "The Logic of Connective Action." *Information, Communication & Society* 15 (5): 739–68. https://doi.org/10.1080/1369118X.2012.670661.

Casanova, Jose. 1994. *Public Religions in the Modern World*. Chicago: University of Chicago Press.

Echchaibi, Nabil. 2017. "Hypermediation as an Argument." Center for Media, Religion, and Culture, University of Colorado Boulder. Unpublished essay.

Foucault, Michel. 2004. "Des espaces autres." *Empan* 54 (2): 12–19.

Hoover, Stewart, and Echchaibi, Nabil. 2014. "Media Theory and the Third Spaces of Digital Religion." Working Paper Center for Media, Religion, and Culture.

Meyer, Birgit, ed. 2010. *Aesthetic Formations: Media, Religion, and the Senses*. 2009 edition. New York, NY: Palgrave Macmillan.

Mouffe, Chantal. 2013. *Agonistics: Thinking the World Politically*. 1st edition. London; New York, NY: Verso.

Raley, Rita. 2009. *Tactical Media*. Minneapolis: University of Minnesota Press.

Rancière, Jacques. 2009. "The Aesthetic Dimension: Aesthetics, Politics, Knowledge." *Critical Inquiry* 36 (1): 1–19. https://doi.org/10.1086/606120.

Warner, Michael. 2005. *Publics and Counterpublics*. New York, NY; Cambridge, MA: Zone Books.

Index